## About the Author

I am just an ordinary person doing extraordinary things.

# Gribet

# Janine Davis

# Gribet

Olympia Publishers
*London*

www.olympiapublishers.com

OLYMPIA PAPERBACK EDITION

A CIP catalogue record for this title is
available from the British Library.

ISBN: 978-1-80074-014-3

This is a work of creative nonfiction. The events are portrayed to the
best of the author's memory. While all the stories in this book are
true, some names have been changed to protect the privacy of the
people involved.

First Published in 2021

Olympia Publishers
Tallis House
2 Tallis Street
London
EC4Y 0AB

Printed in Great Britain

# Dedication

To my brother, Leigh Davis. This is for both of us. You are a
rock star. x

# Acknowledgements

I would like to thank Dr Theresa Barlow and Dan Hogan for all the support you gave me whilst writing this story.

Sarah and Jimmy Johnston, you are the most generous, honest and real-to-the-core people I know. Much love to both of you.

I would like to thank my super strong female friends: Joanne Woodall, Jodi Hooper, Jane Bingham, Stephanie Thorne, Rebecca Pullan, Jane Cordell, Deborah Jane Nichol, Jessica Johnson, Amber Madkour, Peachy Peach, Sarah Dawn, Katy Smith, Faye Jordan, Amy Bletcher and Elizabeth Lord. Along with all my Coastside crew, Phoenix Crew, Just Swim crew; you know who you are. I cannot name you all but I love you. x

Every single one of us has a story to tell. Your story could be someone else's guide to their own life. In today's society, I think it is ever more important that we start to open up about our experiences. Our struggles. Our vulnerabilities. The more we share, the more we realise that we are not on our own.

Life is not perfect.

We are not perfect.

My cards were dealt when I was born. I was born into dysfunction and poverty. You cannot choose who your parents are. Let me tell you, I would trade mine in a heartbeat.

You do have choices though. Do you follow the same path, or do you try to fight your way out of the life you have been born into?

# Introduction

When life has dealt you a tough hand, you think that you are the only one that is dealing with your 'shit'. You know other people have gone through 'shit'! But selfishly you think that your 'shit' is bigger and worse than anyone else's. It's not, of course but the emotional scars it leaves with you, never go away. I have been told many times over the years, 'You are so aggressive, Janine!'

I do not think I am aggressive. I would like to say assertive. I will not take any shit off anyone. I will not be pushed around and walked all over anymore. Not that I have to explain myself but if you understand the journey that I have been on, then you will understand why I am the way I am. I have had no choice other than to get tough and get on with it. Fight, fight and keep fighting, take no prisoners and take no shit! Trusting anyone is very tough. I have a massive barrier around me. I only let people in, once I have figured them out. The trust you have for anyone withers away because you have been burnt emotionally so many times. The abuse, the abandonment, the rejection, the total lack of love and parenting leaves you with a battle on your hands, to make it in this world. How resilient are you?

I now realise that everyone around me has a story. Everyone I meet has had a battle, big or small in one way or another. We live in a society that is afraid to share, in case it shows weakness or you are judged. You never know the journey that someone has taken and that some battles are just a bit bigger than your own.

Growing up on a council estate surrounded by dysfunction and drugs. I should have ended up perpetuating the cycle of single-parent family status. No education. No future. Living off the dole.

There were no dreams. University was never talked about. What were the opportunities? As Boy George once said about state school education, "Give them a basic education and then chuck them in the factories!"

I was on the lowest ladder of society. I was to amount to nothing!

You either get a shit job with a shit wage or as a young woman, you get married. That was it.

Well, fuck you society, fuck you!

I will not be defined by the ideologies in society that have been set out for me as a woman. I will not just be pretty. I will not be quiet and a good girl. I will become strong and independent, which will raise the question, 'How will I ever find a partner?'

I knew I wanted to be someone. I didn't have a clue how I was going to do it but I got on a journey and this is where I am now...

EDUCATION

2014—2016 Bournemouth University
Masters by Research
2012—2013 Bournemouth University
BSc Sports Psychology and Coaching Sciences
2008—2011 Bournemouth University

FdSc Coach and Athlete Development Degree

PROFESSIONAL QUALIFICATIONS

- Exercise Therapy International Sports Science Association (2019)
- Strength and Conditioning Coach International Sports Science Association (2018)
- Sports Massage Therapist Level 3 (2018)
- British Weightlifting Coach Level 1 (2016)
- Youth Fitness Trainer International Sports Science Association (2012)
- Diploma in Nutritional Medicine Rusland College (2008)
- Specialist in Martial Arts Conditioning International Sports Science Association (2006)
- Diploma in Sports Nutrition Rusland College (2003)
- Thai boxing Instructor Red/Yellow Kruang Ruang Bulldog Gym (2001)
- Specialist in Performance Nutrition International Sports Science Association (2000)
- Certified Fitness Trainer International Sports Science Association (1999)

Qualified First Aider
Team Teach UK Skills

SPORT ACHEIVEMENT

75kg European Weightlifting Champion (2015)
75kg British Masters Weightlifting Champion (2013, 2014 & 2015)
English Weightlifting Champion (2013)
75kg Bronze Medallist British Seniors Weightlifting (2013)
BPC British Power Lifting Champion (2009)
WPC World Power Lifting Champion (2009)
BPC British Power Lifting Champion (2008)
British Power Lifting Silver Medallist (2007)
British unequipped Power Lifting Champion (2007)
World Muay Thai boxing Champion (2003)
Southern Area Thai Boxing Title (2002)
British Kick Boxing Champion (2001)

This is my story.

# Chapter One
# Wallisdown, The Beginning

My first years of life were the 70s. Dad was at home. My memory of him being around is intermittent or very vague. There are some stand out moments that I do recall though. He was a coach driver; I was five years old. We were putting together chocolate spread sandwiches; I was so buzzed about the chocolate spread sandwiches. I did not really understand what was happening, I was five! What I did know though is that I was going to spend the day with my dad and chocolate spread sandwiches were the best. We had to tell Leigh, my brother, that Dad was taking me to the doctors so that he wouldn't get upset that he wasn't coming. The front seat of the coach is where I sat for the whole day, picking up passengers, until I was too tired to say, 'Hi,' anymore and curled up on one of the seats and fell asleep.

Dad would read to us at bedtime. This was a time that was nice, safe and comforting. His book of choice was Kenneth Grahame's 'Wind in The Willows'. Those memories evoke a good time, a happy time. I do not remember Mum ever reading to us at bedtime.

Mum, from what I remember, didn't work when my dad was at home. We were often at home with no heating or electricity because mum didn't have any money on her to put into the 50p meter. We were often in the front lounge with candles, making shapes in the shadows on the wall. As a kid you just find the joy in what you are doing. As long as there is play you just get on with it.

A really early memory is Leigh as a baby. He cried a lot! I would have been around three. Mum had this bright yellow, baby-holder seat that she would put him in and then just leave him in the garden, unattended to cry, a lot! I would just play out in the back garden alongside him. I'm not sure where Dad was. Leigh would cry, I assume until he could cry no more, is that right? I ask myself as an adult is that what I would do and the answer is no. It was a different time back then though. I think it was common practice to leave the kids in their chairs or prams outside in the garden with the door shut. You would never get away with that now!

There was a lot of arguing between Mum and Dad. I vaguely remember them standing either end of the hallway. The hallway ran front door to back door. They would be launching whatever they could find and throwing it at each other. One day in a mad hustle, my mum couldn't get us outside of the house quickly enough. I was thinking about grabbing my shoes but Mum said, "NO, OUTSIDE!" Me and Leigh were out in the front garden all bewildered. I didn't know what was happening. Once she got us outside, we had to run and run as fast as we could up to the common. There was a cycling track, I think. That's how I remember it. It was fenced in and it had an outhouse in it. My mum sat in the alcove of the outhouse and me and Leigh had running races round the track to amuse ourselves, until she felt it was safe for us to return home. Mum did mention later on when I was older that Dad was into taking drugs: 'acid'. He would regularly come home out of it.

Dad always thought it was funny to put Dr Who on

because it frightened me. He had his friends round one time and put it on in front of them to watch me start crying. I would run to the back of the settee and hide. They would all stand there laughing at me! I HATE DR WHO, still to this very day!

Christmas, when Dad was still living with us was exciting, like it is for most kids. My Great Granny Miles lived in Boscombe and we would frequently visit her. Apparently, she was a tough Scottish lady. You did not mess around with her. I think that gene has been passed down in the women from the Davis side! I remember sitting in the back of the car on the way home one time from Granny Miles' and thinking about Santa making his journey across all the houses.

Somebody asked me the other day, "Do you have any happy childhood memories?" It is difficult to pick out the good times. There were good times I suppose. I don't remember much of my dad being there. I was so young. There was one Christmas Eve when Dad was still around. Me and Leigh were so excited. We had just put out the carrots for the reindeer and wrote a note to Santa. We were just getting ourselves into bed. I heard bells from downstairs. Mum and Dad told us to quickly get downstairs and say, 'Hi,' to Santa. I could not move my butt fast enough down those stairs. Me and Leigh were straining ourselves out of the back door to see if we could see Father Christmas. Of course, he wasn't there. I love remembering that though. It was fun and joyful. Just a touch of happiness from that one Christmas Eve when he was around.

Then he was gone. I was six years old. Leigh was three and a half.

Life after he was gone was tough, to say the least! It is very difficult to say when Mum started with her cruelty really. I was so young. You really do not have the understanding and comprehension as a young child, because she is Mum. It is only as you grow older that you start to question the behaviour because your instincts are telling you it just doesn't feel right!

Mum had to work. You didn't get all the benefits you get today. We were left on our own a lot! We were always told to not leave the house when she went out. Me and Leigh would get pretty creative at playing games. Making camps with our bunk beds and sleeping bags were the best. We would make the biggest camps ever! We would also get to the top of the stairs, climb inside the sleeping bags and slide down the stairs, hours and hours of fun. We would put the sleeping bags on us like royal capes so that we imitated being kings and queens, so funny.

The bunk beds were used as a tool for pretending that it was a bus. I was the main bus driver, of course. Big sister rights. I would sit at the end of the bus (the top bunk, feet through the railings) and rock that bus backwards and forwards as hard as I could. I would halt it, ask my brother where he wanted to go and then he would get on and we would then both shake that bus backwards and forwards. How it never came apart is amazing really!

Mum would always be out on a Saturday morning (for hours!) and we were told if we wanted our pocket money, we were to tidy our rooms. "Yeah, yeah..." was the answer but our heads did not move from the television set as we were glued to Saturday morning kids' TV. Quite a few hours later and we had not moved at all! We would see her pull up after being out all morning and race up those stairs so fast. I would get all the toys and whatever else was on the floor and launch it onto the bed, cover it with my duvet, kick whatever there was left under the bed, step back, check the room and think,

Okay, all clear. She'd come in and ask if we had tidied our rooms. Of course, we would say, "Yes". She would inspect, never look under the duvet and we would get away with it every time. Of course, when I went to bed, I would pull everything out onto the floor and it would be right back to the state it started in.

My mum used to go out on a weekday evening. Darts night. I would have been eight, maybe nine. She told me never to answer the phone but of course I would. The one time I did answer, it was a dirty caller who started asking me about my vagina and boobs. I didn't really know what he was talking about. I was so young. I didn't really understand it. I did tell her though. I don't remember how but I did because I know that he called back and she dealt with him, or so she said anyway. On those nights she was at darts I would stay up 'til really late and watch 'The Young Ones'. I loved that show! I have since watched it as an adult and don't really get it but at the time I loved it. Oh, and Miami Vice. Loved that too.

A memory that is really clear to me after Dad left us, I was getting ready for school. Mum was screaming at Leigh and dragging him into the lounge. He was screaming the house down. I'm not sure what she was doing to him or even what he had done to warrant getting belted as much as he was but the screaming was blood curdling. I ran into the kitchen; I thought the safest place for me was curled up in a ball under the kitchen table. I was six. That was a common occurrence with Leigh. The physical violence with Leigh was relentless, he got it bad.

The early years growing up on the Canford Avenue estate was the best. There was always a big group of kids to play with. Mum would yell, *"OUT, OUTSIDE, GO ON"*. *"But mum there's nothing to do!"*. *"GO FIND SOMETHING TO DO!"*.

21

Off I would trot, go knocking on friends' doors, '*Can Julie come out to play please?*', '*Can Emma come out to play please?*', '*Can Tracey come out to play please?*' You would keep knocking the doors until you found someone. There was always 'block', 'what's the time mister wolf' or playing up the dump (a patch of grass round the back of the buildings that we called the dump). One day we had decided as a group, to see if we would float down with umbrellas. We had watched Mary Poppins. We wanted to see if it worked. I volunteered, of course. I can't remember who did it with me. A friend from the estate and myself climbed to the top of the garages, fifteen feet maybe twenty, could have been higher. We opened our umbrellas and jumped off! Of course, we didn't float! How we didn't break anything is unreal. We brushed ourselves off and off we went to find something else to do.

If you couldn't find a friend to play with, you'd put your roller skates on and take off round the block. There were a couple of big falls mind you. One when I fell on my coccyx: Oooooo, I went down so hard. I could not sit down properly for a good week. Another time I was round the block that ran alongside the main road and I went down hard, my legs, oh my, were in such a state! One was stretched out in front of me the other tangled up behind. All I remember is seeing this van driving passed and the men in the van laughing so hard. It must have looked very amusing to say the least.

Next door to us was a lovely couple we referred to as Nanny and Grandad. They weren't our biological grandparents but I assumed they were from a very young age. I always called them that. Doreen and Alf. Alf was a carpenter and had a shed at the bottom of the garden. He made Leigh the coolest go-kart ever! All out of wood. Painted green. A great seat at the front for two people to sit. A space at the back for you to stand. You could run with the kart and then jump on the back to hold on. Rope at the front to steer. Leigh loved that go-kart. All the boys on the estate loved it! They were always round knocking for Leigh to come out on it.

When Mum wasn't around, I always knew Doreen was next door if I needed her.

We were on our own again and I thought it would be a good idea to take my guinea pig out of his cage, bring him into the house and put him on the side in the kitchen! Why would I do that? Of course, he scurried off and fell down behind the oven that was on! I was screaming! Oh my, I was screaming. Doreen came running in from next door and helped me get my guinea pig out. Unfortunately, he died a couple of weeks later. I think from shock!

Funnily enough, I bumped into Denise who was her actual granddaughter, just yesterday. She's fifty now. I started to talk about Nan and Grandad, how I use to hang off the fence and shout for them. I told her I don't have any contact with Mum anymore. She seemed to understand. I told her that me and Leigh are close though. She confirmed that you always were. Funny really, you think no one else can see what is going on. But people see, it's just that they are not in a place to say anything. We both reminisced about growing up on the Canford Avenue estate and how good it was. The right side of Turbary Park Common, that is! The other side was West Howe and East Howe, built originally for the gypsies in the 50s. It was rough!

One day my brother was out playing. He was maybe four years old. I think like most little boys and girls at a young age they just sometimes can't be bothered to get to the toilet.

Instead of thinking, 'Oooo, I better go to the toilet', they would rather play around with shit in their pants than leave the fun and go! Leigh was one of them. If I remember rightly, he used to do it a lot.

When we got in, I was in my box room. I had enough room in there for a four-foot bed and a very small bedside table and the window was a letter box size at the top of the room; I had to stand on my bed to look out of it. All I could hear was Leigh screaming the house down, again and her dragging him into the bathroom telling him she was going to rub his face in it. I don't know what went on in there but I knew Leigh was getting it! I did suffer some of the physical violence from her but not like Leigh, he got it the most.

She favoured the bamboo stick! She would actually go out of her way to Homebase to collect packs of bamboo sticks to hit us with. That's premeditated thought! *'Hmmmm, what have I forgotten, ahhh yes that's right, I have to go and pick up a pack of bamboo sticks to hit my young children with'*. She actually shared this story with me! I was eleven or twelve when she told me the story about the buying of the sticks. When he had to get changed at school for P.E. He had welt marks all over his back where she had been beating him with the bamboo stick. The teacher asked him, "Where did you get those from?" He said, "Mum." "What did you do?" the teacher asked. "I stole a £1 note from Mum's purse," Leigh said. The teacher replied, "Well you won't do that again, will you?"!

I know times were different then in the 70s but if you saw a five-year-old kid with welts across his back, would you not question it?

I have looked after kids in different capacities as an adult and I can tell you the thought of grabbing an instrument to inflict pain to a child of five, is beyond my comprehension.

She fluctuated so much with her mood; you never knew what you were coming home to. Most of the time we were well fed, clothed and kept warm. But there were times when we had nothing. I remember going to school with a bag of digestive biscuits because that's all she had in the house for us. I had to ask the teacher if it was okay to eat at break time because I had had no breakfast. Another time the cupboards were so bare, we had Bovril for breakfast, it was horrible! Thank God for school meals, that was my favourite time of day.

Margaret Thatcher became Prime Minister in the UK in the 70s. Before Thatcher came into power, we were having hot meals, it was awesome! There was a dinner lady that always gave me extra and always let me come back for seconds. I loved it. Then the Conservatives decided to change all that. No more hot meals. No more apples and milk at break time. If you came from an affluent family your packed lunch would be full of all the things that you liked. I was part of the free school meal gang because we were part of the poor. Free school meals consisted of a stick of celery, plain crisps, a shit spam sandwich and a tomato. The dinner hall was full of primary school kids aged from five to eight, crying their eyes out because the dinner ladies would not let them leave the table until they had finished their food. I'm one of the lucky ones, I can down pretty much any food. It just wasn't enough for me and I was going home with really bad stomach pains because I was so hungry. In one of her more caring moments, she told me she went up to the school to talk with Mrs Dauncey, our headmistress. She asked her, "What the hell is going on? My kids are hungry. I am going to have to start sending them to school with food, which defeats the object of free school meals." I'm not sure what happened but the celery went and the packed lunches became a little better.

Mum dipped in and out of being caring and just being one hundred percent awful. She had gone out one night, again. I was probably nine, Leigh was around six or seven. We had a Calor gas fire; Leigh was obsessed with the flame. I don't know how many times he had been told to leave it alone. But there we were on our own. Leigh decided to lay down paper in front of the fire to protect the carpet. Obviously, the thinking is there to try and protect the carpet, but paper, fire, you know where this is going. I said to him you need to stop doing that but you know, he is not going to listen to me. So, he carried on, he was having a great time. Once he had decided to finish what he was doing he cleared all the paper away and then we both saw the melted burn marks in the brand-new, brown, shit carpet we had. The 70s, everything was beige and dark brown, with pampas grass in the house and wood chip wallpaper!

Of course, when she came home, she called us both into the living room and wanted to know what had happened. I lied and said I was upstairs. I can't remember what Leigh said but I remember what happened next. We both got the bamboo stick. She took the skin off the back of my legs, I remember that. What a bitch!

She had several different jobs when we were kids. Carer in the retirement home on our estate, shoe shop attendant, I remember that one because if I was ill, she would take me to work and I would have to sit out the back in the staff room until she finished work. Another one of her jobs was a car parts delivery driver. When she had that job, she did try and get us into Holi- care. This was a day care facility for working parents. It was cool. We would have to take a packed lunch. Egg and salad cream sarnies. Me and Leigh had no control over ourselves and would always eat before lunch and then have nothing to eat at lunch!

One of the mornings before Holi-care, I found myself covered in spots all over my body. Mum brushed it off and told me to get ready as per usual. We were in the kitchen putting my hair into a ponytail and all the blood rushed from my head, I was going to pass out. I'm a pretty tough individual, this wasn't normal for me. I did lose my legs from underneath me and she just held on to the top of my head with my ponytail. I was just dangling there. She barked at me, "Go and sit on the stairs. Put your head between your legs and breath." I staggered over to the bottom step and did as she said. There was never any mollycoddling. Just get on with it. Do not fuss. You'll be all right.

Mum would always bring up the fact that I wouldn't cuddle her. I don't know why? She would try and I would push her away. She would always give us a kiss goodbye before school, I hated it! I would always wipe my face down afterwards and she would always say, "You know you'll never get a boyfriend being like that!" I didn't care, I did not like the wet, sloppy kisses on my face from my faggy-smelling mum!

A very prominent dream I had from living at Wallisdown, was me and Leigh sharing a room at the back of the house. Before I went into the box room. I woke up in a dream and I could hear a monster down in the hallway. I remember the dream today as if it had happened last night. I ran out of our bedroom in the dream to look through the bannisters to see what the monster was doing. I knew it was coming to get me and Leigh. I was scared, I wasn't sure what I was going to do. It was big and red and making a horrible noise. It was moving

27

down the hallway. How was I going to protect me and Leigh…?
I woke up.

Dinner time was always just me and Leigh. It was a rare occasion that she ever sat with us. Me and Leigh would always be on our own in the kitchen. She would always take her dinner and go sit in the lounge by herself. If we were playing up, you know squeezing mash potatoes through our teeth, pulling funny faces at each other and God forbid that his fried egg should be complete and mine not, because if that was the case I would reach across that table and smash it up. He, of course, would do the same to me. We would hear this voice bellowing from the lounge. "If you two don't cut it out I'm going to bang your heads together!" We would then carry on in silence. There was always a battle with Mum and Leigh eating his food. You could put anything in front of me and I would shovel it down. Leigh, well, Leigh did not like his vegetables and she would force him to eat them. We were out for dinner not so long ago and his plate came out with tomatoes on it. He said, "Get them off my plate! I still can't stand them." He's forty-four. "Mum use to force feed them to me!" I do remember her losing her shit on a regular basis and mashing his vegetables into his mash potato and shouting, "There, there you go, you can't see them now! EAT them, or you are not leaving the table!" Leigh would continue to sit there sobbing because he didn't want to eat them.

I loved stew with dumplings. Fried rice and banana custard. Those were the best. I'd always be in the kitchen after school. "Mum, mum, what's for tea?" When she replied, "LIVER!" Oh no. not liver! I don't like liver! You knew never to complain. I'd sit down, try and sift my way through the dinner. As she wasn't sat at the table, I would wave the liver around under the table for the dog. That was always a get out of not eating it. Or I would shout through to the living room, "Muuuuuuummmm, can I leave the table for the toilet please?" I'd get a 'yes' back. I would fill my mouth up as much as I could with that horrible stuff, run upstairs and spit it down the toilet, she never found out!

Mum would sit and draw all the time. She was an amazing artist, always drawing me and Leigh when we were kids. We would be sat there watching the television and she would be sketching away. She loved to draw horses. As we got older, I think the resentment at the life she could have had grew worse. She had told me that she wanted to go to art college, but her mum said "NO. You get married, you have kids, that's your life!" So that's what she did. Aged nineteen, married my dad, had me and then two and a half years later had Leigh. By the time she was twenty-four or twenty-five, she was on her own with two kids who were a handful. I know it would have been tough and she was so young. I've tried to understand her behaviour as an adult. But there are just no excuses for some of it, just none.

Growing up I would spend a lot of time at my Nan's house. Usually when Mum couldn't cope. My memories at my Nan's (her mum) are good ones but on reflection, my Nan had no life. She spent her whole day in the kitchen. She used to bobby pin her hair at night, to keep the curls in. I never understood how she slept with all those grips in her hair? She had a teas-made by her bed that would wake her up in the morning with a cup of tea before she got downstairs. I would go into her room and sit with her on her bed whilst the teas-maid did its thing. Nan always made sure that she took an extra cup up for me at night for the morning. We'd share a cuppa and a chat. Once she was up, it was pinny on, downstairs to the kitchen, more tea!

Making tea in the Treggiden house was very important! God forbid you had teabags! Tea leaves only please, never ever use tea bags. Boil the kettle, just before the boil you put some in the teapot to warm it up, pour that out. Tea leaves in. Now, pour in boiling water. Tea cosy on, leave to brew. Cup and saucer, never a mug! Milk in, pour tea, no tea strainer, ready to drink. You would always forget about the tea leaves at the bottom of the cup and get a full mouthful of them!

Her day would start, oh and there was always the plink, plink of Solpadeine, a pain tablet. I realise now that my Mum and Nan were both addicted to it. Mum ended up getting headaches from taking so much. Nan would then spend hours in the kitchen drinking more tea and stretching out jobs she had to do, washing up, boiling Grandad's long johns so that they were double the size. We would always laugh when we saw them on the washing line. In fact, she boiled everything in Biotex. Boil it, spin it and then put it out on the line. Even when she got a top loader washing machine, she still boiled everything before she put it in the washing machine. Never made any sense really but that's how she wanted it done. That was her life at Leedam Road living with my grandad, in the kitchen! She did tell me stories of growing up and all the dances that she would go to. She would often tell me not to settle with the first guy you meet, have a few on the go Janine. I always thought that sounded like hard work. I was never interested in boys anyway and boys were never interested in me.

She would get out to the shops on a Tuesday and Friday for food supplies. Unfortunately, she died in the kitchen, had a massive stroke. It was Boxing Day. Me, Leigh and Mum were there. I would have been seventeen. It was pretty horrible. She was puking up blood. Me and mum had to carry her up the stairs because her body would not take her weight. There was only one toilet and that was upstairs. I think her body was just shutting down. It was around the time of the ambulance strikes, so the ambulance took forever to come. It was an army ambulance in the end. I don't think anything different would have happened had they got there sooner; she would have been completely broken. So, the best happened really.

You never question your surroundings as a kid, you just accept the way things are. You don't care as long as you feel safe and loved. My Nan's house was basic. Even into the early nineties she still had no central heating. The only heating the house had was the coal fire. Winter was the only time you could get a bath because the fire used to heat the water tank. You would find ice on the inside of the windows it was that cold in the house. In the summer, we had to fill the bath with the kettle and pans of boiling water. Up and down the stairs, it was like a game really.

Unfortunately, my grandad was a raging alcoholic, every night except Sundays because that was the only day he was at home. I used to go out with him when he worked for a bakery. That all stopped sharpish because he was always pissed up. I didn't know any different, I was looking forward to the bakery and seeing what cake I could get. I remember also that I used to sit on his lap and he would stroke my hair and tickle my back. I would have been eight. I liked it, who doesn't like getting their back tickled? But I think Nan put a stop to it. As a kid you don't understand but as you get older, you start to try and piece things together and realise there might be more to this story. My grandad always soaked his feet in a bucket in the living room when he got home from work. He would fall asleep and his teeth would fall out, that was always amusing. I can't say I enjoyed watching him soak his feet though.

I've always been an early riser. I would always be up before Nan. There was a couple of times when Grandad had horror films on. I hate horror films. I can't remember the name of it but I knew I didn't like it. There was blood coming out of the walls and everything. He made no attempt to switch it off. I was eight or nine. He did make good cheese on toast though or kippers on toast...

My bed at my Nan's was a fold-up, canvas camp bed. Nan would put a bit of foam on the canvas to make it comfortable for me to sleep in. One blanket and then loads of coats and a hot water bottle to keep me warm. I was snug as a bug in a rug. I didn't give it a second thought that it wasn't a bed. It was what it was and that was where I was sleeping. Hot cocoa, biscuits before bed and a hot water bottle for my feet. What more could you want? I was safe. I was warm and I felt loved.

Nan and Grandad would snore soooooo loud. You could stand at the bottom of the stairs and try to guess who was the loudest!

I did love staying at Nan's; it was a break from home. I would have Coco Pops for breakfast. Massive wedges of crusty bread with thick cuts of cheese on. Cake, home-made fudge from the Women's Institute, cocoa, chocolate bourbons. She would set me up in the morning with sewing, knitting or rug weaving. James Bond in the summer holidays, running round to the corner shop to get my quarter of bonbons or cola cubes for the movie. Playing out in the garden or in the field at the back of the house. There was always a swing made up on one of the trees down there. I still have a rag doll that I made when I was four years old. I can transport myself back to the days I made that. I can picture the conversations we were having about how to sew the body and do the hair. It looks pretty raggedy now but I cannot get rid of it.

Writing our Christmas list and calling for Santa up the chimney as kids. Hilarious! When the fire got going, Nan and Mum would say to me and Leigh to call for Santa up the chimney. You would stick your head in far enough so as not to get burnt and call for Santa. They would say if you were quick enough you might see him at the window. We would go back and forth calling for him and then when they said just let the letter go, you would call one more time and let the smoke from the fire take the letter up the chimney. Let me tell you how many times as a kid I would run as fast as I could to that window to see if I could see Santa; so funny. My face smashed up to the glass, craning to see Santa. Of course, we never did, we were never quick enough!

On reflection, I think I was lucky really because I did spend a lot of time with Nan. I spent a lot of time over there. I had a nice time. It was quiet. I amused myself. I had to, there was nothing else to do and no one else to play with. My Nan had a massive back garden that had different ledges. I would go out on one ledge with the umbrellas and do singing in the rain performances to an imaginary crowd. She taught me to sew, knit, garden and bake.

My Uncle Nicky lived there at that time. I loved my Uncle Nicky and wanted to go everywhere with him, just wanted to hang out. He was my hero. He would bring home all his music: Soft Cell, Gary Newman, Human league. I would plug myself in with the headphones on and dance around in the living room. I would fill my days up with building houses for my Barbie doll, knit clothes for her, generally let my imagination fly.

Uncle Nicky used to come to our house in Wallisdown to have a bath. It would always be when Top of the Pops was on. I loved Top of the Pops. Uncle Nicky would be outside messing around on his Capri. He would always ask me to let him know when the dancers were on and to make sure I shouted him in. He would then come running up the pathway to watch Pans People. The female dancers would dance to the music on Top of the Pops with next to nothing on for that time in the 70s.

When I was at Nan's I would often think about Leigh and what he was doing. I would get jealous of not being included. I felt like I was missing out. He would be off seeing Dad's mum, Granny. Nan couldn't cope with Leigh, so we were separated a lot of the time. He wanted to be where I was, I wanted to be where he was. I suppose we both felt like we were missing something. That we were being shut out of each other's lives. I feel that my mum used to play me and Leigh off against each other.

I'd get home from Nan's and Mum would say to me, "You're fat!" I mean I wasn't fat but had I continued with what I was eating at Nan's, I could have potentially ended up with a little more chunk. What kid doesn't love eating all the fun stuff! Back to cornflakes. I hate cornflakes, soggy, taste of nothing, boring old cornflakes. Give my mum her dues though, she was militant when it came to what we were eating and we never had any money for the fun stuff. The only time we had sweets was on a Saturday with our 50p.

I think Mum always resented the fact that she had never been able to follow her dream of art school. My nan had put paid to that, her mum had dictated her life. I honestly feel that given a choice she would never have had us kids.

Infant school is my first memory of running races. I loved running races. I was always running races with the boys, girls, whoever. I loved it. On our estate playing bulldog with the older kids. I was probably four. An older boy made fun of me, 'You're not fast enough'! I thought, "Oh yeah, I'll get you one day'! I used to run everywhere. To the corner shop. To the park. With the dog. My love of sport and competition was inherent. Going into junior school, the sport got a bit more serious. No more egg and spoon race. 100 metres and the relay race. I loved the relay. Me and Rachel Cross were the fastest girls. She always just beat me though. I made it into Town Sports in junior school. If you made it to Town Sports you knew you were something, I loved it. I don't think Mum ever came to watch me in junior school. She came and watched me once in senior school, told me I run funny. It wasn't said in a way that I would have laughed about it. Those were the first words out of her mouth. No praise, no well done or Janine, you did so well. Just, I run funny, you run on your tip toes. I said, 'I've got spikes on and that's how you run when you sprint!' I thought to myself, I'd rather you didn't come, you're not really that bothered anyway.

We had a conversation around when I was thirty-six and she said she always thought I was jealous. She did not even consider that I was competitive, sporty, that I loved sport and had a skill for sport. Jealous! I mean where does that even come from, who would I have been jealous of?

I started to play netball in junior school and the P.E. teacher, Mrs Carpenter, asked me to try out for the school teams. I was elated that she had asked me. I got through and thought I was going to be in the B team. As it turned out, I had made it into the A team. Me? The A team! It was amazing. When I got home, I told Mum and asked if I could stay for after school club. She said no! I thought right, we'll see about that.

We were on our own when we got home from school until she got home from work, so I decided that I could go to netball and get home before she even found out. I had to make the decision to either walk the long way up Daws Avenue which would add time to my journey making me late. Or walk up Turbary Park Avenue to the side of the common which was known for having bad men that would jump out of the bushes and show their penis to you. I always picked the common way, it was quicker. I would stand at the edge of it. Figure out my path, tighten my bag and run across that common like my life depended on it, pumping my arms, hair flowing behind me, chin up. I did that for quite some time, she never found out. I'm not sure what happened with Leigh. He always made it home safe, somehow. I was ten.

Me and Leigh had been walking to and from school for quite some time, due to my doing. I had been found out for taking the bus money which cost 11p and keeping it to buy sweets and walking to school in the morning, instead of getting the bus. When she found out, I was told that I was deceitful. "Do you know what that means?" Of course, I didn't. "Go get the dictionary and look it up!"

That was the end of the bus journeys and walking to and from school began; three miles every day.

Kingsleigh Junior, now that was an experience and I can assure you that anyone that went to that school in the late 70s and early 80s would remember the headmaster, who was known to the girls as someone you do not want to get caught up with. He was known as a pervert. I had not long been at junior school, so was around eight years old. He was teaching us. I don't remember what subject. But I do remember him calling me out and making me sit on his lap. He proceeded to start stroke my hair in front of the class! It was weird! I did not like it one bit! I knew something was wrong, it felt wrong even as a young girl.

If you were told off and sent to the headmaster's office, the girls would talk about the fact that he would bend you over his knee and pull up your skirt to spank your bum! I told my mum this when I got home. Now, she did tell me she went to some offices to speak to some officials and inform them of his behaviour. The headmaster was a magistrate back then, so they couldn't touch him or something. I know I was left alone after that. Although, this is the mentality of the same headmaster back then. Leigh struggled at school. They did not recognise dyslexia back then and just assumed he was stupid. He was really disruptive in class which meant he got into a lot of trouble. Mum had been called into school to see the headmaster. He asked "Ummm…Where is Mr Davis?" Mum replied, "Mr Davis is not around." "Ahh, really… single parent? Hmmm, Janine seems so normal?" Just outrageous, just because the male was not present in our situation would mean we were demented or something. Those were the attitudes back then I suppose.

I was what you call a dally day dreamer. That's what Mum called it. "You dally daydreaming?"

I was always in a different place. A lot of the time completely out of it. Those places were much better to be in than being at home most of the time. She would make fun of me all the time because she would try to talk to me and I wouldn't hear her. I would often dream about how I would take care of me and Leigh if she were to die. I remember thinking that quite often on our walk home from school. I have to feel sorry for the people that lived on Daws Avenue, because every day without fail, me and Leigh would have got into a disagreement and by the time we got to Daws Avenue, I would be ahead and Leigh would be crying and shouting up the road "WAIT FOR ME! arrrrrhhhhhhhh… 'sob', 'sob', 'sob'… WAIT FOR ME! arrrrrhhhhhhhh…" I said, "No way!" I knew we would get into a physical fight had he got any closer so I would push forwards until we got home. Not too far away though that I couldn't see him, just enough to wind him up. The evil sister that I am, it would make me laugh that he was shouting so loud…

There was a massive green field that we had to cross. He would still be shouting, "WAIT FOR ME!" when we got to that area. One day the grass was so long that it towered over my head and I ran into it. It was so much fun, like hide and seek. I could still hear him in the grass shouting for me but he couldn't find me; such a mean sister!

Another one of the days we were crossing the green field and the grass at that point had been cut. There was a main road that followed it all the way around. As he was chasing me, I looked back and he had decided to stop right in the middle. I saw that he was taking a piss where everyone could see him; it was like aim and fire! Like, he was seeing how far his piss could get up in the air. All these cars were passing, there was not a care in the world from him.

Another time, I do not know how it happened but he got me. The grass had been freshly cut and there were piles of grass clippings everywhere. He managed to pin me down to the floor and shove grass in my face, down my shirt and pretty much everywhere there was an open hole, it was horrible. I never let that happen again. Serves me right, karma for not waiting for him!

Responsibility was thrust upon me from a very young age. Mum made me start cooking from a young age. I learnt how to prepare a chicken and roast it at around seven years old. I was cooking eggs, beans, sausages and chips around nine-ish, maybe earlier. Baking was standard. I was making scones and Victoria Sandwiches for Brownies and Cubs from seven-ish. I would always be tasked with making the Vic Sponge for Leigh's Cub trips. The mixing used to make my arms ache! There was no electric mixer back then, I had to cream the butter and sugar together by hand.

I did like Brownies but all that badge getting was a bore! The best part of the Brownies was the camping. I did learn how to do hospital bed corners for making beds and polishing silver. I think that was the only badge I ever received! I don't know how she managed it but I ended up in a different Brownie camp, that I didn't belong to. I remember being driven out to the middle of nowhere and being left with a group of people I didn't know and feeling lost and worried. Watching her drive off from a big glass window and thinking I didn't want to be there. But you know from a young age, I was probably nine then, I learnt how to get stuck in and make friends.

Back home and back to duties. Tea making duty started when I was really young. Every morning SHOUTING from her bed, I would hear, "JAAAAAAAANINE! TEA!" That was my cue to get up, make tea and bring it to her in bed. Every morning!

Leigh, for a time, would be locked up in his room. It was

to stop him getting up to mischief in the morning whilst she slept in her bed. She put a lock on the outside of his door. Until SHE decided it was time for her to get up, he would scream the house down, of course. Beating the door, kicking the door, absolutely losing it. I know that he just took to pissing on the carpet floor. He did wet the bed for quite some time. That could just be a young child thing or it could have been related to what we were living in at the time. She went through a spell of getting him up at night before she went to bed to see if that would help him and he pissed right in her face. THAT MADE ME LAUGH A LOT.

We often changed rooms around for whatever reason. I remember having to carry wardrobes with my mum when I was young. Like it was nothing. I never questioned it, we just got on with it. She'd order "JANINE! grab that end". I'd pick it up and we'd move it from room to room. Was I naturally strong or lifting heavy shit from a young age made me strong?

Me and Leigh shared a room for quite some time. Those council houses were just thrown together in the 70s. The walls were so thin you could hear next door talking in their living room. You can imagine what the walls were like room to room. My bed was right up against the inside wall, right next to her room. When she had a boyfriend over to stay, I would hear everything. It was like they were fucking right by my head. It was fucking horrible. I can still hear that now. I would have been eight-ish. As I got older, she decided it wasn't right that me and Leigh shared. That was when I was moved into the box room. Thank god for that!

There was a time when I was in that front bedroom and me and Leigh were playing, that I started to see Victorian women clothed in bright yellow and pink bustle dresses coming out of the floor. That's the main thing I remember. There were also horses, merry go rounds, maybe cartoon characters. I can't remember how long it went on for. But I do remember telling mum about it. She was very much into 'black magic', you know, being psychic. She would talk about that all the time. She would often refer to the fact that she had it and that her mum had it. She also always talked about this man called Jeffery and that he spoke to dead people. She told me that if there was a funeral and he was walking past, he would be able to chat to the person that had just died. I never met Jeffery funnily enough. I do wonder now if he ever existed. I remember telling her about what I had seen coming out of the bedroom floor and that then instigated her to tell me that I had a psychic power. I never really took that all too seriously. Although, when you have your mum talking about it enough and asking you if you see things, you start to believe that you do see things. Or was it just a figment of my imagination that would run away with itself? I never did have another experience like that in the bedroom and now that I am older, I do wonder if she had spiked me with something that made me hallucinate, which is probably more to the point!

When we lived at Noble Close, Wallisdown she did try in her own way to teach us about money and saving. We had 50p pocket money at the weekend. Me and Leigh would race around to the Spar and get as many sweets as we could with that 50p. She did ask, "Why don't you try to save 10p a week and spend the rest on sweets?" We tried but we were both rubbish at it!

She sat me down around nine or ten and drew a vagina and explained what was going to happen. I thought, 'What the hell she going on about?' We then had to watch a documentary on how babies were made and born. Leigh was definitely not paying attention and I just thought again, 'I don't get it!'

I don't remember me and Leigh fighting much at Noble Close. I remember us playing a lot when we were left on our own, playing camps. We were always building camps; it is amazing how we never hurt ourselves. We were too busy belting down the stairs in the sleeping bags, me dressing him up as Adam and the Ants. I thought it would be a good idea to put nail varnish across his face to have the lines like Adam from the Ants!

I used to get him on the end of the couch and would throw him across the couch like superman using my arms and legs to launch him, which was always great fun. We did find a guitar, bad move really! We were using it as a bridge from the sofa to the floor, funnily enough it snapped! That was very quickly put back in the bag and back behind the sofa. We never spoken of it again, until it was found. Of course, neither one of us knew anything about it!

I have a flashback of preparing dinner; I would do that quite a bit. The gas oven I would have to light with a bit of burning paper with a flame. I would have to put the gas on and stick my head inside the oven to light it! I would have been around nine or ten!

Chopping up onions, they were always really strong back then. I was only thinking the other day how onions don't make me cry as much as they did back then! Why are they not so strong these days? My eyes couldn't take it. I thought it would be a good idea to put a snorkel mask on to protect them. Mum and Leigh came through the back door to find me preparing dinner with the snorkel mask on. Mum asked, "What are you doing?" I said, "Peeling the onions!"

She did have real moments of really caring for us, I suppose but it was fraught with instability that only got worse as we got older. You just never knew what you were coming back to and I honestly feel that she just didn't really like us in the end.

She would always show me her body and say "LOOK, LOOK AT WHAT YOU HAVE DONE TO ME!" I thought well, it's not my fault I was a big baby. I was huge apparently. For her size anyway, 5ft at best and I was 9lb 3ozs. I think maybe a little heavier. She gave birth to me naturally. Apparently, she said that she strained every muscle in her body. She then proceeded to blame me for all her stretch marks and the way she had been left. How was that my fault?

Leigh was a handful. I think we were both a handful but we needed stimulation. We never had that and when you don't get it, you get up to trouble because you are looking for stuff to occupy yourself with. Leigh would drink neat squash. Back in the 70s, that stuff was loaded with all sorts of E numbers that would send him through the roof. She had to stop buying it. I also remember he used to work his way through a bag of sugar in no time (sugar sandwiches: white bread, butter and granulated sugar poured over the butter, yum!). She bought a bag of brown sugar and said to me she had to find a way to stop him getting through so much of it. She bought the brown sugar knowing that he would do the same and that it would give him the shits! It did! She said that little shit is upstairs shitting, he won't be eating too much of that anymore!

I suffered terribly with shyness growing up. It can still crop up from time to time now. I don't know where the shyness came from for me or what was a trigger for it. I know that it was debilitating. I loved to dance. I would put my Nan's kitten heels on and pretend to tap dance in the kitchen before school, so funny. That was pretty much every morning! Mum took me to a ballet class. I couldn't do it, I just couldn't join in. What stopped me, why? An overriding sense of fear, fear of failing, fear of people laughing at me, fear of not being good enough!

Mum took both me and my brother to judo classes as well as a kid, I hated that too! I always ended up with the big boys and felt like they were laughing at me. Again, I just did not feel good enough to be there. That has carried through the whole of my life. Just not being good enough at anything!

I started going to Kempo at the YMCA with a friend. I did not hate that. I looked forward to it. But like most things, mum didn't have enough money for kit and the ongoing costs of continuing the training, so that was the end of that. I wonder if she agreed with it. I remember telling her when I was sixteen years old, I wanted to do kick boxing. She questioned it. It was a boys' sport, which is funny really because she was a 5ft articulated lorry driver! She squashed that idea in no time.

I wasn't shy when it came to my athletics. I wasn't shy when it came to playing netball in junior school. Maybe because I knew I was all right at it. I'd been validated by the schoolteacher Mrs Carpenter, who'd said I was good enough to be in the A team, which I could not believe. Me. I was good enough for the A team? Goal defence 'GD'; I was good at it as well. I would meet women in town in my twenties and they would say, "I remember you! I played netball against you! You were tough!" I took my position and competition very seriously even as a ten-year-old girl. P.E. at school was everything to me. I remember forgetting my kit one day in junior school — I would have been nine. I couldn't believe it, what an idiot! I started crying and the teacher said it was okay and that I shouldn't worry. But she didn't understand, it was my joy! I LOVED P.E. It meant everything to me.

At infant school, you would always find me doing running races with the boys. I LOVED RUNNING RACES… I would run as fast as I could which would mean sometimes losing my feet from underneath me and face planting on the concrete floor, face all smashed up and gammy!

Mum's response was, "Look at you! What have you been up to now?" There was never a compassionate response, not disgust either but not a caring one, just inconvenience, yeah, inconvenience.

I remember making it into the school play in infant school. The Three Little Pigs. I was the wise pig with the brick house. I never told her about it. Never mentioned anything. Don't you think that's strange? I would have been six or seven years old. I was having a great time. We were taken over to the school dining hall and given tomato soup and a big bread roll and I just got on with my position in the play. Apparently, I hadn't come home on the bus, so she was looking for me. Mum ended up at the school and there I was on the stage doing my bit. So weird, why didn't I tell her?

Dad's input was nothing. I mean nothing. The Child support agency wasn't around then and he certainly didn't dip into his pocket any time soon, to help with the costs of bringing up two children. We were lucky enough to get a phone call at least once or twice a year telling us how much he loved us. What a complete loser. We would be so excited speaking to him.

You realise as you get older about the lack of input. The calls were to nurse his own guilt. He contributed NOTHING: money, guidance, love, overall parenting. NOTHING!

One year my Dad had called. He had asked Leigh what he wanted for his birthday, Leigh would have been six or seven. Leigh specifically asked for a, "BMX, Dad!"! "Okay son!" I don't know how the conversation went but Leigh was expecting a BMX bike. Around his birthday he got up every morning and watched the postman come up our path waiting for a delivery; NOTHING! Nothing came, no card, no sorry son, no phone call, no wish you a happy birthday, nothing! He did that every day for two weeks at least until he gave up looking for the postman. Who does that without any remorse? Who does that and then when he gets round to calling again says, "I love you two, I've always loved you, you know?"

These memories stay with you but as children you forgive, you never forget but you do forgive. Because you hope the next time round, this will be the time. Yes, he's phoned again, yes, we do mean something, yes it will be different this time.

This is what happens. NOTHING, nothing is different, everything is the same. He has nothing to offer other than the same behaviour than before. The same selfish behaviour he has displayed time and time again. It takes you until you get to your adulthood to recognise the repeated selfish behaviour and to stop looking for the parent you want him to be.

All you want is your Dad to be your Dad and love you enough, to just be there for you. Words are cheap and they mean nothing.

He appeared one Christmas, 1982. The year E.T. came out at the cinema. I remember because he bought Leigh an E.T. woolly hat. Dad tried to take us to the movies to see E.T., but the line was humongous! That was the end of that. He took us round the shops instead. I talked him into a Barbie and some super, dangly earrings. I remember him giving us a massive bag of presents. Of course, we were excited, what kids aren't excited about a big bag of presents? But do you know what, the presents mean nothing. I do not remember one of the gifts. All kids want is time! Time doing anything! Reading, playing, talking, hanging out. The material shit means nothing!

I don't remember anything else from that Christmas. I know the following year we were shipped off to the United States for Christmas, now that was an adventure!

Me, eleven years old and Leigh would have been eight and a half years old, flying across the Atlantic by ourselves. Never been on an aeroplane before, flying solo, two kids, eleven hours! Would you do that? I don't think I would feel comfortable letting my kids fly on their own that young. The poor guy sat next to us; we fought the whole way over. Leigh couldn't sit still, up, down, up, down, blankets, drinks, he was out the back with the flight attendants the whole way! I have some precious books that were given to me by my Nan that I have kept all these years. One of them is The Jungle Book. Inside is written: -

Christmas 1983

To Janine, lots of love Nan.

I decided to take it with me. I have never read the book but in the back of the book, I decided I would start to write about the trip. The following is what I wrote in the back of the book. The spelling is as I wrote it then on the plane going to America:

*At the airport and setting off.*

*We woke up at 4am in the morning and got dress set off at 5.00 in morn. Took us 2 hours and five mins to get to HEATHROW. We had a look around and at 9.15 we had to leave I nearly started crying. When we got going my stumock up turned and I felt horrible. BUT GOOD SO FAR.*

*LEIGH AT THE START HE WAS ANNOYING HE KEPT ON HITTING ME AND WOULDN'T LEAVE ME ALONE. BUT HE IS ALRIGHT NOW.*

*We are in America and have to land at losangly's. Then get going to San Francisco. We are have a movie now.*

It's funny seeing my young handwriting. I can just about take myself back to that flight. It was scary. I did not like landing in Los Angles, I remember starting to feel very sick when we had to take off again to fly to San Francisco. It was all just very disorientating.

We stayed with the Mapa's. That was the family my Dad had married into. The house was in San Jose and the house was like a mansion in comparison to the council house we had come from. I was amazed at the double front doors they had and the stone staircase that led up to a balcony that overlooked their sitting room.

I had a Walkman at the time. I was plugged into Wham very loudly and got told off for it by Mr Mapa. "Turn that thing down!" I loved Wham; the only way to listen to them was very loudly!

I remember not spending a lot of time with Dad, he continued to work. Nothing stands out, other than the trip to TOYS R US. Oh, my goodness, it was HUGE. I wanted a Cabbage Patch Doll; they were all the rage back then. But I couldn't get one of those, so of course the next best thing was cheerleader pompoms. One red, one blue. I spent my time prancing around with them.

I also remember my dad telling me to change my clothes. Adamantly, I said, "NO I don't want to." He then tried to reinforce it. "Go change your top." I said, "NO," again. I liked

48

what I had on and that was that.

I know that I am super stubborn and once I have made my mind up about anything, you will not move me, not one bit.

His response was, "You're just like your mother!" I didn't care at that point. I was wearing what I was wearing and that was that!

Oh yeah, the trip to the Natural History Museum in San Francisco, I remember that… I saw a two headed snake! It was real, I told my biology teacher about it in senior school. In front of the whole class, he told me it was nonsense, told me not to be so ridiculous, humiliated me in front of my friends. I know what I saw though. It was a two headed snake and it was real!

Of course, in the US we were showered with gifts, what kid doesn't love that? But all you ever want is time; the gifts come and go, they mean nothing. What are you going to remember, the time your mum and dad spent with you or the gifts you got when you were a nipper?

We phoned my mum on New Year's Day, I was excited to speak to her. We were telling her everything we had seen. They had cable channels. There was a box on top of the T.V. A and B, you would switch it to either and get soooooo many T.V. programs I couldn't believe it! We were still on three channels back home: BBC 1, 2 and Granada, that switched off at night. America had T.V. all night long! As we went to say goodbye, it would seem that we couldn't get mum to put the phone down. I didn't really understand what was happening. Mr Mapa was shouting Jane. Jane put down the phone to get her attention. This went on for a little while. I think they just put the phone down in the end and hoped my mum would do the same.

My mother told me when I was around thirteen that she had tried to commit suicide and that she was unconscious for two or three days. What parent tells their daughter that? She can't have been unconscious for that long anyway; she would have been dead. But, as a thirteen-year-old I took it on board. I'm not sure that I felt anything but that type of information resonates with you. Tucks itself away in your psyche, moulds you and stays with you.

Granny came out to the USA when we were there, my Dad's Mum. The funny thing is, my mum had done a good number on us not liking her and she was always known as horrible Gran, why? Why did she do that? From what I can remember, Granny was never horrible to us but we had been brainwashed into thinking that she was horrible Gran. Mum always referred to her as horrible Gran and said that she would end up a lonely, old woman, all on her own.

Gran was from Aberdeen; she was funny and cheeky and loved us kids. We just didn't know it, we just thought, yeah, you're horrible Gran!

Granny made homemade fudge. Oooooo… it was like eating sugar velvet and it was so good! She had made a load and it was in the garage cooling down. Of course, me and Leigh were always up to mischief and individually we were out in that garage chipping off pieces from the outside because we couldn't wait. She would ask both me and Leigh. "Oi, you two rascals, you stealing the fudge?" Of course we would deny it but our little faces gave everything away. She knew, never really scolded us but in a cheeky way told us to stay away from it, otherwise we'd get none! The fudge consisted of two blocks of butter, condensed milk, sugar and vanilla essence… melt in your mouth, sugary dream; it was the best!

After Dad had left us, we still had a good connection with Granny and Grandad. I loved Grandad. Grandad Chick, he was the best. Always playing with us; Snap was the favourite. I always cheated to win. He would always reprimand me for it as well. I would laugh my head off and continue with the cheating. Granny had a piano, keyboard, electronic piano thing that had all kinds of beat buttons on it. I was always on it, trying to play Chopsticks and press all the beat buttons, with no sense of beat to it.

At one point, Granny and Grandad had a dairy farm out in Cranbourne. I loved going out there. We were always playing in the barn and being told not to. Climbing in the hay, finding eggs. Petting the cows, getting up with Grandad in the morning and walking the fields to the other farms either side. It didn't matter what I was doing, I was hanging out with my Grandad. The cows scared me if I'm honest, they were huge compared to my little eight-year-old frame but I was with Grandad, so I was all right!

Granny reared a goose egg and Donald was born! He was better than any guard dog you could have and the only person he liked was Granny. One year we were out on the farm and it had snowed. Me and Leigh were out in the snow making a massive snowball. I was pottering along and thought Freedom the dog was fussing around me, so I shushed him away without looking. It turned out it was Donald and he was having none of that! He got hold of my kneecaps with that razor-sharp beak and was not letting go. I started screaming and Grandad like a superhero, got hold of Donald and flung him as far away from me as he could; I was safe. I loved Grandad! I had massive blood blisters on both kneecaps from that bloody bird.

When I get hungry, I get angry, my tummy hurts and I can't think straight if I go without food for too long a time. I have always been like this, right from a baby. Apparently, so mum told me. The nurses had to give me sugar water when I was fresh out of the womb. I was hungry! That hasn't changed through the whole of my life. I need to be fed regularly! I would ask Gran, "What's for tea Gran?" She would always tell me, "Shit for nosey!" So, funny! As a young girl, I thought it was eggy bread because every time she replied with that, we would have eggy bread. I would skip around the cottage singing, "Shiff for noseys, shiff for nosey!" I loved eggy bread, no mind to me. Of course, in her Scottish accent, it was, "Shit for nosey parkers." I loved my Gran.

Unfortunately for me and Leigh, Grandad had a massive heart attack when I was eight and didn't survive. He was the driving force behind us keeping contact with the whole side of my Dad's family. Granny and Grandad would turn up at the infant school to make sure that they saw us. Now he was gone, that was the end of that. Mum started with her 'horrible Gran' campaign. Little by little, me and Leigh were isolated from Dad's side and Mum's side. We saw nobody and no one knew the extent of what was happening to both of us. Mum had a very good front at looking like she was fun and caring on the outside. That's when you never truly know what is happening behind closed doors. No one believed us.

We would visit my Uncle Miles (my Dad's older brother) and Aunty Charlotte. We would visit them regularly. They had a tiny flat in Boscombe. Thinking about it, it was a bedsit really. My Uncle Miles was into Elvis. I was always pinching his Elvis badges, I thought they were so cool. We were visiting one time and I got curious about the red wine that was in the fridge. I was obviously poking my nose around in the fridge looking for food! I don't know how it came about but I had asked for some of this wine and they gave it to me. If I rightly remember I had quite a lot. I know I ended up feeling very dizzy and lightheaded. DRUNK! I was eight, what was that all about? I still don't like wine to this day. Maybe that was the reason for it.

Miles and Charlotte moved from that small flat to a bigger house off Castle Lane. We rode our bikes down there one time. It would have been two or three miles back from their house to Wallisdown. One of the bikes got a flat tyre so we had to walk back with it. It was really late, had to be past 10 p.m. and the sky was really clear. Mum started to tell me all about the different constellations, which was a pretty cool bonding moment. Just a little bit of light in amongst the dark!

Anyway, they upped and moved away, I think back to Sheffield where Aunty Charlotte was from, so that was the end of that connection.

My Mum said some terrible things about my Uncle Miles as well. She said he had to move because of a connection to messing around with kids. I thought at the time that's weird. But what do you do when it is coming from your mum? You take it on board and don't think about it again. But that family connection was dissolved. One less person to have on mine and Leigh's side growing up.

I found out many years later, at my Gran's funeral that I went to, that Miles and Charlotte had tried to take us. They said, "We'll have the kids." They could see my Mum didn't really want us and Dad was long gone. My Mum said, "No way, keep away from my kids."

She didn't want us but she sure as hell wasn't going to let any of the family take us either. Maybe that's where the story about Uncle Miles came from, to turn us against them.

After we returned from the USA, the connection with

Dad's side of the family broke down completely really. I only saw Gran on one occasion and even then, I was so brainwashed into thinking she was a horrible person I had no time for her. I feel bad and angry and ashamed of my behaviour. But again, what do you do when it is your mum? You believe her. I also found out at Gran's funeral that she had a treasure box by her bed at all times. In that box were pictures of me and Leigh as kids. I mean, what the fuck? Why would one person want to do that? My mum didn't love us and she was going to make sure that no one else was going to love us, that was for sure!

We were often taken to see doctors of some sort when we were living at Noble Close. Special doctors, I think. I know we were taken out of school for it. I assume we were being assessed and mum was asked questions about our development. I know me and Leigh used to just play and amuse ourselves whilst we were there. We went there a lot. Thinking about it as an adult, was she being assessed and watched? I know social services were involved as we grew up. Were they involved when we were younger? She told me that the doctor would ask how I got hurt when we would go and see him. Later on, in my teenage years she told me that Dad had picked me up at some point in a fit of rage and threw me across the room. I apparently hit my head against the wall; I don't remember any of that! It would be interesting to see my doctor's notes as a young child. I have the biggest dent in the top of my head, it's really big. Is that a childhood injury or just the way my head developed, who knows?

Mum did get involved in single parent groups. We would go camping in the local area and do social stuff but that never lasted too long. She just never maintained friendships for very long. We had one holiday as a family when we lived at Noble

Close. A caravan holiday to Wales. She bought the current boyfriend; he was an absolute prick! Me and Leigh made it our mission to torment him as much as possible, especially when he was taking a poo in the outside toilet that we had to use when we were set up on a farmer's land. We would be shouting kid's things through the cracks in the door to torment him. He didn't like it. He would start yelling at us to go away. That just made fuel for the fire because we knew we were getting to him.

I had a falling out with the boyfriend on this holiday. We were probably having words. He was barking out some orders that I didn't like. I think I had probably slapped him first. I was nine, how hard could it be on a grown man? Open palm. He walloped me, left his handprint on me, leg or arm I can't remember, not the face which is a blessing I suppose but I hated him, that was for sure. Dick!

I do remember that they had both been out and me and Leigh were at home on our own as usual. There was a massive thunderstorm. Mum would love to go out and watch the thunderstorms at the beach. She was obviously feeling guilty because she came back and got both me and Leigh. The storm was pretty big, I suppose it can be kind of scary. If I rightly remember, we would just take ourselves upstairs and curl up with the dog, who was petrified of storms. He'd got lost in one, that's another story! So, I would curl up with my Bruno to keep him feeling safe under the bed.

Mum always smoked and the boyfriend smoked as well. It was horrible to be around. Another thing you get used to because you don't know any different. Nothing worse than having your mum say, "Come here," and spit her smoky, horrible breath onto a tissue and use it to wipe your face. Both me and Leigh hated it. Spit and wipe the face, why? I do not want your gammy, faggy saliva all over my face!

Anyway, me and Leigh were in the back of a car during a trip and both of them were smoking. All the windows closed. I could barely catch my breath. You were too afraid to ask to open the window. So, I made myself as small as possible on the back seat and tried to search for an airway where I could catch a bit of freshness. I fucking hate smoking! It is a horrible addiction that has no worth to it. It stinks and still to this day I cannot bear it in my face. That isn't to say that as a teenager I didn't do it. What did I know? Everyone was doing it around me. But I saw sense and ejected that from my life very early on. Horrible. When I see parents smoking with their young kids, I feel sorry for them. For the kids. They haven't asked for it but are being exposed to it anyway.

I don't remember what happened to him. Probably wanted shot of us two. He certainly wasn't interested in bothering with me and Leigh. One day he was gone and that was that. GOOD, HE WAS A DICK!

After the USA trip I was moving up to secondary school. I was getting older and bigger. I needed a bigger room apparently. To be honest, my frame would have outgrown that box room I was in. I don't know how she did it but she got us moved into a brand, new build. A three-bedroom house in East Howe, Pearl Gardens. That was where it really started to change. The behaviour from her just deteriorated!

Or maybe I was growing up and was just understanding more of what was happening to both of us.

# Chapter Two
# Gribet

It was exciting being in a new house, my own room big enough with a proper sized bed. A bedside cabinet and it had a built-in cupboard for all my clothes. We were allowed to choose a colour for our rooms. I chose baby blue paint, with a baby blue patterned wallpaper. It was our job to decorate our own rooms. I thought it was fun. I like the process of starting a project and seeing it through to the end, even though I did not have a clue about the wallpaper but I got the job done! I liked it. I was eleven years old. I was in my own room and it was big enough to swing a cat around in it. Leigh on the other hand, was not that one bit interested in that process at all. He had a bed, bedside table and dark brown wardrobe. When Mum had asked if he had finished in his room, he said, "Yes," and was out the house like a shot. Playing outside was far more interesting than painting his room. On inspection he had painted around everything. Nothing had been taking down or moved out. Bright green, all round his curtains, around the bed frame, around the wardrobe, painted the wardrobe door (obviously had a creative moment then). It was so funny. When you moved the curtains there was a beautiful line where he had painted around them. So, that was that. Leigh's room done and that's how it stayed.

Pearl Gardens is where we had moved to in East Howe. It was a small cul-de-sac with maybe twelve houses in it. We soon realised that the kids and teenagers in this area were not like the ones we were friends with in Noble Close in Wallisdown. No sooner had Leigh got his go-cart out, the kids from Pearl Road and Sunningdale Crescent which was round the corner from Pearl Gardens, were round sniffing about and causing trouble. Bullying the little kids off the go-cart along with Leigh and then proceeded to destroy it, smashed it up! Leigh was devastated. You quickly realised that you had to toughen up.

All the Kingsleigh schools (nursery, annex, infant, junior and senior) were in the same road, Hadow Road. When we moved to Pearl Gardens it was great because it was a ten-minute walk up the road. No more three-mile hikes to school. The friends at Noble Close didn't all go to Kingsleigh, I can't remember where they went. But the kids in East Howe did. There was no let up from getting away from them. At school, follow you home, in your road, living a few doors down!

The bullying and name calling started pretty early on for me. Junior school I got laughed at for having boy's legs. I suppose because of all the sprinting I was doing, the quads were developing and looking more developed than some of the young girls at school. I also got referred to as a Jamaica woman. Mum told me that when I was born, she said, "Oh my, she's got a tan!" Olive skin, I think. In the summer I do go pretty dark. Leigh does too, which is unusual because he has blonde hair and blue eyes. I have light brown hair with green eyes. Mum doesn't have olive skin at all and Dad has bright red hair, blue eyes and fair skin. So, who did we inherit the skin from? I do not know. It used to really bug mum. She would sit out in the sun, go bright red and then be the same insipid colour the following day. Every year growing up she would always say,

"Look at the colour of you!" in the most disproving manner. Another reason not to like us. Jealous, bitter, who knows?

Going to senior school at Kingsleigh was fraught with all sorts of unkindness. If you were a little bit different you were singled out. The older boys were horrible. Even the teachers did not want to get involved with them. They pretty much did whatever they wanted to. Most of those boys came from West Howe, they were not nice!

From what I understand, West Howe was built in the 50s to house the travellers. Put them in one area. Mum used to live the other side of East Howe Lane, the better side! She said she used to ride over to West Howe as a kid and go down what use to be called West Howe Lane. Kids were running around barefoot, there were burnt out cars in the road, front doors of the houses hanging off, just carnage everywhere. It was rough! If the kids didn't go to Oakmead School, which was right off that estate, they went to Kingsleigh. The school was rough! The teachers were burnt out as well. Most of them had been there since the late 40s. I know some of them had taught my mum's older brother, right the way through to my mum and her younger brother. Any of the school friends I bump into now, will tell you the same as me. The school was diabolical. They did not care.

One day I was in the playground, just minding my own business, daydreaming on my own. It had been snowing and I would say there was a good twenty inches on the ground or more. There was definitely enough on the ground for the older fifth year boys to single me out, trip me up and bury me in the snow. There had to be about six of them kicking snow over me. Whilst it might sound funny, it's not, trust me. Having your legs taken out from underneath you by surprise for no reason, when you are twelve years old and then being buried in the snow by boys that are sixteen, not knowing when it's going to finish is not 'FUN'!

I got called 'gribet 'a lot. That started quite early on moving into East Howe and at senior school. I apparently have big eyes. So, the gribet is associated to frog eyes, 'gribet, gribet'. To be honest, I am not a petite person. I was bigger than most of my peer group and at twelve years old, that would have been another thing to being different to other kids at school I suppose. Anyway, there was this local boy. I did not like him. He was mean. He had come round into Pearl Gardens. I was playing with some friends on our roller skates. He didn't have any on, so I told him he couldn't play. I didn't want him to play. He was much older than us anyway, fifteen or sixteen. He referred to me as 'gribet' and kept on saying it. I suppose I bought it on myself but I didn't like him. I told him if he called me that again I was going to hit him. I was twelve, what was I going to do? But he was picking on me, so I had to back myself up. He said it again, so I thought, 'Shit, I better go and sort him out'! I went over and punched him on the arm. I don't know why the arm? I felt bad punching him in the face! He then cracked me in the face and took off running. I chased after him on the roller boots. We are now scuffling in the road outside my house. It was all a bit chaotic. I realised he had got up and I was trying to get myself back to my feet. My hand wouldn't work; it wouldn't take any weight. I finally got myself around and looked at my arm. My forearm was at a ninety-degree right angle. I started to scream and scream and scream. It turns out that a neighbour had been at the window putting her kid to bed when she saw the whole thing. She saw him stand up and stamp on my arm! Broke both bones. It turns out there was a lot of abuse happening in his house. He ended up in foster care because of that incident. I got compensation; I think around £1500. Mum did say that she was going to put it into a trust fund or something. I could have it when I was eighteen. I used to daydream about it. I would try and figure out how much interest it was earning and how much I would get. Of course, it was never put into anything. She used the money to pay for her HGV licence. You could say that was a good thing because she would be in a better paid job, so that we had more. That just wasn't the case.

The slow trickle of her giving up as a parent started happening around the age of twelve to thirteen. I was marched up to the local newsagent at twelve. "She needs a job!" "She's too young, come back when she's thirteen." At thirteen years old, I was told that was that. You work, you earn money because she was providing nothing from now on. There is tough love but isn't that just a bit extreme?

So, that was the start of the work ethic; I had two paper rounds. One in the morning walking round the East Howe neighbourhood and one in the evening walking round West Howe. I hated them! What other choice did I have? I had to do them!

As for her job as a truck driver, she was a driving instructor before the truck driving; she was earning good money with that. She did keep a roof over our head I suppose but then she had to do that for herself anyway. I saw the truck driving as a means to spend as much time away from me and Leigh as possible. She was never home. She would leave the house at about three or four p.m. and then get back around eighty-ish in the morning.

Being referred to as a boy or a man started very early on

in junior school and continued on into secondary school. Mum said to me one day, "You need to change your walk!" I said, "What?" "You need to change your walk, you walk funny!" I thought to myself, 'How do I change my walk? My walk is my walk, if I change my walk, I'll look weird!' I didn't change my walk; I never really knew what she was referring to if I'm honest. Although, there was this boy, Craig, in the fifth year that used to hang out in our area. He was from West Howe. He really wasn't a nice person and would regularly have it in for you in one way or another. I think he may have asked me out. I probably thought he was joking as I never thought anyone was interested in me. I didn't think I was attractive enough for anyone to fancy me. I may have said, "Ah, no you're all right," or, "No that's disgusting!" He had hair like pubes and a big, black, front tooth; I was not one bit interested in him at all.

That is the only reason I can think that he took to following me home from school every day for eighteen months, singing, "She walks like a man, she talks like a man," in my ear. I have tried to understand it over the years and the only reason I can think of is because I rejected him. All because I rejected him. If I rightly remember I just used to walk down the road and let him get on with it. I didn't like it but if you ignore a person long enough, they go away. I HATED HIM.

If you decided to walk through the school field to get home, you were basically asking for trouble. I don't know why I just didn't walk the long way round. I would see the older boys playing football, the pube hair boy would be in that group. I would see them and think if I move fast enough, they won't see me. I was a nothing, why would they want to bother with me? Wishful thinking on my part! Before you knew it, a football booted straight at your head. They would all be laughing. I hated them too. They would have been the same boys that buried me in the snow! Why me? Why was I singled out?

God forbid if they found out it was your birthday at school! The tunnel of death, there was no way out of it. Two long lines of kids. You would be cornered in at one end and you would have to run through, whilst they punched, kicked and anything else they could do until you came out the other end. Thankfully I never got that.

There was a local youth club that use to be at The Annex, that was the first school I went to. I still don't understand that school, maybe it was reception? Who knows? It was turned into a youth club and quite regularly pube hair boy and one of the other shithead boys would be up there tormenting me. I was referred to as trap jaw from HE- Man. I never understood that one either.

I was walking into school one day. There was a gangway to walk up and you could walk past the games huts. They were pretty big. The whole of one side had been covered with pornographic pictures of vaginas, women with their legs spread open and boobs. I mean you name it, it was up there. Written in big capital letters across the pornography was, 'JANINE WISHES'. I don't remember crying or being too upset about it. I did however think, 'I'm going to get you!' I did go back to the huts one evening, not long after it had happened. I drew some legs with an asshole, wrote Craig's name and said that he took it up the arse! I felt satisfied with my comeback! I got caught by the local policeman that night. He asked me if I had done that. I said "No!" He asked what my name was. I gave him a fake name. I was with my mate Michelle. She looked really nervous but kept her mouth shut and followed my lead. He just sent us on our way.

When I reflect on myself as a teenager and a young adult, I just thought I was a pig. Not attractive, not worth anything. Certainly, didn't think anyone would be interested in me. The drip, drip of name calling and the association to being like a man did have an effect on me as a young woman.

Whilst I had that inside torment going on with myself, I did just get on with things. I don't suppose you have any other choice really, other than starting to abuse yourself; like so many young adults do. Self-harm, anorexia, drugs, drink. I would ignore the older boys as much as I could. Try to stay out of the way of getting that football kicked at my head! The boys of my year group, I would generally beat up if they were annoying me. I would get out of my chair, walk round to where they were and wallop them as hard as I could, on the arm! I would then casually walk back to my desk and get on with my work. The girls left me alone as well! I somehow seemed to hold my own. I got a reputation as being tough. I never really understood that one, because I didn't think that I was.

There is a story of me in junior school where Mum had come up to see the headmaster (the perv!). She could see me from the reception. I was sat at the back of the class. She saw me telling off some boys in front of me. Apparently, I got my ruler and was hitting them side to side with it on their shoulders. I then saw the teacher, told on them and they got told off! When the teacher turned away, I then gave them another what for. If I rightly remember, they were being annoying! Stealing stuff off the table, just wouldn't leave me alone. So, I sorted them out. She sat in reception watching this, amused.

I was bullied a bit in junior school by a girl who had

decided to single me out for not having a dad. I don't remember the ins and outs but it did get to a place where I did not want to go to school. Mum said, "Right! I've had enough of this! If anyone starts on you, you give them what for, you wallop them!" I thought, 'Right, okay'. So, this girl had been giving me a hard time and we were out in the playground. I just so happened to be right in her path, so I tripped her up; clipped her feet out from underneath her. She fell and landed face first and chipped her tooth. I skipped off satisfied with a good job done. She left me alone after that. In fact, going into senior school she was part of the girl group I used to hang out with.

Back into senior school there was this boy in my registration class. He was SO ANNOYING. I'm not sure why but one day when we had just come back from lunch, I had my head resting in my hands on the table. This boy decided to seek me out and wallop his school bag on the top of my head! WHY? I stood up and thought, 'Right, I'll get you!' Once the registration was done, I sharked my way through the kids to get outside to find him. I got my bag which had really sharp corners, swung it high above my head and nailed it right round his nut. Floored him! He was on the floor crying, holding his head in his hands. I ran off as fast as I could. I had no comeback. He left me well alone after that.

Another boy in my peer group who use to annoy me on a regular basis, thought it would be funny to call me 'nigger' one day. Like I have said, my skin can go pretty dark in the summer. We were in a metalwork session. He was on the opposite side of the table we were working on. I told him to hold his hand out on the table. The idiot did it, so I hit him with the hammer on the back of his hand. It sounds pretty awful when I tell the story, hitting someone with a hammer. But it was do or die in that school. I then went and told the teacher that he called me a 'nigger'. He was told to get out of the class and wait outside.

He recently found me on Facebook and sent me a message: 'Fancy a fuck!'. What an absolute dickhead. I said, 'It's nice to see that you're still the knob-head you were at school!' I did not friend him!

Moving forwards a couple of years from the Facebook contact, he found me again on a dating website. His message to me: 'Always fought...' (fought! spelt with an F, I mean come on) '... you was a lesbian. Hi, how are U, only playing, LOL.'

Uneducated, abusive, racist, misogynistic asshole!

I deleted my profile. I did not respond. When does the abuse stop?

My girl-friendship group at school somehow was good enough to become Prefects. I don't know how I managed that but we were certainly not part of the goody group that was getting work done. We were a handful and I certainly had an attitude about me. I was angry and cooperation was not always part of my agenda.

Slowly but surely mum just gave up. We were on our own more and more once she had become a lorry driver. She worked night shifts, leaving early afternoon and not getting back sometimes until after we had left for school in the morning. We had to get on with it. I don't know how it came about but we had this Social Worker that used to come and visit us. I was around thirteen. I thought it was great because I would challenge Mum's made-up stories about me and Leigh. The Social Worker would tell her that the behaviour was not right. Mum would sit there and just berate me and Leigh, make us out to be the worst children ever. I thought, 'No way, I'm not having that!' I would say, "That's not true," and I would relay the story as it actually happened. It was great! Then the Social Worker was gone. She couldn't come any more so that was the end of that. Social Services didn't replace her, we were just left to get on with it. Homework, schoolwork, anything I had to take to school, reports, she just wasn't bothered. I never had any food to take to school for cookery class. Teacher would always ask the same thing, "Where are your ingredients?" I would answer in an attitude because I was embarrassed that we didn't have enough money for the food to bring in, "I don't have any." I would then be pushed off to work with someone that had the ingredients. Teacher would huff!

Mum would be insistent on going into Oxfam when we were kids. I would dread it if I was out with her. My girl group would ridicule people with Oxfam clothes or jumble sale clothes. You would be ripped apart if anyone from school saw you going in there, you would get it! Most of our clothes were from Oxfam. I had to keep that well-hidden.

I got free school meals at school. In senior school I had to go and collect my tickets for the week on a Monday and hand one ticket in each day once I got my meal. They were worth £1. I would sell them and go hang out with my buddies at the fish and chip shop at lunch time. I did not want to sit on my own in the dining hall by myself. I wanted to be where the fun was, having a fag. The school found out about this. I had to go and sign for the tickets daily. Nothing changed, I would still sell them!

Sport was the only reason I would go to school. That and art; everything else could just do one. I wasn't thick but I just really didn't have an aptitude to want to learn or be bothered with anything else. There was no support at home and the behaviour from Mum was getting worse, so I had no respect for anyone in authority. But sport. I loved sport. I achieved outstanding achievements in P.E. three years on the trot. I still have the certificates. The school held a big assembly to collect the certificates. Mum never came to any of them; I went on my own to collect them.

The school would run after school athletics club. I would turn up eager to get on with practice and learn. Nobody, including teachers, would turn up. I would run around the field on my own doing my own practice. I would have loved to be part of an athletics club, but Kings Park where they had an athletics club was so far away from where I lived. Getting the bus over there would have been a nightmare. I had no money to get over there anyway, along with the fact that I did not have the confidence to go into a group on my own.

My trainers were always a shambles as well. I would be at town sports with trainers I had tried to glue together because they were falling apart. Some of the older girls were watching one time and called me over to swap shoes with one of them, so I had a better pair to run in. It was so demoralising. I still ran though whatever I had on my feet and I would still try to do my best.

One year I had really pushed for a pair of spikes. She had initially agreed. I was so excited. I knew with those on I would run faster and I would not have to wear my glued together trainers. It was the week before and I knew town sports was coming up. I was really pushing for these spikes. At the finale push she said, "NO." I lost it. I had never lost it like I lost it then. I was so upset. I lost it so bad, I was at Nan's. Maybe Nan backed me up a bit. She gave in and I got them. One battle achieved. I got my spikes. I was so happy. I was growing up as well. I was starting to challenge her.

At the age of fourteen, Mum decided I was having sex! I wasn't. I had no interest in boys. But she decided that I was so that was that. I was marched up to the doctors and put on the pill. I sat in that room with her stood in the corner. No privacy, or questions asked of what I wanted. The doctor was talking but I was not listening. I was thinking to myself, 'I don't know why I'm here. I'll check out the instructions when I get home.' He finished talking and said, "Do you understand?" I said, "Yes." I just wanted to get out of there. I got home and looked at the pack. It said, after your first pack take a seven-day break. So, I took the whole pack. It did not say after twenty-one days have a seven-day break. I took three months' worth of contraceptive pill. I still had a period. I didn't think anything was weird. Of course, I blew up from all the fluid being held in my body. My tits grew humongous. Mum, then told me I was pregnant! I wasn't. I wasn't even having sex! I knew enough to know that I needed to be having sex to get pregnant. She marched me back up to the doctors. We are all in the same room again. She just stood there, lips pursed together in the corner of the room, telling the doctor that I was pregnant. I said, "I am not!" She repeated, "She's pregnant!" I repeated, "I am not!" The doctor started to ask me questions and soon realised that I had been taking the pill wrong. He took me off it. I had to let my body settle back to normal for six months. My mum was a fucking idiot!

As I had ballooned, it did mean doing any kind of running was awkward. I didn't really have an issue with it until my teacher told me that I had to get a sports bra. All the boys would stand at the end of the 100m track and watch your boobs bob about as you ran down the track. It was embarrassing and you felt a little violated. So that was the end of that, I stopped trying. I was too self-conscious of them watching me run. I could not concentrate on winning. I never asked my mum and she certainly wasn't going to buy me a sports bra.

Around fifteen, the girl group I was hanging out with had started drinking, smoking and hanging out with boys from East Howe and West Howe. That was the demise of my sporting achievements at that time. We had started to venture into town as well. We were going to nightclubs at fifteen. We would get the last bus home. So bad. We would be trying to drink neat gin, vodka or whisky from the bottle. It always used to make me wretch. I didn't like it!

We were also as a group going into town and shoplifting stupid shit, like pens, pencil cases, mousse for our hair, suntan lotion. Just teenage, worthless, stupid shit! There were six of us all together one day in town. We all got caught. What were we thinking? A group of six teenage girls bumming around town. Not looking inconspicuous! The police collected us from the store in a meat wagon. Took us to the station. We were separated into cells. We had a mug shot taken. I refused to give my name. I knew Mum was going to kick the shit out of me. There was no way I was giving a name over. The police were getting frustrated with me. I dug my heals in and refused. I think I gave the name of the Social Worker that was coming round the house.

Eventually we were allowed to leave with a warning. I must have handed over my details in the end. Mum came to collect me. I'm not sure if the police had spoken to her but when we got into the car, she said to me, "Why not a TV or a video? Instead of all the stupid shit you were getting!" That was the end of that. My girl group all got grounded. I was left alone. Just carried on as normal. She wasn't around to enforce the grounding anyway!

Me and Chell, one of the girls from my peer group decided to go into town one night. Westover Road in Bournemouth in the 80s and 90s was like a racetrack. Cars would circle the block all night long. There was a wall outside The Pavilion Theatre that runs along the top part of Westover Road. A group of young teenagers was always hanging out around there causing trouble and getting up to no good. Me and Chell were walking past, when one of the young men beckoned us over. We went of course, curious of the group of guys. We ended up in the back of a car. One of the guys had asked if we wanted to come for a drive. We both agreed. Naïve, stupid idiots that we were. Before we knew it, we were flying around the back streets of Bournemouth. He must have been doing 60 plus. Driving straight through junctions without stopping. I honestly thought we were going to die. I said to Chell, "We need to get the fuck out of here." It was like he was playing chicken with a car full of kids. So fucking stupid. We did make it back. I got out of that car quick smart and we both did a runner as quick as we could. Famous saying, 'curiosity killed the cat', springs to mind.

I did try to start up my sport with the county netball team. They used to practice at the youth club I went to. I was curious, so I approached a woman and asked if I could come along. She told me to come to the school sports hall for a training session. I turned up, had a great session and never went back. I just didn't have the confidence and no one behind me telling me that I was good enough. That was the end of that.

The local newsagent next to the fish and chip shop as you

went into school, was selling singles to all the kids. Terrible. 10p a fag. We'd go in there and buy singles all the time. What hope did we have? Never mind about the people on the estate that were smoking weed in front of us. I would hang out at a neighbour's house and they would all be smoking weed in the front room from the age of twelve. Mum would buy it too. She would hide it behind the couch. Me and Leigh would find it and smoke it when she was out working.

Along with the neglect came the abuse. Leigh was still getting the stick. I was getting the psychological abuse. 'You're shit, you're no good, you need help, you're evil and you need to see a councillor'. That was pretty much all the time. She wouldn't speak to me for weeks on end as well. I never knew what I had done wrong.

One day she was losing her shit about something, we were summoned into the house. After she was done yelling, she said, "Get the stick," Leigh boldly said, "NO." I looked at him and then looked at her. She screamed, "GET THE STICK!" Leigh coolly said, "No." She dived into the cupboard under the stairs and was rampaging around in there looking for the sticks. Leigh looked at me with a big smile and said, "I've buried them in the garden!" So cool, I laughed! She came out all bedraggled and said, "Get out of my sight." We both thought, 'cool' and got out of there quick smart.

My mum in company was charming, funny and sociable. But me and Leigh knew who she was. It was hard getting other people to understand that.

As she was working nights and we were left to get on with it, we had free reign to do as we pleased. Leigh, at one point had put a tent up at the bottom of the garden and was staying in that. He would appear with bags of biscuits, sweets and pop;

you name it, he had it. I couldn't figure out where he was getting the money from. It turns out he was going house to house on a fund-raising scam! That soon ended when somebody figured it out and chased him down the road; he was eleven years old!

I was hanging out with the local, horrible mob who would end up in my house until god knows what time of night: three a.m. or four a.m. On occasion they would come round and just rampage in the back garden just because they could and mess all the shit up, just create havoc. I never really liked them; I don't know why I spent time with them

My girl group hung out with them, so I suppose I just followed. If we were not at my house, we would end up at houses in West Howe that belonged to one of the boys' parents. We were also hanging out in the local pubs. The Thatch or The Smugglers that were right smack bang in the middle of West Howe. It always had the police there for one reason or another. It was rough. I would be drinking lager and lime. I would then go through this whole charade when I got in to disguise the fact that I had been drinking. Mum never gave a shit; she was never that interested in what we were up to.

Some of the girls ended up dating some of the boys. I didn't like any of them or even had any wish to be with them. The girls were pretty promiscuous. They would end up all in the same room having sex. I didn't want anything to do with that, so would get out of there sharpish. I was still very shy. Maybe boys were interested in me, I just couldn't see it, or even want it.

There was this one guy. Tony. All the girls fancied him but for whatever reason he took a liking to me. I was, of course, amazed that he was even interested in me. I would bunk off school to go and hang out with him. I was fifteen, he was seventeen. I had never even kissed a boy at this point. I was so unbelievable shy that I just couldn't bring myself to do it. He would try and get me to kiss him but I just couldn't do it. What if I got it all wrong? I don't know what was stopping me. Of course, he went off me. I wasn't putting out. I made up this story about my dad abusing me and told him that's why I couldn't put out. What a terrible thing to say. The story of course was founded by my Mum, who had put the thought in my head. I thought there would be some kind of forgiveness for me, maybe a little bit of understanding for why I couldn't put out. Dad had never done that of course. I was looking for an escape root out of facing the truth; that I was ultimately terrified of failing.

We were all drinking and smoking weed quite regularly. We were at a party one night; I was probably fifteen. Drinking and smoking weed. Doing buckets: a bucket full of water and an empty two litre cola bottle with weed in it. It messed you up. Anyway, I thought, 'I've had enough. I'm going for a lie down'. I found a room upstairs and settled down for a sleep. What you don't understand when you are fifteen and stupid, is that there are predatory older men that are seeking out vulnerable young girls that don't know what is going on. This guy, I knew him, was from around the estate. He was 22! I wouldn't call him a friend. He found me in the room and before I knew it I was having sex. Did I say no? NO, I didn't. Did I really know what was happening? No, I didn't. I was drunk and high. Was I raped? I don't feel like I was but I know as an adult, I was taken advantage of and it was my own fault.

Of course I blame myself, I should never have been there. Had I not been there I would not have been taken advantage of. Those pieces of shit men that prey on young girls, they are never held accountable for their behaviour because of course, I was asking for it!

My first sexual encounter; horrible. I do tuck that one away as it fucking upsets me. It's not one of my proudest moments.

Mum didn't have a clue what was going on at all! She did say to me one day, "Don't you think it's time you had a boyfriend?" I said, "I don't want a boyfriend!"

Me and Leigh really fought when we lived at Pearl Gardens. Not just siblings shouting at each other, we were chasing each other round the house with screwdrivers, knives, forks, you name it! I would run through the door and shut it as fast as I could. When I opened it, the attacking utensils would be stuck in the door. He had punched the screwdriver in so hard that it created a massive hole! We knew we were in for it. So, we ran upstairs, took the bathroom door off and was going to swap it for the door we had damaged. We soon realised that the door wasn't going to fit, so put it all back into place and I decided I would take the rap for it. Leigh was going on a camping trip. We covered up the hole with all his packing. I got him out the house. I took the telling off.

When she was home, she would have complete irrational outbursts of anger. I could hear her downstairs smashing plates, cups and whatever she could get hold of against the wall. I never knew what that was about either. She had a boyfriend that I did not care for around the time I was fifteen. I thought that they were all dicks. But I was a teenager — I thought all adults were dicks! This particular boyfriend finished with her and she lost it. She went round his house with a hammer and beat his back door in. Got arrested for it. She then told me a story that with her mental powers she knew that he had placed a letter that she had written to him in his glove compartment in his truck. She willed it to catch on fire and it blew his truck up. I mean what the actual fuck! She would also tell me that she could put out streetlamps when she was driving home in her truck at night! She did go as far as telling me that she could move stuff around with her mind. This is what we were growing up with!

We would have very rare moments of mother and daughter togetherness; I had offered to do her hair. "I'll dry your hair mum." "Okay," she said. Then, it turned into a nightly job. Mum shouting my name from upstairs, "JANINE! HAIR." I then had to dry her hair every night. I did not want to do that. I purposely held the hairdryer on her head to burn it. Her response, "What the fuck are you doing? Go on fuck off!"

Satisfied with my job well done, I very quickly fucked off like she asked me too.

She was always either perming or highlighting her hair, something else I had to do with her. The perming was a nightmare. Those little bits of paper that had to go round the curlers. If I wasn't doing it right, I would get it. "What the fuck are you doing? Go on fuck off!" What would I have been, fourteen or fifteen? What the fuck did I know about putting in perming rollers? And those fucking highlighting caps with the crochet hooks. You would put a cap on that had pre-made holes that you would have to hook hair through. God help me if I wasn't doing that job properly either!

Cleaning round the house was a given. She would leave jobs for me and Leigh to do. Obviously, Leigh was not interested in doing his. So, I would do all of it, just to save the peace. We quite often had cat shit or puke and dog shit around the house that she would just leave with paper over it! Why didn't I clean it up? I would bring my friends in like it was normal behaviour.

I don't know how she managed it but she got Leigh sent off to the naughty boys' home, at Slades Farm. I don't even know why? It was bad! She told him if he didn't like it, he could come back. She had no intention of him coming back.

I was booted out of the house quite regularly from the age of about fourteen with nowhere to go. I just didn't know what to do or where to go. I can't remember why I just didn't go to my nan's. But for some reason, it just wasn't an option.

I don't even remember how it came about but she drove me round to a friend's house. She told the parents that she could no longer deal with me. I was in the living room hiding behind a massive house plant. I was so embarrassed. I just couldn't believe it. I was pretty good friends with the girl but I didn't know the parents at all. Mum put on such a convincing act as well. So, there I was left at this house that I did not want to be in, feeling the lowest of the low. The parents looking at me like I am scum. I was carted off to my friend's sisters house over in Bearwood. She had a spare room, if I rightly remember. I just held up in my room. I had no school uniform and I had to get to school from there. I don't remember those details. But I do remember turning up at school in just my jeans and T-shirt. I think I explained the situation to a teacher and then just tried to get on with my days. One teacher who I was delivering a message to, decided to pull me in front of the whole class and reprimand me for not having a uniform on. "Where is your uniform?" I told her to mind her own fucking business! As you can imagine I did not have a great deal of respect for any adult at this point!

Mum would then resurface and say, "I think we need to talk." Of course, you go along with it because she's your mum. She picked me up and we drove to a hole in the wall, got burgers, went down to Shore Road right by the beach and sat there talking. She was asking me all kinds of weird questions. She kept implying that I had suffered sexual abuse. I kept saying 'No, I didn't know what she was talking about.' She implied that my behaviour was a classic case of child abuse.

At that age I just didn't know what to make of it. Not long after that meet up, she said I could come back home. So off I went back home with 'MUM', back to the mad house because it was home and it was all I knew at the time.

I had asked her if I could go to The Academy, it was a nightclub in town. Acid house was huge then. All my friends were going. She asked what time I was going to be home. I said, "Two a.m." Surprisingly she agreed. She was out driving all night anyway. She would be back around six or seven a.m. So, it didn't matter what time I got back in. I went; it was really cool. Everyone was jumping around with the big, yellow acid house smiley face on their T-shirts and it was great. So, all my friends were going the following night as well. I thought, she's not going to know if I go or not so I went. Unfortunately for me she got home early. I was running round the road and saw her car in the drive. I thought, 'Shit, what am I going to do?'. I styled it out and went straight in. I said, "Sorry for being late!" It was three in the morning. She chased me up those stairs so fast and then proceeded to hurl whatever she could find at me: punches, shoes, clothes, whatever. I stood on my bed and held up my duvet as a shield. I mean what did it matter, she didn't give a shit and she was never there anyway?

I got thrown out again, not for the night club incident, I'm not sure what for. Maybe because I couldn't pay rent. Once again, I didn't know where I was going to go. I phoned a buddy of mine and went and stayed with her. The mum of the buddy was trying to get me to be an au pair. If I had been a bit older, I would have done it. I wasn't ready for that. I could barely look after myself, let alone look after someone else's kids in a foreign country! Thinking about it, I would have been fifteen or just turned sixteen. I was doing Y.T.S. (Youth Training Scheme). What an absolutely bag of shit that was. I ended up on that because a careers advisor told me I was not clever enough to become a P.E. teacher. 'I'm not clever enough' resonated with me well into my late thirties! I left school with no exams. I had a B in art. Grade 1 in English Language. I did turn up to the other exams. I just couldn't be bothered to engage. I had no application whatsoever at school. So, the careers advisor in her infinite wisdom decided I was stupid!

I sat there and thought, 'Shit what am I going to do?' All my mates who were into make-up and hair themselves, were doing Beauty Therapy at Bournemouth college so I thought, 'Right, I'll give that a go'. So, off I went to Bournemouth College to become a Beauty Therapist. You need to understand something. I am not cut out to be a beauty therapist and I do not belong in the beauty therapist world! It was a couple of days at college, the rest of the time at a work placement. It was slave labour: £29.50 a week. Basically, the workplace would have you doing all the shit jobs, mainly cleaning. Start at nine a.m. and finish at five p.m., cleaning for £29.50 a week, it was terrible.

Mum wanted rent out of that £29.50 a week, fucking bitch! I think I had told her what was happening at the salon with me cleaning all the time. I am sure she called the college to complain. That was the end of that work placement. They did not have another work placement so I was pulled off the course until one became available. That meant no money, which meant no rent, which meant chucked out of the house, ended up at my friend's house!

When I had my interview to go to college to become a beauty therapist, Mum did not come with me and she certainly did not provide me with the bus fare to get there. I raided my copper jar, and scraped together the bus fare in coppers, to get down there.

I'm at my friend's house with no work. I know that they used to talk about me. I could see my friend, her mum and sister all sat in the garden talking about me. I always felt like a spare part. I knew I did not belong there. I did not want to be there. I had nowhere else to go. I needed a job. I had started working at The Suncliff hotel as a chambermaid. I thought Sunday was God's day; no one worked on Sundays. My stupid little fifteen-year-old mind! I had only been at the hotel three or four days. I went back to work on the Monday and the housekeeper asked where was I the day before? I told her, "I didn't think anyone worked Sundays!" She said, "Here's your money for the days you have worked, goodbye! Sacked!" I thought, 'Shit, what an idiot I am. What am I going to do now?'

Mum was somehow on the scene. Maybe I did not want to go home or I was not allowed to go back home? She would be there playing the dutiful parent! I needed a job. Mum pointed me in the direction of a factory: Millers in Poole. Mum would quite happily send me to the worst job ever but had no interest in seeing me go to college!

It was a sausage, quiche, pasty making place. Clock in

clock out, I HATED IT… I did what I was told, off I trotted for the interview; I needed money! I ended up in the quiche department. Most of the time packing quiches. No hats, no gloves. Quiches on the floor, picking them back up getting them packed, it was pretty disgusting. I was sent to the conveyor belt on one occasion and put on the dough section. I had to stand on the same spot for four hours before morning break and place tiny pieces of rolled up dough on baking sheets in consecutive lines. It was like taking Valium; the work was so monotonous. I struggled to keep my eyes open. I would find myself staggering about because I thought I was literally going to fall asleep.

There was a report whilst I was at the factory that a cigarette butt and broken off bits of nail had been found in a quiche. The officials from Sainsbury's all came around to check what was going on. We were all on our best behaviour. Hats on, gloves on, all spick and span. As soon as they left it all went back to normal. Hats off, gloves off, picking quiche off the floor. I have never eaten a shop-bought quiche, pasty or sausage roll since then. I hated it there; I left after six weeks. I would question myself, 'There has to be more to my life than working in this shit hole?'

I left my friend's house and moved into a house in Pearl Road just round the corner from Mum's. This woman was quite a bit older than me. She was a nail technician and had her own business. I did work for her for a short time over in Boscombe when I was fifteen. I had to pretend I was eighteen. I would do Saturdays in a hair dressing salon, doing people's nails and piercing ears! Anyway, she wanted to play the saviour and look after me, so I moved in there. I didn't want to go back to Mum's house. This woman offered me a room, so I took it.

All this time I was waiting for the college to get back to me with a placement for my beauty course. Leaving the factory was probably a bad idea because it left me with no money. I had applied to the council to get my rent paid at the house. That took weeks and weeks to sort out. It did buy me some time, so I was able to wing it for a while whilst I was waiting for the council to sort the money.

I eventually heard from the college; they had a placement for me out in Swanage! Swanage from where I was living was no easy journey to make. To get to Swanage I had to leave the house at six a.m. to make it to the salon for nine a.m., all by bus. One bus to Poole bus station. Another bus to Swanage. It was a nightmare but I did it. I managed to salvage the funds to get there. I don't know how I was doing it but I was.

Whilst I was working in Swanage, the woman I was staying with went on holiday for two weeks. She filled up the fridge for me with food and put ready meals in the freezer for me, so I was set for the two weeks she was away. Her brothers would frequent the house: one I went to school with and the other who was three years older than me and I ended up sort of dating. They came into the house and ate all the food, everything! I could not believe it. I thought, 'You fucking twats'. What was I going to do? I didn't even challenge them on it. I had nothing and no means of replacing it either. I wanted to keep my placement in Swanage, so any money I had was for bus fare. I started searching around the house for money or anything I could use in order to have some funds in order to feed myself. I found this woman's cheque book. I wrote myself a cheque I think for £20 and went and cashed it with my grandad.

Looking back on that is so weird. Why didn't I ask my nan or my grandad for help? I was sixteen years old! I was in a position that my mum had made me feel like I was the enemy, that I was the person that was in the wrong. I didn't feel like I could ask for help. I knew I was on my own.

One morning after the woman had come back from holiday, I heard her on the phone. She was having a conversation with the bank. They had called her to say that a cheque had been used out of her book. I went into panic mode, 'Oh no, what am I going to do? Shit, shit, shit, shit, shit'. I couldn't figure it out and I was so ashamed. So, I went round to Mums' house, I broke in and went up into her room and took her bottle of sleeping pills. I went back to the house and downed the lot of them with a load of alcohol. I thought it was the answer to everything. Let's just get the fuck out of this world. I don't remember anything after that. I had said I didn't feel well and the woman had given me more painkillers, whilst I was delirious and flat out on the couch. All I remember is waking up in the morning and thinking, 'What did I do?' Shaking and amazed that I had woken up, I went straight downstairs crying and confessed everything. She walked me down to the bank. I had to stand in there and look shamefully at the teller whilst she explained what had happened and said that she was not going to make any further charges. I don't know how Mum came back into the picture but like before, she was playing the part of picking up the pieces, taking on the role of being the mother. I moved back into the house.

Walking back from the shops one day, not long after me trying to end my life, I saw the local shit bags that I used to hang out with, all hanging out in the street. They all stood there looking at me, shouting down the road that I didn't try hard enough! I didn't try hard enough to kill myself! Bunch of horrible cunts!

Whilst I was living in that house before I had tried to kill myself, I dated Darren. He was the brother of the woman whose house I was living in. He would knock me up by banging on my bedroom window, climb through and expect sex. He would get sex; I was sixteen. I didn't know my arse from my elbow in how I should expect to be treated. He would hurt me, I would ask him to stop, he wouldn't. He would just bang his penis in and keep going and going! I would be in tears whilst he was doing it. Second sexual experience, fucking horrible! Apparently, one occasion he tried to wake me up and I told him to fuck off, called him all kinds of names. I never remembered any of that; I was asleep when I was doing it! He would be in a mood in the morning. I would ask him what was up and then he would re-tell what I had said to him. I thought it was hilarious, never remembered a word!

I bumped into him not long after I had left that house in a club called The Venue. I was seventeen at the time. He said he was sorry and that he had treated me really badly. I just looked at him and shrugged my shoulders. I thought, 'Fuck you. I don't need your apology. Fuck off!'

Back at Mum's house I remember that she and the woman that I had been living with would get together and talk about me. The woman said I owed her money, which I probably did but I was not in any position to pay anything. I had nothing! I lost my placement at the beauty shop in Swanage. That was the end of that career. I was jobless, no money and back at home with 'Mum'! For whatever reason, she decided around this time to get a padlock for her bedroom door. She locked all the food away from me so that I couldn't eat it. She didn't speak to me for three months. No explanation, nothing. I hid out in my room and when she went out, I would run downstairs and see what I could find to eat. Porridge, raisins, the odd jacket potato. It was a horrible, horrible time. I went through all the family pictures and threw out all the pictures with me in them. I thought, 'Fuck you. You don't want me, then I will make sure there is nothing to remind you of me'. I did keep a diary as well. I do remember writing in it that I wanted her to die. She found it — that note. That could have been the reason she started talking to me again. Years later, I found a photo album when I was round her house visiting. I did not know that Leigh, separate to me throwing away the pictures, had cut his head out of every picture he was in. I did not know that. She had stuck his head back in the pictures. Surely that screams out that there was a problem in our house. I remember Leigh being around at this time, he must have been back from the horrible boys' home that she sent him to. She would give him the keys so he could get the food out of her room. He didn't know what to do.

We were both trying to figure out our own way to survive what we were living in.

There was never an explanation as to why I had three months of silent treatment. I think maybe I had found myself a job so I could start paying rent! I was seventeen years old.

These days I hate sulking or people that can't communicate. You got a problem, sort it out. Good or bad, whatever you have to say, say it! Otherwise, it is like torture.

This was the year that Nan died. We were round there on Boxing Day; she basically died in the kitchen. I have spoken about that already. I did use to walk over to her house to visit. It was only ten minutes from our house in East Howe. I would literally be at the bottom of her garden before I realised, that's right, she wasn't there anymore! I think Uncle Nicky and his girlfriend Mandy blamed us for her death. They didn't speak to us at the funeral. I saw how Mandy was looking at us across the church hall. I haven't really seen my Uncle Nicky since then.

I don't think I was depressed. Mum assumed I was, she told me! Hanging out with the local shit heads was out of the question. Staying in was my only option at that time. I didn't have any friends and I didn't have a job so making new friends was difficult. I am sure she didn't know the total story of what I had done at that house. I certainly wasn't going to speak to her about it. Mum said I needed to get out. She was probably right. I don't know how it came about but I went out on this blind date. In for a penny in for a pound, let's see what happens. I did not fancy him at all. Smaller than me, possibly five feet six. Very round and ginger, which for some people might be nice but for me, no. We went off to The Venue, a club at Tower Park. I'm up for fun but I did not want to touch his penis, thank you very much. I knew he was trying to get me drunk. Idiot. Kept buying me double gin shots with no mixer. It was disgusting, straight gin, horrible. I bumped into an old school friend who then said come with me and meet my friends. I thought, 'Fuck him, idiot'. I knew what he was up to, so I sacked him off.

I had the best night and made friends with a group of girls that were a bit older than me. These bunch of girls became my new group of friends. They were all working together in a hotel in town. One of the girls was the housekeeper. I had mentioned I was desperate for a job. I was fabricating the fact that I had no money. I was making up stories. I would tell them that I'm waiting for money to come in, blah, blah, blah. I was lying because I was ashamed. I was fabricating my truth because I wanted them to like me. The housekeeper friend said that if I could get myself down to the town and to the hotel, there would probably be a job for me. I thought, 'Right, how am I going to do this?'. I took myself off to the social services and pleaded with them for some money. I wasn't going to get it from mum, so I had to find another way and that was what I came up with. They fortunately gave me a fiver. I got on the bus, made it to the hotel and got that job. Chambermaid. It was bloody hard work let me tell you. But I now had money. I told Mum I had a job and she asked, "Right, how much are you earning?" It was £75 a week. She wanted £25. So that was that. I paid her rent to keep her off my back. I was sort of back on my feet. I had some independence back. I had a tiny bit of control back to my life.

I had a new group of friends that were cool and liked me. I had money to buy clothes. I could eat the food I wanted to! I needed fun in my life and I now had money in my hands to go and find it.

# Chapter Three
# The Summer Of Love

Working at the hotel was hard work. The hotel had three floors including a basement. I had rooms on all three floors. Departure day was a bitch but I liked the hard work. I felt like I was getting fit, running up and down the stairs, changing all the beds and getting the rooms all tip top for the next guests to arrive. It was great fun, all us girls working together, we had such a laugh. One of my buddies, Mandy, had a room downstairs in the basement and would quite regularly slope off when no one was looking and curl up in the downstairs toilet that was big enough for her to sleep on the floor. I'd ask, "Where's Mandy?" Michela who was the housekeeper always knew where she was. She would reply, "Probably slacking, asleep downstairs!" I'd laugh and go looking for her.

We would all get paid on Saturdays, go into town with our wages and get new outfits and fill up on toiletries from Superdrug. Impulse, body cream, maybe a new lippy. We would then plan what our night out was going to be.

There was a pub in town called Pumphries. Everyone who was everyone would go to Pumphries on Saturday afternoon. I was seventeen but managed to get in everywhere without I.D. I looked older than I was when I was younger. Men that I would meet around that time would always assume I was in my twenties. We would sit in there and either be drinking Holsten Pils or Diamond White and Black. You would hear chitter chatter from different groups in the pub about what party was going on and where everyone was going to go Saturday night. Madisons! That was the place to be in the early 90s. There was Madisons and Kev's House. Us girls were Madisons crew. That place was amazing!

It was the early 90s, the clubs were playing Happy Mondays, The Stone Roses, Primal Scream, Inspiral carpets. Then it changed! House music turned up and the rave scene erupted. We were right in the middle of it. It was so exciting and so fun. Everyone was so happy and cuddly and just looking to have a good time.

In the beginning we would end up at beach parties and late night after-parties. I would witness some of the older crew taking pills. I wasn't sure what was going on but they all assumed because of the size of my eyes, that I was on something as well. People at the party would come over and ask what I was on. I had an abundance of energy so staying up all night was not a problem. I would always answer, "Nothing!" At that time, I wasn't sure what that was about, nor fully understood what was going on around me. But I knew I was having fun and everyone else was having fun too. I was curious. What were they taking? Everyone seemed so happy and looked like they were having the time of their lives.

We were at Whiskeys one night, another nightclub that was in vogue to be at, in Bournemouth town in the 90s. Whiskeys was a bit more underground though, not so mainstream as Madisons and Kev's House. Us girls were invited by Olly to go to a rave, of course we jumped on it. It was my first illegal rave.

We arrived at an old shack in a field, in the middle of nowhere! I could not tell you where we were. It was dark and three a.m. We had walked through quite a few fields to get to the shack. There were a few hundred of us in this shack with decks set up and a generator out the back of the shack. We danced all night long on dried up mud. It was amazing. You can imagine dancing on dried mud though, dirt dust everywhere. We were just hanging out, taking in the environment and Olly offered Mandy a load of speed. He held it out in his hand and she took the lot. We all went, 'No!' Not all of it!' We then watched as she proceeded to stay on the same spot for at least three hours, just dancing away, she was what we say, 'right off her tits!'. Daylight descended on the party and it came to a close. We all piled out the shack, looking at everyone in daylight. We had all looked so pristine when we came out at the beginning of the night. Wasting so much time getting ready, do your hair, put your make-up on, outfit looking sharp. Then the night happens. By the end your make-up is down your face, hair all sweaty, clothes all filthy.

Mandy, who was off her tits, had snot trail marks all up her face where she had been rubbing the snot from her nose. She had dirt and snot trails all over the side of her cheek. I found it difficult to look at her because it made me want to retch. I tried to tell her she needed to sort her face out but every time I looked at her, I wanted to be sick. She was saying, 'Please help me' but I couldn't, it was horrible. Poor Mandy. We then as a group had to figure out where we were and get to work. Us girls jumped into a taxi and went straight into work as we were. Sundays were regularly like that. Saturday was departure day, loads of work and Sundays was a quick whip around the room, not much to be done and get out of there. I'm sure everyone that worked there knew what we were all up to but as long as we turned up and got the work done, they never questioned us. We would all be in our party gear from the night before as well!

One Sunday, I had finished all my rooms bar one. I had a couple of hours to go before we could leave. So I thought it would be a good idea to lay down for a bit. The door was wide open. The room had people staying in it! Fortunately, they were out because once I laid down, I passed out for two hours! Oh my god, how did I get away with that one? The girls were all asking where I was. One of them came and found me, woke me up. I was really disorientated and grumpy. I had been out cold for two hours on that bed!

The dance scene really took off and drug taking, speed and E's, was a massive part of that. Every weekend, Pumphries, Madisons, Rave.

Madisons would shut at two a.m. and we would all be outside trying to find out where the rave was. There would always be a massive convoy and most of the time we would be in cars of people we had never met before. Massive convoys of cars all driving around the middle of nowhere in Dorset, trying to find the field that the rave was in. It was a great, great time. I was still just seventeen. If there was no rave happening, we would end up down the beach. This was when I tried my first experience with drugs. We were all hanging out in this caravan, talking shit and being stupid. Speed was being passed around. I said, "Let's try some." My buddies were like, 'no, you're a handful as it is, you don't need it'. I was like, "But I want to try it." I was curious. Everyone looked like they were having fun and I wanted to see what it felt like. So that was that. I did a little bit and felt on top of the world. No inhibitions, no fear, no insecurities, just an 'enhanced Janine'.

I watched an interview the other day of an ex-heroine user.

He was asked why he used. His response was for that time he was high, it was just utter bliss from the demons and life. He could just forget all the abuse and the struggle with everyday life.

On reflection of why I wanted to take drugs, I was curious! I always alluded to the fact that I was just having fun. I was having fun that was for sure! But I can definitely associate with the heroine user. I felt calm, confident, powerful, not afraid and in control when I was taking the drugs. I lived for the weekends. Everyone was living for the weekends. It was very tribal being in the clubs at that time. Everyone dancing as one energy, there was nothing like it. It was powerful and addictive.

I know Mum had an inkling what I was getting up to. She used to speak to me about her younger brother, Uncle Nicky, taking speed. She never asked me outright. I was working, paying my rent and not causing any trouble, so she let me get on with it.

I was always the last one up. If there were no parties and everyone else wanted to pass out, I would quite regularly end up at home dancing in my mum's living room by myself because I was still high! Mum was passed out upstairs.

I'm not sure where Leigh was at this time. I was so caught up with my buddies that I really wasn't interested in what was going on with him. I know he was around at home; he was always stealing my stuff. I was always getting mad with him. I really don't remember what happened with Slades Farm home. I've never asked him and he does not want to talk about it. Sometimes you just want to forget the bad shit and just get on with your life.

For me the priority was getting out every weekend and scoring drugs. Pink champagne (speed) was the flavour at this time. It made me feel invincible. I loved the music. I loved to dance. I loved the fact that it took all my inhibitions away. You would get what was called rushes through your whole body. They would start at the bottom of my feet and would travel all the way up to the top of my head, making my nipples hard. It was the best feeling in the world. Most importantly we were having the most fun!

With the high though, there had to be a down. Sunday come-down. If I was at work in the hotel and the come-down was kicking in, you would always find me in the hotel kitchen drinking copious amounts of fresh milk. I don't know why. I just wanted it and fancied it!

Monday felt the worst ever! Then again, Tuesday felt even worse than Monday; like your life was over. Thursday you were through the worst of it, by Friday you were feeling pinky perky and the weekend was back around again.

The rave scene was huge. Everyone you knew was in it. Well, everyone I knew was in it! My friendship group outside of the girls was starting to grow bigger. We had started meeting lots of like-minded people. The rave community was about everyone just out, loving life and loving the music.

This is when Terry turned up. Terry infiltrated our group; he was sniffing around the girls. He set his sights on one of the girls and she blew him out, thought he was a bit weird. He then started sniffing around me, paying me some attention. Of course, I lapped it up. I was craving love and was clueless at seeing any form of idiosyncrasy and dysfunction that may be a bit off. I generally ignored that and went with what I needed: attention.

Mum was being a bitch again, unreasonable and unpredictable; I needed out. Terry suggested I go to live with him at his parents' house. We had a couple of rooms upstairs and the parents had the rest of the house. They were very affluent, middle class, had a bit of money. They were certainly not council estate.

I found that out at a dinner one evening when Terry introduced me. We sat at the dinner table with his parents, sister and brother-in-law. The brother-in-law proceeded to talk about how council estate people were just the worst. I was still very shy at this point so wasn't saying too much, for obvious reasons. I kept my mouth shut tight about where I grew up. Fortunately, they never asked me where I was from. It was horrible sitting there listening to them talk about council estate people that way.

I also had so many knives and forks in front of me that I thought what the hell am I going to do with this lot! I waited and watched what everyone else was doing and followed suit.

Terry's mother kind of took me under her wing. I had started opening up about my mum. Mum certainly didn't know where I was. She did not make any contact with me to find out how I was or what I was caught up in.

Terry thought it was funny to spike my tea with drugs. His choice was acid and speed. We would be sat there watching T.V. and he'd go off and make tea. I was unaware of what he was doing. I would drink my tea and start to feel weird. He would then start laughing, like it was a joke! Fucking asshole! His parents were clueless.

Along with the drugs comes the sexual experience. What do I know at seventeen? I am guided by what the young men introduce into the sexual journey when you are starting out at that age. I'm not asked about what I like. How do I know what I like? I realise now that your journey will be dependent on how much porn the men are watching at that age! This will also mean they will instigate certain sexual acts they have seen in porn. You, as a young, naive girl, will not question it, because you think that you should be doing it! Everyone was doing threesomes. That's all that anyone could talk about in the 90s. If that's your bag, I am happy for you. It's not mine. I do not want to have sex with another woman to keep my man. Does that make me a prude? No! That is my choice. That is my right. Anal sex as well. These mother-fucking men that think that all women want their dicks shoved up our asses, are out of their fucking minds! I do not want to do that either. Have I had an ultimatum dished out to me as a young woman? Yes, I have. Was I strong enough to say no? No, I wasn't. As young women we end up in these situations that we cannot get out of, for fear of reprisal or being called a prude. Well, I say, "Fuck you now." I have a right to my own choices. I have a right to say no without thinking you are going to leave me or refer to me in a derogatory manner just because I will not let you stick your dick up my ass!

I fell pregnant with Terry; I was still only seventeen. I did not believe it at first. Dismissed it. Went into denial. After a week of doing that, I thought to myself, 'What the fuck are you doing? Get your shit together and sort this out!' I knew even then I was in no position to have a child. I could barely look after myself, let alone bring a child into this world with a guy that was putting drugs in my tea for kicks. So, I got an abortion. I did this all on my own. I do not ever feel sad or feel like I should never have done it. I made the right decision at the right time under the circumstances I was in. I have no emotional connection to this decision. I do not feel sad, or bad. I did what I had to do with the choices that were available to me.

Terry's mum was always dieting. I suppose that rubbed off on me. I also thought I was massive and not very attractive. So, if I lost the weight, I would be more acceptable. I did not have any education on health and what was right for me. I had seen a government guideline table that said five foot eight in height should be nine stone. I went and weighed myself. I was around ten and half stone. I was healthy. I realise that now! But, at the time I thought, 'Right, you need to drop weight'.

These guideline tables do not take in to account your body type and how you are built. I am a mesomorph. I am not built to be nine stone. To achieve this, I lived on eight hundred to one thousand calories a day; basically, starved myself. I lost the weight, got to nine stone. I looked emaciated. My friends were starting to tell me to stop. I couldn't see it. I was starting to spot-check. If you are unsure of what spot-checking is, all women do it, especially people that are suffering with an eating disorder. You start to see places on your body that you identify with as being fat. For example, I needed to lose fat from the inside of my legs, I needed to focus on the back of my arms and I needed to focus more on losing fat from my belly. If you are in a position where you are obese, you generally have to deal with a lifestyle change that has got you into the position that you are in. If you are already very skinny and emaciated, losing fat from the inside of your legs is not a priority, being healthy and have a healthy image of yourself is far more important than spot-checking your body.

I would reply flippantly and say, "Yeah, yeah, I will once I have lost the fat on the inside of my legs." Not healthy and just crazy. Of course, I did stop and started to educate myself on what my body type needed and started to work at seeing myself in a much healthier way.

Terry's parents had a warehouse in West Howe, I'm not sure what they did. Engineering of some sorts. I had left the hotel and had started working in the warehouse full time, I was making a bit more money. But this did mean that I was around Terry all the time because Terry worked there too.

Terry's parents pushed for us to move out. Instead of renting, they pushed for us to buy a place. There was a scheme at the time where you could buy half the property and pay the mortgage of the half for a certain amount of time and then look at buying the rest of the property once that time was up. I remember looking at a new-build in Meyrick Park and then we decided on a place in Westbourne, Snowdon Road. I was eighteen and had my first property. My memory of this time is vague. I remember having to lift a bloody washing machine up five flights of stairs! It had a bloody cement block in the bottom of it. It was so heavy! Once we got it into the flat and set it up it wouldn't bloody work; typical! Our relationship was starting to fall apart once we got into the flat. His behaviour was becoming more and more erratic. I was extremely unhappy and I do remember crying myself to sleep one night, for fear of being pregnant again. Fortunately, I escaped that one.

He was extremely possessive and behaving really oddly. I think he thought I had someone else. I didn't but I think I was starting to distance myself from him. I was spending more time with my girlfriends and he was spending more time with his friendship group. There was a house key incident that I remember. I had forgotten mine and needed to get into the flat. We were both at work and I asked him for the flat keys because I had forgotten mine. Instead of giving me his keys of which I knew he had, he told me that he didn't have his either. He followed me home with a step ladder strapped to the top of his van and climbed up the building to get into the flat. This house was five storeys, it was super-high. I remember standing down in the courtyard convinced he had his keys on him. Why would you go through all that trouble to climb up five storeys on a rickety old step ladder? I thought the behaviour was very strange. He definitely thought I was going home to be with someone.

Around this time, there was a new nightclub in Weymouth called Maximes' everyone that was anyone was going there. Me and the girls had started going down there. I was in there one night and was dancing on the edge of the dance floor. I saw this guy. Blonde, curly locks. I fancied him. I don't know what drew me to him but I kept my eyes on him for the whole night. He knew I was watching him. It was so out of character for me to do something like that but when I was high, I was invincible. I started to see him in Madisons. I made sure that he knew I was looking. One night he came up to me and pulled me to a quiet area of the club. He asked me how old I was and I said 18. He then asked me if I wanted to go out. Of course, I said, "Yes." I don't know how I wangled it because I was still with Terry at this point but I think we were living very separate lives.

Pete was his name and he took me to the Avon Causeway, a lovely pub in Christchurch. It had an old railway carriage outside in the front of the building that you could sit in. Very quiet, a good place to have a first date in. We hung out and must have got on well because he asked me out again. He took me on a beach walk with the dog, asked me what music I liked to listen to. I was very much into soul music. We went back to his house, he asked me upstairs and he played, I think it was

Marvin Gaye, so cheesy but I felt wanted, cared for and not taken advantage of. He left in the morning for work, let me sleep in. He let me wear his jacket home. I was so happy. That following day I asked my friend Michela if she wanted to get a flat with me. She said yes and that was me out of Terry's life.

Mum had reappeared at this point, I not sure how or why. I had probably reached out to her, like I did; she was my mum. I went round at Christmas time with a poinsettia as a peace offering. She had moved out of Pearl Gardens and was living in Throop. I was eighteen and always thought she had my best interests at heart. She told me to just up and leave Terry. Leave the flat, just take what I needed and get out. So, that's what I did. Left with nothing. I'm not sure what happened to the flat. Does Terry still have it? I doubt that from what I heard on the grapevine; not long after I left he got into taking very heavy drugs. Some of our friendship group that he was hanging out with, from what I understand, said he was still spiking people in that group with drugs. But not the fun stuff, the heavy shit, heroin; but that is just hear-say!

Unfortunately, knowing how he was with me I would not be surprised that he did that. My friend Tina who was part of that group turned up around that time and had lost it. She just wasn't present, talking nonsense, could not string a sentence together. I think she had a complete breakdown. Such a shame because she was larger than life, had a great voice. She was working a lot in London with different music groups. All gone. I was lucky to have the mindset to get out when I did.

Leigh was living in Throop. He would go missing all the time. I never thought to ask where he was. This one particular time he had been gone for three weeks. She had not even batted an eyelid to think where he was. He would have been around fifteen. Mum then had a phone call from the police to say he was in Dorchester prison; so weird when I think about it. I don't suppose they would be able to do that these days. It had taken the police three weeks to get in contact with my mum. He had got caught up with a bad group in town. They had been arrested for beating up foreign students. Leigh can't fight his way out of a paper bag. He was in the wrong place at the wrong time. Mum didn't even care. I decided to go and check on him. I drove to Dorchester, sat with him for five minutes and he said, "I'm in the middle of a film." I thought, 'Yep, he's all right'. So off I went.

Michela and I moved into a flat in Winton, Edgehill Road. It was a basic flat, nothing posh. It was the upstairs to a house. The landlord lived downstairs. We had two bedrooms, a very small kitchen and a living room. I had managed to secure a job at a hotel next door to the old one that I had worked with the girls. Michela was still working there but the rest of the girls were now in relationships and working elsewhere.

Me and Pete had fun. We were young and liked each other. It wasn't crazy. He didn't abuse me in any way. He was young though and had a preoccupation with most girls, especially his ex-girlfriend, who was pretty, blonde and came from money. It did make me feel very insecure, especially when he was being very close with her when we were out partying. But I know now that I was caught up with my own insecurities of never being good enough and spent a lot of my time avoiding doing anything, that would expose the fact that I didn't think I was good enough. Making dinner, I didn't want to cook. I was afraid I would get it all wrong. Sex: very, very shy. I would always feel very insecure about that. Not good enough, getting it all wrong, all up in my head. I didn't come from money, so

I couldn't afford nice clothes or shoes. I was in a shit job. It goes on.

Working in the hotel only paid me £75 a week. I think the rent was £70 a week between me and Michela. I needed to earn more money, so I started working in Asda behind the cake counter. I hated that job. White A line dress that had poppers up the front. A tabard that went over the top with orange and white stripes. A trilby hat that was not big enough for my head. I have a very large head. According to the paper strips you can get in Halfords to measure your head, I have a man's sized head. Asda did not source a hat that was correct for my size. They insisted that I wear the one that I had so it just perched on the top of my head. I looked ridiculous. I was meant to wear tights. I never did!

At the time, the Asda cake counter made little tarts that were big enough to swallow whole. Jam tart, lemon curd, Bakewell and treacle; yummy, yummy. I would grab one, go out of the door to the left of the serving counter and round the back of the bakery and shove it down. By the time I came through the door on the right it was finished. Stealing or just perks? Whatever was not sold was chucked into trays anyway and squashed down to be thrown out! I mean, just terrible when you think of the food poverty.

One night at work in Asda, myself and a colleague were sent to fill up the cream cakes. We dipped everything into that cream. Gingerbread, chocolate fudge cake, biscuits. Whatever we could grab, we dipped it in that cream! I was sick as a dog when I got home. I have never touched a cream cake since.

That job gave me an extra £30 pounds a week. Just enough to give me a little bit extra to live on.

The drug taking did settle down a bit at this time. The

relationship with Pete was a bit more stable. I had looked into taking my GCSEs again. I signed up for English Literature and also started a Spanish speaking course. The Spanish course lasted a day. I cannot roll my Rs at all! The teacher was making us stand up individually and do it in front of the whole class. I left promptly. I was not in a place to be humiliated at that point. As for the English Lit., I did it for a while but I just wasn't in a place emotionally to see it all the way through.

It was the early 90s and raving was massive. A club called Sterns opened up in Worthing, it stayed open until six in the morning. Me, Michela, Pete and all his friends would all get together and make our way up there. We'd get into the club around nine p.m., take an ecstasy pill and you would not see me then until it closed at six a.m. I would say, "Catch you later," make my way down to the dance floor in the bottom of the club and dance and dance and dance, nine p.m. 'til six a.m., non-stop. I would have the time of my life. Meet some of the best people, be best friends for those hours you were in there, never to be seen again. You would have that special bond and connection for that time and that time only.

I don't really know why me and Pete broke up. I have tried to think about it over the years. I have always blamed myself. I was moody, I was trying to figure myself out. He asked me to move in with him. I turned him down. That for sure would have made him feel rejected. At the time I was thinking about my time with Terry and I didn't want the same thing to happen. I was thinking about myself and not about how that might have hurt him.

One morning he drove me home and told me that was it! He was never coming back! No explanation! Nothing!

I was eighteen. I then proceeded to lose my shit, shall we

say? The breakup with Pete was definitely the catalyst to me going off the rails completely.

Our lease at the flat in Winton was coming to an end. Me and Michela were both in a bit of quandary as to what to do next. The landlord was being a bit difficult. We had mice in the flat and she was blaming us, saying we had bought the mice with us! We didn't have a lot of money between us so looking for somewhere else to stay was a touch difficult. Agents fees, deposit, months' rent in advance is a lot of money to find.

Up pops 'MUM'. She turned up at ours and asked us to move back in with her. We could share the front bedroom and pay £25 each a week (to share a room!) until we had found somewhere else. I always thought she was looking out for me, always. I was still with Pete at this time. It must have been another kick in the teeth for him, as far as rejecting his offer of living with him from me as well! I was moving into Mum's and not into his! I ran it past Michela, she said, "Okay." So that's what we did.

What was I thinking?

Maybe I was moodier when I moved back in there. Maybe, without me realising she had started to work on me. She was such a bitch. She sat down one day and said, "I'm struggling with the bills!" When I think about it now, it was such a crock of shit! She was working as a driving instructor, cash. Working as a lorry driver, night work, £15 an hour. She was also claiming. How was she struggling? When I reflect on it now, it makes my mind boggle! She was raking it in!

Me being me, I felt bad; it was my mum! I said "Well, I'll just pay you more money." Me and Michela paid £35 each a week for a room we were sharing. £70 a week. We had a two-bedroom flat with a bathroom, kitchen and a lounge for that price before I had made the idiotic decision to move back in with my mum. Mum was also charging me money for food as well. My mum's behaviour had started to unravel like it always did. These are a couple of standout moments from that time.

I had been to get my hair cut by a friend of mine that was a hairdresser. Mum had mentioned that she had seen Raquel Welch with a hair style that she liked. I said, "Why don't you go and see my friend. I tell you what I'll treat you for Christmas."

So off she went, picture in hand. My mum has thin, dead straight hair, Raquel Welch thick, wavy hair. The style was never going to work. The style that she liked was a short, curly cut!

She came back from the hairdressers and did not speak to me for two weeks. She hated the cut and it was all my fault, clearly! The two weeks she didn't speak to me was the two weeks before Christmas. I decided I was going to get her a gift to open on Christmas day. I bought her a potato masher. I thought fuck you! I wrapped it up and stuck it under the Christmas tree. I made sure I passed it to her on Christmas day and watched her open it. Her reaction was priceless. I knew she hated it and I knew that she knew I'd done it for effect. Fuck you, you bitch.

After this incident, it would have been a couple of months later, one evening I was paying my £35 for the shared room. But I didn't have the £5 to give her for the food she had bought. I said, "Leigh owes me £5, can you get it from him?" She flew off the couch and booted me in the shin with her steel toe-capped boots on. At this time, I was five foot eight to her five foot nothing. I lost it! I grabbed her and threw her on the floor and then proceeded to ground and pound her. As I held her down to the floor, I said, "This is going to be the last time you ever hit me, ever!" I knew then that I had to get out of that house, it was time for me to start looking for another place to live.

Leigh was around at this time and had moved into a squat where he spent most of his time. He would phone Mum's house and leave messages on the answer phone, high on acid. I thought it was hilarious. But really it is just sad. Fifteen and living in a squat. Although the squat was not a crack den, which is something you think of when you think of a squat. The group of people he was hanging around with would scope out buildings that had been empty for a while and then find a way in. They had set up camp in John Lennon's Aunt Mimi's house in Sandbanks. It was a fun house to be in. From my understanding there was a bouncy castle in one of the rooms. DJ decks set up in another room. A total party house from top to bottom. This is where Leigh was forming his family around him.

My friend Michela told me one day, that she had asked my mum why she didn't have any pictures of her kids around. My Mum's reply, "Why would I want them on the wall staring at me all the time, no thanks!" At that time, I just thought it was nothing more than expected.

Whilst I was back at Mum's, I was trying my hand at an insurance broker's. I did not have one clue about what I was doing. They stuck me in an office with piles and piles of files to go through, about insurance! What did I know about insurance? Every day I would go into that office and sit in front of that pile of files and try and figure out the easiest way to get on with. I had to dictate letters to a secretary as well! I was blagging it all the way.

Pete throwing me away unexpectedly meant that I was spiralling out of control. The separation from Pete definitely kicked up deep-rooted rejection feelings I had about my dad, along with what was happening with my mum. I was very confused and not happy. Me and Michela lived for the weekends and the drug taking was paramount in what we were getting up to.

I had found a room to rent in the centre of town. The room was right at the back of the flat out of the way of the rest of the rooms and right by the front door. I would not have to contend too much with the landlord because she had the front of the flat. I was still working at the Insurance Brokers but had also taken on working at a veg shop on a Saturday. I was cleaning toilets in some offices three nights a week and then had looked to take on cleaning at five in the morning. I realised at that point I was doing too much, so cut back on the morning clean.

Once I was in the flat and away from Mum, I seemed to settle down a bit, got my head down and got on with working but that did not last long. The partying and drug taking was taking its toll. I regularly would not eat all day so that when I went out in the evening, everything I took would get straight into my system. On quite a few occasions I had drank a whole bottle of wine before leaving the flat. When we got to the club, I would have a wrap of speed, an E and some acid. That was supposed to be taken throughout the night. I would say, 'Fuck it' and take the lot, all in one hit and then black out, no clue of what I was doing in the club or if anyone was doing anything to me; very, very dangerous. Anything could have happened to me.

One of my buddies back then, Pippa, was on the beach one day. We were hanging out, just bullshitting when one of my mates Zack turned up. He was talking about his mate coming over from sunseeker with his speed boat. I probably asked to go for a ride in it. Zack's response was, "You sure, he goes really fast!" I replied with my usual Billy-big-bollocks, big mouth with, "Yeah, it's going to take more than a speed boat to shit me up!" Famous last words. The boat turned up, me and Pippa swam out to it, climbed into the back and sat on the plastic ridge at the back of the boat. The boat really was a two-man boat. The engine size was triple the size of the boat. I sat at the back, wedged my feet in under the seat and gripped onto the back of that seat like my life depended on it. My buddy Pippa held on to me like she was going to die. I gripped hold of her so as not to let her go. That boat took off so fast. I had my eyes shut the whole time. I know the driver nearly lost it. If we had hit that water that would have been it! I opened my eyes and saw the pier. I immediately thought, 'Okay, okay, we are just by Bournemouth Pier, not far'. But of course, we were nowhere near Bournemouth, we were by Boscombe Pier a mile and half away from where we needed to be. I wanted out. I shut my eyes again and prayed we would make it back in one piece. As soon as he stopped at Bournemouth Pier I was out, jumped in the water and swam to shore relieved I was still alive.

I hated it at the Insurance Brokers. I popped a letter through the door one day and told them that I was not coming back. I think I had been out raving all weekend and the thought of going in there to trawl through those files that I knew nothing about with a massive come-down, was something I did not want to get into. That was the end of that job. Back to the hotels I went. The hotel jobs were easy to find and they had no responsibility. I could do it high if I needed to. I didn't care about the hotel job. There were no aspirations. I needed money and that was the easiest place to go. I found a job as a chambermaid in no time. Living in a beachside town there is always work in the hotels.

My head space was messy and I wanted out. I found an article in the local newspaper that said come and grape pick in France. Live on the farm, get paid, have fun! I phoned up and booked myself on. I was getting out of town. I was running away. I thought all my problems would sort themselves out if I wasn't in the town and around my mum.

I still had some kind of connection with her at this point. I remember going round there to tell her what I was doing. Excited, I thought she might be excited for me. No! Mum's response, "You'll be back in a week!" You could maybe see that as reverse psychology, making me think, 'I'll show you'.

There was no reverse psychology, her tone was bitter in its response. She never had anything good to say to me.

I would be camping at the vineyard. I did not think to take anything with me. I took a holdall with a sleeping bag in it that looked like my nan had made it. No tent, no cooking utensils, nothing. I had my passport and £70 in my pocket. Off I went to the coach station. It was an organised trip so there was a coach waiting for us at Bournemouth coach station. Everyone that got on the coach had massive backpacks that looked like they had everything in it. Tent, cooking equipment, proper sleeping bags. Me, a crappy old bag with a shit sleeping bag. I was really nervous. I didn't know anyone, what was I doing? When we arrived at Southampton, I was going to get off the coach and come back to Bournemouth. I didn't though. I thought if you don't do this now, you'll never do it. I started to make friends and started to chat to this girl called Lisa. The conversation started on about how we were going to be in tents for three weeks. I said, "I didn't know where I was going to stay? I didn't have anything!" Lisa said, "I'm on my own, you can stay with me." I was sorted. I didn't need a tent and I was going away to earn money, so that would soon be a turn-around from me being skint.

All I was thinking about was myself. I wasn't thinking about the mess I was leaving behind. Michela had moved into my room at the flat. I left her to deal with all the shit, thinking if I run away, it will just go away. The bank (who I had let a bounced cheque for £15, turn into a £150 pound bill and rising every week, as I just couldn't see any way of getting on top of it), I had rented a T.V. at the time and left Michela to deal with. I didn't pay that either. I should have warned her but I didn't. I just ran away. I feel bad for that because it cost my friendship. I did what I did without thinking about the consequences. I was selfish and I am sorry.

# Chapter Four
# The Grape Picking Adventure

The coach journey seemed to go on forever. Everyone on the coach was drinking. There were a group of young lads at the back of the coach that were downing everything they could get their hands on. One of them ended up being sick at the back of the coach everywhere, it stank!

On the ferry crossing, the drinking continued — they were drinking brandy! My head was starting to spin, I suffer with sea sickness so the channel crossing was not great. The smell of brandy was making me feel really nauseous. I thought it would be a good idea to be on the upper deck, outside, breathing in the fresh air. If I was going to start throwing up, I could do that over the side of the boat. I sat outside on my own for the channel crossing and made it across without throwing up, bonus. Once we had reached France, we had to get back into the sick-stench filled coach and make our way to Dijon.

The vineyard was in a tiny village in Dijon. We set up our tents and then figured out the village we were staying in. It had one tiny little bar and a boulangerie. The fresh chocolate-filled croissants in the morning were amazing! I think we had a couple of days to settle in and then it was up and get ready to work. The truck beeped the horns around seven a.m. We had to be up and ready to go, otherwise they left without you. No work, no pay. Before you left in the morning you were handed a bucket, and secateurs. You were then pointed to the vans where we were piled into the back. We were driven to a field and given a row of grapes to pick. It looked a mile long to me from where I was standing. I thought, 'Okay!', plugged myself into my Walkman that was playing house music and said to myself, 'I'm pretty fit let's crack on!'

Apparently, the further south you go, the closer the grapes grow to the ground. The further north you go, the higher the grapes grow, up to head height. In Dijon they were waist height to my five foot eight, which meant using the knees to start with. Squatting up and down, up and down. It wasn't long before my knees started to hurt. I know, I thought, I'll keep the legs straight and use my back, up and down, up and down. Of course, my back started to hurt! Looking back up at the row of grapes seemed endless. I'd just sit and hide for a bit, have a fag!

It was hard work and physically really demanding. I would get so far and sit down on my bucket and hide and wait for the Polish that were in the picking group, to come and help me finish my line. I did that on a regular basis.

We would have a break around nine a.m. The French helpers would bring round red wine. I was like, "Oh my, at nine a.m.!" Everyone else on the trip was like, 'Cool'! The whole English crew along with the French would start drinking at nine a.m.! It was the same every day. Pissed all day, every day! Not only would we get wine at nine a.m., we would go back for lunch and there would be more red wine on the tables. Of course, the French are very casual. The English were like animals, like they had never seen it before and would never see it again. Copious amounts of red wine all day long. I didn't care for red wine so much. I would just watch the rest of the crew go back out for afternoon work, completely out of it. It was funny to watch. I would be peering over the vines to watch some of them rolling down the hills because they couldn't stand up!

I mean the work was really laborious and incredibly hard so, for the most part it was the only way to get through the days.

I was always observing what everyone was doing. I am what you call a 'people watcher'. On our first day, we were curious what we were going to be fed. The Brits on one side were eager, the French on the other side all looked very relaxed. Our first course came out. Although we didn't know it was our first course! We were grabbing and devouring everything that we could get our hands on. What we did not realise is that there were at least another four courses coming out. This still didn't change the behaviour of the Brits though. I remember looking over at the French. They were casually chatting and were still on their first course, where the English had devoured three courses to their first. Again, we looked like animals that hadn't been fed for weeks!

We had one shower between at least twenty of us. Coming back from working in the fields was always a race to get to the shower for hot water. It was an experience at the vineyard that was for sure. Lisa had put up the tent wrong. The outside cover was touching the inside cover. The poles were on the inside and had to be on the outside. There was a massive downpour of rain one evening! Everything inside the tent was soaked. We had a massive pool of water right in the middle of the tent. There was no way we were sleeping in that for at least a couple of days whilst it dried out. There was a couple of guys in the crew that had an eight-man tent. It was pretty big to our two-person tent. They very kindly said we could sleep in their tent whilst ours was drying.

The evenings at the vineyard site consisted of either drinking down the local bar or drinking, all cooped up in the eight-man tent. There were no assigned spaces to sleep in. You slept where you slept. I was renowned for just passing out wherever I was. We would all be inside the big eight-man tent, laying all over the bags and kit. One minute I would be in the group drinking, laughing and chatting, the next minute I would just pass out on whatever was there and go to sleep!

One of the group would ask, 'Where's Janine?' There I would be just passed out in the group whilst they continued to party around me. I think I would just get to a point where I had had enough, make that split decision and just lay down and go to sleep in whatever position I was in.

The final day of picking the grapes, the vineyard had a party. Along with all the drinking and eating that day, me and Lisa got to tread grapes in an old fashion wooden barrel. Maybe four of us stood at the top of the barrel and very slowly, barefoot, started to push the grapes down. So, weird. You sink into the grape juice right up to your neckline. The smell is intoxicating. I felt like I was getting drunk just from the vapour. You then continue to squish the grapes with your feet. You are just swimming around up to your neck in grape juice!

Lisa asked if I wanted to go home. I said, "No way". She suggested we go looking for more work. We decided to travel to Colmar and try to pick up more grape picking work. Colmar is in Northern France. We were trying to follow the grape picking trail. We figured there would be more grape picking work in Colmar. A girl we had met in Dijon, Melissa, had mentioned that her Dad had a hotel in Spain. She was making her way there in November. Me, Lisa and Melissa had all arranged that we would meet up there. We had a plan. Go to Colmar, get work. Fly down to Spain. Meet Melissa. Sorted. Of course, our plan wouldn't work out to be that easy.

We figured out our train journey to Colmar. That only took a few hours, so we made it there in a day. I had to purchase a backpack because carrying around a holdall was not practical. The backpack took a big chunk of the money I had earnt at the vineyard but the bag was a necessity if we were going to be traipsing around Northern France on foot. We both figured out the employment bureau in Colmar. That was the first port of call. See if we can find work! Apparently, what they were doing was giving out work on the day. If there was work on a vineyard, we would find it there.

From what I can remember we did not get much joy. Two very young, British girls in France looking for work. Let's say the French were a touch dismissive towards us to say the least.

So, the next best thing was, find a bar and go have a drink to figure out our next move. It just so happened there were some British guys hanging out in the bar: Pete and Chris. Pete told me and Lisa about a camp site they were staying on. These guys were cool. They didn't give off any bad vibes. We decided to stay with them and follow them to the camp site.

The camp site was cheap per night but I was not earning any money. I needed to think about how I was going to survive. Pete told us they were moving across the road. There was a riverbank with a nice grass verge we could all set up camp for free. We stayed one night on the camp site and then packed up our stuff and off we went. The four of us soon turned into about thirteen of us. I can't remember where everyone else came from. Me and Lisa would get up early each day and head to the work office to see if we could find work. Nine times out of ten we would end up meeting more British guys. They would follow us back to our camp and set up home. It was great, our own little British commune.

Lisa and me decided one morning that we would head off to vineyards, to try and talk to the farmers direct. We went from vineyard to vineyard to find work but nobody would give us anything. I was soon figuring out that the French were not too keen on us. We must have been on the riverbank for coming up to two weeks. I was living on cans of beans that I would cook on the open fire in the tin and two litre bottles of Kronenburg. Not a great diet but it was cheap and the beer would help me sleep at night, because I was drunk and would not feel how cold it was getting.

To get washed, we would sneak onto the camp site opposite at night and use the showers when no one was around to get cleaned up. There were the bushes to pee and poo in.

I was running out of money, fast! No work, no money. The police turned up one day as well and told us all that we had to leave. They very kindly gave us a few days to figure out what we were going to do. Sleeping in a tent when the temperature is dropping is not fun. I was sleeping fully-clothed with my sweatshirt as a hat to cover my head a night. I would have the arms of the sweatshirt coming out at my ears. I looked really funny. I also had my Naf Naf puffa jacket on (Naf Naf was the brand to wear in the 90s!) because it was getting so cold! Me and Lisa were in a quandary as to what to do. The plan hadn't really worked out. We did not have the money to fly down to Spain. We did not really want to go home but we were closer to Calais than we were to Spain.

There was this Irish woman, Susan, that had set up camp with us. She pulled me and Lisa to one side around the fire one

115

night and said, "I can see that you are both trying to figure out what to do." Me and Lisa had spoken about hitching down to Spain from Northern France. It was a long way. We were both questioning whether we could do it or not. Lisa said, "If you don't try you will always question whether or not you could have made it. It would be better to try and fail than to not try at all!"

We decided to sleep on it and make our decision in the morning. We both woke up and said, "Right come on let's do it." We went and bought a map. I said that my mum had mentioned when I was growing up, if we were going to hitchhike that we should do it with the lorry drivers because most of them would be pretty decent and it was their job. So, we should be pretty safe. Lisa spoke of an international truck stop in Beau where we could pick up a British lorry driver and he could take us all the way down to Spain. It was a good plan but a bit delusional to think it would be that easy. We packed up our kit and set off on our adventure. We made our way to the Autobahn and started to stick our thumbs out. I haven't mentioned yet that I could not speak a work of French and Lisa was rudimentary in her language skills. We had a French translation book though, so we were sorted. Have you ever tried to use a translation book? It never works.

It wasn't long before we picked up our first lorry and he was heading towards Beau, or so he said anyway. The lorry driver we had picked up was a big, fat, French man who did not speak a word of English but we had communicated with our broken French that we wanted to go to Beau. He agreed and we jumped straight in. Lisa was in first and made a bee line to the back of the cab and settled down in the sleeper part. I stayed up front. She was asleep in no time. I thought one of us had to stay awake as anything could happen!

It can get very monotonous on the motorway. My head was starting to droop. I'd been sleeping in a tent for six weeks. I was a little bit sleep deprived. I was a bit dozy when I looked up and across at the driver. I couldn't believe what I was seeing. He had his dick out and was wanking himself off with a sleazy, big smile on his face. I averted my eyes immediately and looked out of the window. I thought I was seeing things! No, he couldn't possibly be doing that. So, I looked back again. Oh yes, he was still doing it. Dirty, fucking, old shit bag. I shouted for Lisa to wake up. He didn't understand what I was saying but he did very quickly put his dick away. I explained to her what he was doing and that we needed to get the fuck out of this cab.

What were we going to do? The very first lorry driver that picked us up was a fucking pervert! I couldn't believe it! I couldn't even look at him. I was trying to rack my brains as to what to do. I can't remember how much longer we were in that cab for but I do know that he pulled over in a truck stop that had a toilet in it. It was like a services, without any services, just a toilet area. I got out of that cab quick smart. He spoke with Lisa and basically suggested that we tend to him and then he will take us wherever we wanted to go. I said, "No fucking way!" Lisa on the other hand was easy breezy. She was like, "It's just a blow job!" I said, "No fucking way! You do what you want, I am out of here!" I wasn't sure what I was going to do but getting out of there was definitely the plan of action. Lisa decided against fucking the fat, greasy, dirty, old, French perv and left with me. I decided I needed a pee. It turns out this was the first experience of pissing in a hole in the floor. I had never tried to piss into a hole in the floor before. Before we knew it, we were both laughing about how we were going to deal with not pissing all over ourselves and the fact that there were dug out placements for your feet. One minute I was trying to survive a perv, the next I was trying to place my feet precariously in the dug outs so as not to piss all over myself, laughing our heads off.

We got ourselves back out onto the Autoroute, not deterred by the perv and tried again to pick up our next lorry driver. We were successful in picking up a Spanish driver who could speak a little English. He was super-friendly and took care of us. He drove us all the way to Beau. We had made it to the international truck stop on the first day! There was a cafe, so we decided to get a cuppa and a bite to eat. My eating at this point was all over the place. I don't think we had eaten anything all day. I was probably pre-occupied with surviving! It was getting pretty late. We both decided that we should probably try and get some sleep as we were not going to pick anyone up at night. We then had to figure out where we were going to sleep. Lisa wanted to bed down under a picnic table right in sight of the cafe. I certainly did not want to do that. It would have been weird, being right in sight of all the drivers. I felt a bit shameful to be honest at sleeping out rough. We went round the back of the building and found a doorway that was not in use, got our sleeping bags out and set the alarm for sixish. It was really strange setting up in the doorway. I felt really exposed and vulnerable. I could hear rats running around and felt really unsafe at just falling asleep. Lisa was asleep again in no time. I dipped in and out, not really feeling comfortable enough to fall asleep for any length of time.

The alarm went off and we got ourselves together. We used the toilets in the cafe to brush our teeth and then set off to see if we could pick up our next lorry driver.

We picked up a really quiet, French dude. He could not speak a word of English but he was cool. He took care of us and drove us all the way to Avignon. He radioed through to sort out our next driver who could speak a little English and drove us all the way to the Spanish border. He treated us to a hot chocolate. He also radioed through and sorted out our next driver, or drivers I should say. There were two drivers and they wanted to split us up. I said, "No!" I was a little unsure of getting in the trucks. They reassured us and I thought, 'Right, if he does anything or tries anything on I will do him in. I'll just smash his face up.' These drivers took us all the way to Barcelona. It was around two in the morning. They asked us where we wanted to be dropped off. I said, "A camp site." We had our tent and little money so staying in a hotel was out of the question. The drivers were not prepared to just drop us off at two a.m. in Barcelona. They said we would be raped and killed, so kept hold of us until we had figured out where we could go that was safe. All our correspondence at this present time was over the radio that the drivers had in their cabs. I was racking my brains again, where were we going to go. Lisa was useless at this point. I knew it was down to me to think about where we were going to go. I said, "Take us to the Airport!" I thought that would be the safest place for us. They wouldn't kick us out because we may very well be travelling and I thought we could get cleaned up. So, that's where they took us. We were now in Spain.

We made a beeline for the toilets when we arrived at the airport, had a sink wash and brushed our teeth. We then found our way to some benches and made ourselves comfortable. The airport was dead, only the odd person wondering around.

We set up camp on the benches and fell asleep. When we woke up it was a different story altogether. There were people everywhere! It was really disorientating. Neither of us could speak Spanish and we were both really tired. We were starting to gripe at each other. We needed money, Spanish money. We both fancied a cuppa but didn't know how to ask for it. My shyness kicked in. I didn't want to make a fool out of myself so did not want to go and ask. Lisa didn't want to do it either. We were both being a pain in the arse about it. I think Lisa went up and sorted it in the end. We then had to figure out how we were going to get out of Barcelona and to the autopista. There was a shuttle train out of the airport where we could pick up a main train that travelled across the country. We decided to jump the trains. We were limited on funds so had to be sparing on how we were spending our money. We would take our chances and hope we didn't get caught. Using our map, we figured out where we wanted to get off the train and made our way to the autopista. At this point of the journey, I had taken to just eating brie cheese and drinking beer. I liked it, so I had it.

We had arrived at a spot on the autopista where we stood hitching for quite a few hours. We were grumpy and really starting to bite at each other. We were not having much luck so made a plan. The decision was to jump the train again and make our way back to Barcelona. Fortunately, we didn't get asked for a ticket and made a snap decision to get off before we got back to the city and hitch at a different place on the autopista.

It wasn't long before we picked up a lorry driver that was from Holland, who could speak perfect English. He was driving all the way to Alicante. Lisa jumped into the back of the cab straight away, again! But this time it was a hammock! I sat in the front of the cab in a big, old seat that was nice and comfortable. For the first time in three days, I felt safe and relaxed. The Dutch driver was really cool and my instincts were telling me that everything was okay. Me and the driver just chatted away for a while and then he asked if I smoked weed. I said, "Sure." He said that he had some Thai weed that was really nice. He lit up a smoke and we watched the sun come down over the Spanish mountains. It was majestical. The sun just slowly disappearing behind the mountains, lighting up the sky with the red, orange and purple hazes. Time for a little reflection. Me and Lisa had almost made it. Funnily enough, he got his camera out and as I turned to look at him to see what he was doing he took a picture of me, so weird. Just savouring the moment, I guess.

When we made it to Alicante, the driver invited us to have some food with him. Lisa, when she got out of the back of the cab was complaining about the fact that the hammock had been bouncing around and making her feel sick. I thought, 'Well that will teach you'. She had not at any point of the journey offered to swap or stay awake to make sure we were safe. On the inside I was laughing a bit, good that you suffer a little because I'm exhausted. I've been awake for three days making sure we were safe!

We had our food with the driver and then made our way to a camp site that was in Alicante. It was so amazing to set up the tent, have a shower and get clean, get tucked up in our sleeping bags where it was nice and warm and safe. I was looking forward to having a restful night's sleep. We woke up naturally, no time schedule, packed up our belongings and made our way into Benidorm. By midday we were standing on

Benidorm beach.

We had done it! We had made it! I couldn't believe it. I was so happy and surprised and proud of myself. Whilst we sat there on the beach soaking up the sun rays, we had to figure out what we were going to do next!

# Chapter Five
## Sticky Vicky and Her Magic Fanny

We both decided to have a wander down the promenade of the beach and figure out where Melissa's dad's hotel was. We figured that if we went there and explained that we were friends of his daughter, he would help us out a bit, maybe give us a place to stay. As we were chit chatting, an old dude decided he was going to start chatting with us. He seemed friendly enough and was definitely in his seventies so seemed harmless enough. You assume because they are in their seventies that they can't hurt you. Old doesn't always mean friendly, just sayin'! We told him we were looking for this hotel. He said he knew where it was and then offered to make us some food, if we wanted to go back to his apartment. Once we had eaten, he would then take us to the hotel. We both thought, deal! Free food. I had no money and Lisa was running low.

The plan, of course, back in Dijon with Melissa was to meet her there in Benidorm but things just hadn't worked out that way. We had arrived in Benidorm three weeks early. We were just praying that her dad would help us out.

We made our way to the old dude's apartment. He was very hospitable and fed us well. We both thought great, we could maybe get some free meals out of him whilst we figured out how we were going to survive. He told us we could come round any time and then walked us both to the hotel.

The dad of Melissa, I mean, the poor guy. Two teenage girls turn up on his doorstep saying they are friends with his daughter and that we were supposed to be meeting but we were early, because we couldn't find work in France. What was he meant to do? He could have turned us away that's for sure. But he didn't, he gave us a room, for free! We were both so happy. A proper bed!

It was so amazing to not be in the tent. I laid down on that bed and just savoured it. Fresh sheets, mattress, pillow and a safe room with a lock on the door. I then took a look at my clothes and thought I've had six weeks of drinking beer, whilst living on bread and cheese. I had started to pile on the pounds. I needed to sort that out quick smart. I didn't have any money to buy extra food so the weight would start to come off quick anyway. We took off down the main drag of Benidorm, where the clubs and bars were. There were plenty of English guys stood outside handing out flyers trying to get passers-by into the clubs. We started chatting to them, asked them where we could find some work. I had £15 in my pocket and no ticket home. I had to sort something out as quickly as possible.

One of the guys that was handing out the flyers, spoke to the owner of the club. He introduced us to him. The club owner said he would pay us 1500 pesetas a night with free drinks, to come and dance on the dance floor to make it look busy. If we were dancing and having fun, it would attract people to come in. We both said, "Yes'" immediately. I thought great, I'm back earning. I didn't know how much 1500 pesetas equated to. I didn't care. The job was seven nights a week. It was enough money to get me fed. We were living rent free at that moment. So, we both just needed enough money to feed ourselves. I loved dancing and the fact that we were getting free alcoholic drinks meant after a couple, you didn't care what you looked like. Brandy and chocolate milk were my favourite, and the staff were always generous with their measurements.

My memory is a little vague as to whether or not we ever went back to the old dude's apartment for food but I do remember Lisa coming back to the hotel room one night after she had been round there. I must have stopped going because it was a bit weird. Lisa on the other hand had a different set of morals than mine. Lisa said that the old dude had offered to let us stay at his apartment rent free, with whatever we needed. He would pay for everything, as long as he could have sex with either one of us at any given time. I was eighteen years old. The old dude was definitely in his seventies, he could have been in his eighties. He was skinny and wrinkly and old, to my eighteen-year-old self. I said, "No fucking way! That's disgusting!" He'd said we could do it in the dark. Oh my god! Just so horrible. It makes my skin shiver thinking about it. Even with a bag on his head, for me there was just no way. Lisa, I don't know about.

We got moved out of the hotel into Melissa's dad's apartment which was very kind of him. But we were eighteen, selfish and partying. Staying in the apartment felt weird. I never felt like I could move around freely. We certainly didn't feel that welcome there. I suppose he didn't want to just turn both of us out on the street. We both needed to find another living option. Lisa and me just drifted apart after that. I have no idea where she went or what she ended up doing. I made new friends and moved into an apartment sharing with some other English guys that were doing the same as me, dossing, drinking too much and taking whatever drugs were being passed around. One of the apartments I stayed in had thirteen of us. There were lilos everywhere because there were only two beds. First come first served for the beds. There was only one bedroom with two single beds. I never made it to the beds. There was a couch that could be used as a bed in the living area. First come to that as well. We had the balcony where all the lilos were. Teenage kids asleep everywhere! It was madness but so much fun. Always someone to hang out with, drink with, do hot knives with (weed) and listen to Bob Marley as the sun came up.

I moved around a lot in Benidorm because the people that you hung out with were never there for very long. At one point, I moved in with a guy that was all a bit possessive. He was telling me he loved me after only a week or so. I felt like I was being smothered so I got rid of him. I think after that episode I was homeless for three days. That was horrible. I really didn't know what I was going to do. I was still working in the clubs. I would hang out at parties afterwards, take a lot of speed to keep me awake until I had had enough. I would then make my way to an all-night café, take a seat, have a cup of tea, have a wash at the sink and then go down to the beach and sleep it off. It was a touch depressing as well as isolating. I felt really alone at that point. I was, however, good at making friends. There was a group of girls that were looking for a fourth person for their apartment. They knew I was looking for somewhere so asked me to come in. I was straight in. Bed, cooking facilities and shower; luxury!

There was one day that I was feeling really low and I thought a call to my mum would cheer me up. I walked down to a pay phone, called the operator and asked to make a reverse call to the UK I heard the ringing. I then heard my mum's voice and the operator asked if she would accept a call from Spain?

I heard my Mum say, "No!" and slam down the phone. It was like she had just ripped my guts out and stamped all over them. What kind of mother was she? I might have been in trouble, I might have needed her help or I might have just wanted to have a chat. I sobbed all the way back to the apartment. I fucking hated her.

It didn't take long when I was in Benidorm for the boys to start sniffing around. I was young, vulnerable and insecure. I'm sure men can sniff out the vulnerability a mile off. When men paid me attention, I genuinely thought they actually liked me! I bought into the attention paid to me and as I was so desperate to be loved, I went along with it. Of course, stupid me, they just wanted to stick their penis in me and then get shot of me as fast as they could. There is nothing like being used as a piece of meat, it just fills up your soul!

It takes a long time to figure out the shit bags from the genuine men. I always saw the good, never assumed anything about anyone but it turns out I am utterly stupid. I have been used time and time again. It can make you very cynical!

In amongst all the shit, I did however meet a couple of guys called George and Cal. George was from Scotland and Cal was from Barrow-in-Furness. They had both met in Benidorm the season before I got there and had decided to come back out. I took a liking to Cal. As it turned out he took a liking to me. I started spending a lot of time with both of them, hanging out, having fun and getting really pissed. Oh, my goodness George would get wasted! He couldn't string a sentence together and that was every night. They were both trying to look for work and were struggling to get anything. They were running out of money fast and didn't want to go home. I could see that they were struggling and they would not accept any money from me. I didn't have much but they were both not eating. I would buy enough food for all of us and take it round.

There was one night with both of them that stands out. The Spanish cheap wine is horrible. The only way to drink it was to down it. We decided the three of us would play a word association game. Timmy Mallet used to play on kids' Saturday morning T.V. You can't pause or hesitate. Come up with a topic, for example 'your favourite takeaway!' and begin! If you pause or hesitate or repeat something someone has already said, you had to down a shot of the horrible wine. I lost miserably. The more you get it wrong the more drink you have, the fuzzier your brain gets! We finished the game and decided to go out. I wanted to go back to my apartment to get changed. I think the fresh air hitting me in the face was a game changer. I was drunkety, drunk, drunk. We made it back to the apartment where I then was all over Cal. I had taken all my clothes off and was just wandering around naked. I had tried to have a shower and puked my guts up everywhere. I tried to clean it up with powdered Cif. Red wine covered in greeny-coloured, cleaning powder! I then passed out on my bed, face down, legs spread apart, completely nude, gone! Cal and George were still present in the apartment. Cal invited George to come take a look at me passed out. Not a defining moment! George went off out and Cal decided to stay and keep an eye on me. He slept on the sofa. One of the good guys.

I'm not sure if I was with Cal when I did this, or I met George and Cal after?

I had stopped dancing for money in the clubs at this point. I had been offered a job at a cabaret club called Johnny's Bar or something like that. I was stood outside handing out flyers, trying to persuade passing holiday makers to come in. I hated it because I am no good at it, but it was more money and less hours. I am no good at selling. I am very black and white. If they want it, they want it. If they don't, I just do not have a way of manipulating people into something they don't want. I did have the older holiday makers saying I should be in school getting an education. I said, "Na. If I want to do that, I can figure that out later on in life."

One night I was stood outside and a Spanish guy approached me. He said, "I've seen you dancing!" I said "Okay!" In my head I was smiling but on my guard. I had not seen him before and had certainly not seen him around on the club scene in Benidorm. He said, "I like the way you move. I want you to come and dance for me." I was like, "Okay!" He said, "Come to my studio tomorrow, I want to see how I am going to dress you."

I didn't feel threatened by him and I didn't feel like I was in any kind of danger. The curiosity was too much for me. So, the following day I went to his studio. There was a girl present that I had seen around the clubs that use to do some of the sexier shows. Again, I didn't feel threatened in any way. He asked me to take off all my clothes. So, I did. He asked me if my pubic hair was a natural colour which I thought was strange. I said, "Yes." He seemed to like that. I stood there for a while as he circled me, taking in my nakedness. I was then told that I could get dressed. He told me to come back a few nights later. He was going to paint my body in different colours and we were both going to go out into the nightclub and dance for around ten minutes. I said, "Okay!"

It was a pretty brave thing for me to do. I would be there in my nakedness ad-libbing to the music, just going with the flow. I was in. I turned up. I didn't tell anyone about it. I had a double shot of Malibu, Malibu! Like that was strong enough to take the edge off my nerves but that is what I did. He came and got me and we took off into his studio where he proceeded to paint my body in gold, silver and white. I had peacock feathers coming off my hands and a massive, white wig on my head with peacock feathers coming out the top of that. I had high heels on that I had to really concentrate on walking because I cannot walk on high heels. I had a bit of gold gauze over my noo noo and that was that.

We went out and I let go of all my inhibitions and just felt the music and danced. He said it was the best performance he had done with anyone. I felt elated and empowered. After the dance, we were walking around the club and I suddenly realised I had no clothes on. I started to feel a little uncomfortable. The club was really busy and full of Spanish people. I had never been in there before; it was obviously off the track of the tourists' clubs. I asked to go and get dressed.

Back in his studio he said, "Now we have sex?" I said, "NO!" and took off very quickly, money in hand, very pleased with myself.

Once I had done that gig, I got offered to do more of the sexier shows that went on in the tourists' nightclubs. Sticky Vicky and her magic fanny were always a favourite. Google it — she is pretty famous in Benidorm. Another was strawberries, tits and cream. A girl would come out, do a dance, take her top off and squirt whipped cream all over her boobies. She would then pull three guys out of the crowed and put their arms behind their backs and blindfold them. Whoever sucked off the most cream was the winner. Mud wrestling and jelly wrestling. You name it, it was going on. I did not want any part of the more sordid side of the entertainment. I've always found men gawping at women like that and what they think of them, a bit disconcerting. I don't want men looking at me like that and I do not want to be portrayed like that.

Dancing naked for art's sake was different.

Me, George and Cal ended up getting an apartment together. George continued to get absolutely shit faced every night. I can't remember what Cal was doing or even if he found a job. I do remember that we met a group of guys that had been doing building work in Germany and were earning a nice, tidy sum of money. I think Cal was struggling with the lack of money so decided to up and leave with the guys from Germany. I was gutted. Me and George were at a loss of what to do. We moved about a bit from apartment to apartment because we were both trying to survive.

I got collared into doing a kiss-a-gram. I don't even know why I agreed to it. This woman gave me this little speech I had to do. I didn't have the money to get new clothes so that I could look the part. I had it in my head I needed to look sexy! I never felt sexy or desired. I found a small strappy top, mini skirt and pulled some cash together to get some shoes that looked a bit more the part than my trainers!

On the night of the kiss-a-gram, I thought a glass of red wine would help with my nerves. The glass turned into the whole bottle and by the time I got to the kiss-a-gram I was absolutely shit faced. There were loads of people in the bar. It was so embarrassing. I don't think that much of myself at the best of times but especially back then. I pulled it off though. I don't know how. I never ever wanted to do that again, ever! I was so shit faced that when I turned up for work at the club, the manager sacked me. I don't blame him. For the most part you think you have it all sorted and together but I know from working on the door later on in life, you ain't got shit sorted. You generally look a mess and the more you try to hide it, makes it more apparent that you are not holding it together.

I eventually heard from Cal. He sent a couple of letters to a bar that all of our correspondence used to go to, if we had any. It is so lovely getting mail. I still love getting mail to this day. It is so personal, rather than texting and email. We spoke over the phone and he was back home in Britain. I'm not sure if I pushed for the idea or he asked me to go back the UK. I got a flight and flew back to Manchester to meet him. Cal was waiting for me at Manchester airport. The meeting was really emotional. It was so lovely to be met by someone that had not only missed me but was really excited to see me. We drove to Barrow-in-Furness where he lived with his parents. He had initially set me up in a really shit bedsit room in the city of Barrow but then decided against it. He took me back to his parents' house and asked if I could stay there. He stayed in the spare room and I had his room. I started looking for work as soon as I got there and found a job out in Kendall. It was a good two-hour drive from Barrow. It was a live-in chambermaid position. I was taken to my room in the main hotel because they did not have a room for me in the staff quarters. The room I had was bleak, cold, no T.V. and apparently somebody had committed suicide along that corridor. Maybe in my room, I'm not sure. I didn't really care. It was boring. No music, no nothing but I stuck it out for a week. The food was horrible and I felt really alone. The people there were not really that friendly. Cal came up to visit a week after I got there. He bought music and weed.

We were in my room hanging out, smoking weed and

playing the music really quite loud. There was a knock on the door. My first thought was to pretend I wasn't there, obviously because we were smoking weed and I didn't want to get into trouble. There was more knocking on the door. We still pretended that there was no one in the room. The mind of a cannabis smoker! Logic and rationality goes out of the window. The knocking continued, to the point that whoever it was knew I was in there and was not going away until I answered the door. I opened the door and the guy standing there said, "They have a room ready for you over in the staff block." I said, "Cool." He gave me a key, told me the room number and went away. The smell of weed out of the room would have been really strong. I mean, how was I going to get away with the fact that there would have been no one in the room? Idiot!

Me and Cal packed up my stuff and went across to the live-in staff block. It was horrendous! The room was filthy, the mattress was mank. The wardrobe door was hanging off. The sink in the room looked like it hadn't been washed in months. It stank! It was even more depressing than the room I had just come from. Cal said, "Come on we are leaving." So that was the end of that. The idea was to get enough money together to get ourselves back out to Spain. I wasn't going to do it staying there. We made our way back to his parents' home. I didn't get another job whilst I was in Barrow. I signed on and we just hung out. We took off biking around Grizedale Forest. The images that spring to mind are light blues, fresh green everywhere, fells that change colour depending on the light of day. The freshest air you could take in biking around. It started to snow. It was like being in a fairy tale. You just have to stop just for a moment to take a picture in your mind because the beauty of being up there just takes your breath away. We stopped off in a pub out in the middle of nowhere. We didn't have to lock the bikes up, just propped them up outside. A small pub, with a big, log fire burning really bright, for me and Cal to sit next to and get warmed up for a bit. Drinking our hot chocolates, before we set off again around the lakes and fields in Windermere.

I was a pretty needy individual back then and I am sure that Cal needed some breathing space from me. He did try to set me up in the gym one day but I lacked so much confidence in myself, because I didn't know what I was doing. I wouldn't stay. To be fair he chucked me in the gym and left me to it. He didn't even show me around. but he was probably trying to get some space from me.

Cal had decided that he was off and that he did not want this relationship with me anymore. This was after we had ended up at one of his mate's house, where they were all sniffing glue. It was horrible. That was something I wanted no part of. I was devastated once again at being rejected. He was taking off to Spain with or without me. I had nowhere to go. Homeless once again, I didn't want to go back to Bournemouth. I certainly didn't want to go back to my mum, that was for sure. His mum and dad were going to take me to Blackpool once he had gone but I decided to go back to Spain with him. I was holding on for dear life. Basically, making a pain of myself. The poor guy. I wish I could apologise to him. I think back to myself back then and it makes me cringe.

We were now back in Spain. George was still there. It had only been three months really since we had gone. The summer season was starting to pick up again. Work wasn't difficult to find and a new batch of people were coming and going. This is where Sally popped up. I think Cal and George had met

Sally when they first went out there. She had decided to come back and do another stint out in Benidorm. We made friends pretty quickly and started to hang out all the time. We were dancing in the clubs. The manager of the club then gave me and Sally work behind the bars! I don't know how I managed that as I could barely speak Spanish. I did it though.

Whilst I was in Benidorm, I always found time to spend at least a couple of hours on the beach every day. I would make a point of getting up whilst everyone was sleeping. I made sure that I got up and went out into the sun. What was the point of being in the Mediterranean and not having a tan!

We were then asked to dance in the bigger clubs outside of the town. I was doing all right as far a work was going. I was however, taking too many drugs. Cal had left again. I was hard work undoubtedly. Once he did leave, I threw myself into getting more wasted. One of the club owners pulled me to one side one night and tried to speak to me. He was trying to let me know I was going too far. I was young, thought I had all my shit together. I am sure if I could see myself now, I would be saddened by what I could see. But when you are that age you don't want to listen to anybody. I thought I had it all under control and that I was hot shit!

The madness and never having a stable home to live in, all got too much in the end. My subconscious was telling me that if I didn't get out of this lifestyle I was going to die. I knew it was time to come home to Bournemouth and find my next journey. I bought a ticket off a girl that was selling her return flight to Gatwick. She booked in my bags and then gave me her boarding pass. I floated pass the flight attendant praying that they would not ask for my passport and see that the boarding pass was not in my name. No questions asked, I found my seat on the plane and sat tight until we were up in the air.

I landed in Gatwick. I looked out the window of the aeroplane, it was cold and pouring with rain. I felt happy to be on home ground in the UK.

Janine and Leigh 1981.

Leigh and his mate Mark on his sixth birthday. The infamous kitchen table Noble Close.

Janine Town Sports day 1983 ten years old.

Janine sixteen years old 1989 last day of school.

Janine seventeen years old Madisons.

Janine seventeen years old at Terry's Christmas 1991.

Janine eighteen years old nine stone.

Janine. Dijon. Grape picking.

Janine and Sally Benidorm 1992.

Janine and Kerry USA 1996.

Rafael 1997.

Janine and Leigh Alcatraz 1998.

Women Kickin' it 1997.

Janine and Lou 1999.

Janine and Leigh 1999.

Janine Prime bodies 2001.

Janine 2000 first fight end of first round.

Janine won first fight against Gina Stone.

Second fight 2000.

Janine and Leigh after a fight win.

British Kickboxing title win 2002.

World Title fight 2003.

# Chapter Six
## Don't Do Acid On Your Own

Before I left Spain, I had to figure out where I was going to stay back in Bournemouth. I had contacted a friend, Michelle. She was a friend I knew from Pearl Gardens. She had left the neighbourhood too. Coincidently she was in a relationship with one of Pete's very good friends, Tim. She was a hairdresser by trade so regularly cut my hair, she was the one that had given my mum the Raquel cut. I had contacted her from Spain and asked if I could stay with her. She said it wasn't ideal as she had left Tim and was sleeping on a pull-out bed with a friend. But, for a few nights I could stay with her if I was desperate, which I was. I thought, 'Get myself back and then figure out the rest as go went along'.

I was a selfish, inconsiderate, not thinking about anyone else individual at that time. I had helped myself to her clothes, well, a pair of jeans. I just didn't think about asking if I could wear them, I just did. What was I thinking? It upset her, of course it did. Who had I become? I broke the shower attachment to the taps in the bath. Not on purpose, but it was another thing to add to me imposing where I was staying. I needed to go. I knew it and I could tell that Michelle was in a compromised position with the owner and me her friend. There really wasn't room for me to be there. The owner of the flat didn't want me there.

I had just come out of the Town Hall. I'm not sure why I

was down that way. Maybe sorting a place to stay or maybe sorting out signing on as well. I needed some money coming in until I found a job. Just by coincidence, my mum drove past I couldn't believe it. I didn't really want to see her or speak to her. She pulled over and said, "Get in." I did as I was told. It is funny how you revert back to the behaviour of being the child. It is like you lose your voice; you can't speak your truth in that abusive relationship. Also, she was my mum. She drove me back to the house in Throop. We caught up a little bit. I hadn't seen her in a year. She asked where I was staying. I said I had nowhere to go. She said, "You can come back here." I didn't have much choice. I thought, 'All right, back home it is. You never know things might be different'. Before I left to go away, I had stored all my stuff up in her loft. All my good clothes, all my records, cutlery, pictures, my good trainers. I was looking forward to putting on my Adidas Gazelles. I asked, "Can I get my stuff out of the loft, Mum, please?" She said, "What stuff?" I said, "My stuff I put up there before I went away!"

She said, "Oh, yeah, I sold that!"

I sat there, dumbfounded, all my stuff, gone! Why? Why would she do that? She could tell by my face that I was not pleased. Her response, "Don't get angry, I didn't know when you were coming back!"

In my head, I was like, coming back? I am your daughter, why would you not leave it up there? Why didn't you take my reverse charge phone call? You may have found out where I was. You could have just left it up in the loft. It's not like it was in the way!

What was I going to do? I had nowhere to go, I had to suck it up and just let it go. I got my belongings from

Michelle's and made my way back to my mum's house.

Dad. Dad who? He was just not on the scene at all really. I think I had made my decision at that point that I wanted nothing to do with him. Mum was doing a good job at saying things like, "I want you to make your own decisions. I want you to make up your own mind about your dad. But you know he beat me up. You know he did some really disgusting sexual things to me!"

What was I meant to do with that information? She was my mum. Of course, I believed her. I wanted nothing to do with him. He certainly wasn't interested in what I was doing. Or even cared about my welfare. Why should I want anything to do with him at all?

I signed on the dole for a bit, just to get some money coming in. It took six weeks before you could get anything. I'm not sure what you were meant to do in the meantime if you were destitute. Six weeks is a long time when you are desperate! It was guaranteed money though, so if I needed to borrow from someone, I could pay it back. Whilst I was waiting for the money to come in from welfare, I went back to the hotels and got a chambermaid job. Like I have said, there is always a job in the hotels, either in housekeeping or in the kitchen. I wasn't proud, I'd do anything. I needed money.

The thought of bar work before France and Spain, was something I had never thought about but as I had done a bit in Spain, I went and asked in a pub my Grandad (Mum's dad) used to go in all the time. It was right in the centre of town. I managed to land the job and they gave me Sunday night to begin with. As soon as I had signed on, I signed off. I was working both the hotel and the pub called Woodies. It wasn't long before they offered me a full-time position at the pub. I gave up working in the hotels. Chambermaiding was graft. Working the pubs was fun! It did not take long to fall back into drinking a lot. I was working in a pub and everyone was doing it — taking Es on the weekends and generally getting up to no good.

On one occasion I had ended up in Elements, a popular club in town, drinking 20/20. That stuff was like drinking fruit juice but was like rocket fuel in your system. There was a guy from the hotel that I had been working with. He was sniffing around and I was wasted.

In the club I was all in control. I stepped outside of the club and the fresh air hitting me was like a baseball bat. He said, "You fancy coming back to mine?" I was like, "Sure!" I was so naive. I was just going back for a cuppa as a friend. But in reality, he thought his luck was in! We arrived at his house and were sat in his back garden. I thought he had a pool. I had even had a conversation about it with him. He didn't correct me. He must have thought, 'Great she's really out of it. But, talking enough to be consensual'.

He went off to make us a cuppa. I got up off my seat to test the water, it was grass. I was kind of hallucinating. I thought shit, get your shit together Davis. Then an overriding feeling of sickness came over me. I needed to go and straight away! I marched into the house, said, "I am leaving and see you later." He said, "What? Are you sure?" I said, "Yes!" very adamantly. He then asked if I knew where I was? I said, "Sure," and thought to myself I'll figure that out when I get outside. He put a jumper on me to keep me warm and then buttoned my jacket all the way to the top of my neck.

I swiftly walked out of the house and down the pathway. I went on my way. He said, "Turn left." I turned left and soon figured out I was on Richmond Park Road. I recognised the traffic lights at the end of the street. If I could make it to the end of the road, I knew there was a taxi rank where I could get a taxi. I then proceeded to puke my guts up in every single garden in that half a mile stretch of road. I managed to make it to the taxi rank. What the woman must have thought of me when I walked through the door. I must have looked a right state. I made it home though in one piece, goodness knows what I paid the taxi driver. I think I just threw money at him and stumbled out of the car. Once inside the house I grabbed a bucket, took off to my bed as quick as I could and passed out with the bucket next to me.

There was one time when I had been out that I must have blacked out coming home and woke up in the corner of my room, on the floor, bundled up in my duvet. I have no recollection of how I got there. Mum, of course, as she walked past my room would look at me in disgust. I would leave my bedroom door open, idiot that I was. Her passing comment was, "You're going to become an alcoholic." I thought, 'Oh fuck off, you don't know anything'.

I was smoking cigarettes on top of everything else. Such a disgusting habit. There is nothing to gain from it. Other than, smelly breath, smelly clothes, rotting teeth and gums and killing your lungs. I sat at home one day on my bed and thought, 'What the fuck am I doing? I'm contemplating either buying food or fags'. It was a no brainer to me, give up the fags what are you doing! That was the last time I ever smoked a cigarette.

In my little fantasy world I lived in, I wondered what Cal was doing? Would he come and find me? What about if I got myself a job up North so that I was closer to him? I found a magazine that advertised jobs in hotels around the country. I cannot for the life of me remember what the magazine was called. I found a chambermaid job in a hotel that was right on Lake Ullswater, very close to Penrith in Cumbria. I would only be up the road from Barrow and not the other end the British Isles. I was running away again but ultimately, I had to see if there was anything left with Cal.

My friend Sally who I had met out in Benidorm, was back home now and lived in Hull. I planned to stop off in Hull on my way up to Cumbria.

The day before I was due to leave, I met up with a friend of mine, Suzanna, who suggested we go for a drink. Of course, I agreed! A couple of vodkas later and she suggested we go to Madisons. I said, "Oh yeah." We both decided to drop an E. As I was throwing shapes on the dance floor, John Bellows turned up who was a right wrongun'. He danced his way over to me and dropped an acid tab in my mouth. In hindsight, I should have spat it out. But I didn't and just let the night pan its way out. I was flying! We ended up at a house party. I completely forgot that I had a coach to catch. Suzanna reminded me around four a.m. I thought, 'Oh yeah, shit! I need to go'.

I was that high I forgot that I was high. I bustled through the door and Mum was huddled over the cooker with the gas rings on, warming herself, I think. She was not happy for one reason or another, probably because I'd been out all night. I came in and put my arms around her shoulders, goodness knows what I was saying to her. I then had a lightbulb moment and realised how high I was and suddenly let go. I ran upstairs and got all my stuff together. She very kindly drove me to the coach station and bid her goodbyes. It wasn't emotional.

It then hit me. I'm off my tits, on my own, with a two-hour journey to Victoria in London, a three or four hour wait in London and then five hours to Hull. This is going to be a journey of a lifetime. Get strapped in!

I got on the coach and huddled myself up on the seat. The gentleman on the coach that would sell you tea and coffee, took one look at me and said, "I think you need a cup of coffee, don't you?" He had a caring little grin on his face that made me feel at ease as to the state I was in.

I made it to Victoria, got off the coach and thought I needed a cup of tea. There was a cafe just round the corner of the coach station. It was pretty busy and there was a pretty big queue that I joined. I made it to the woman that was serving and asked for my cup of tea. She said, "You need to buy breakfast to get tea."

I said, "I don't want breakfast." I was not in the mood for food. The drugs will do that to you. If I had food, I would most definitely be sick.

She repeated, "You need to buy breakfast to get tea."

I repeated back, "I just want a cup of tea!"

She said, "It'll cost you a fiver for the tea!"

I said, "I do not give a fuck about how much you want to charge me for a cup of tea, I just want a cup of tea!"

I got my tea.

I was starting to feel a bit more level-headed. I vaguely remember sitting and chatting to an old lady, she was ever so nice. Once I finished my cup of tea, I made my way back to the coach station to wait for my coach to Hull.

I had never been to Victoria coach station before. I assumed it was like Bournemouth coach station. You got on the coaches the same place you got off. I went and sat on my bags and watched a lot of coaches come in and could not for the life of me figure out why people were not getting on. I sat there for close to three hours like that. A nice gentleman came up to me in the end and asked me if I was okay, I said, "I do not have a clue what I am doing!"

I explained to him I was on my way to Hull and my coach was meant to be leaving in about twenty minutes. He had a little laugh to himself and said I needed to make my way out of the station and across the road where the departure station was.

What an idiot!

I then scrabbled to get my shit together and get across the road. Another nice man came up to me with a trolley and asked if I needed help. I thought, 'How nice'. I said, "Yes please." My head still quite fuzzy. I thought about these nice people helping me out.

What I didn't realise is that these guys do it for money and not just to be kind. He wheeled my stuff across the road and as I sat down where I needed to be, I said, "Thank you." He then waited around and in front of everyone that was waiting in the area, he barked at me, "Well you gonna pay me!"

Of course, I was shocked, I said, "How much do you want?"

"A pound will do!"

Embarrassed, I threw the quid at him and then just hustled myself down in my seat without looking at anyone. I thought, 'Fucking asshole. Why not say to begin with instead of seeking out the twatted, vulnerable female. Dick…!'

I got on the coach and five hours later I was in Hull with my bud Sally. "Oh dude, I have had a hell of a journey."

Moral of that story: do not drop acid and then spend the day on your own, trying to figure shit out. It was horrible.

# Chapter Seven
## The Beauty Of The Lakes

I arrived at the hotel and my first impression was that it was very posh! There were TV stars and MPs staying there. I had never worked in such a posh place before. I was shown around and taken to my room that was above the main reception. They did not have a room for me in the employee's digs, so I was staying in the main hotel until they did. I knew from working at that hotel in Kendal that the food they give the staff was pretty awful. I told them I was a vegetarian. Breakfast would be all right for the staff because it was fresh. But come evening meal, they would serve up whatever was left over from breakfast most of the time. I, on the other hand, because I told them I was a veggie would get fresh bakes and fresh food made for me every night. Oh, yeah! I was the envy of most of the staff at dinner time. I was just lucky I'd had the smarts when I got there to get that one sorted straight away.

When I was out in the local town area, I had to be careful and not pick up a chicken sandwich in front of the friends I made from the hotel. That would have given the game away! I needed to keep that little secret close to my chest.

From what I remember, working at the hotel it was fun and everyone that worked there was pretty cool. Lake Ullswater is breath-taking! The scene across the lake and on to the fells from the hotel changed every day you looked out the window. It's the same view. But the colours change from dark green, to deep blues and dark browns. You would open the windows when you went into the rooms to tidy. I don't know what it is up there but the air is so clean; like you are breathing in the freshest air possible! Stick your head out the window and take in the biggest breath. Fill your lunges up so that they can't take any more and let it out really slowly. It makes you feel alive! I would then look across the lake at the fells to see what colour it was. Just beautiful.

When the weekend arrived, we would head into Penrith and go to the tiniest club called Blues Disco. I had a tequila drinking competition with one of my work mates on one of the occasions we went there. I drank them under the table and then proceeded to do handstands and backbends on the dance floor. I was told I was of another breed that night. I was a full force of energy, like a steam train coming through. Most people back then would find it difficult to keep up with me.

That particular night, the hotel had given me cauliflower cheese for my dinner. Once I had returned from our escapade from Blues Disco, I had proceeded to projectile vomit all night. I was crawling on my hands and knees backwards and forwards from my bed to my bathroom. I was in such a bad way. There was no way I was going to make it into work. Fortunately, one of my housekeeping buddies knocked my door in the morning and asked if I would like the day off? They didn't need me. I was so relieved! Once I thought I could venture outside a little later, I went downstairs to see if I could get a bit of dry toast to fill my belly up. Every time I tried to speak; I would retch. It was horrible. I found out from one of my friends that the cauliflower cheese had been off! Great combination: gone off veggie food and tequila.

One night we were out playing pool in a local pub. I do

not know how I had Cal's number but I thought, 'Right, this is why I am up here. Let's give him a call'. He answered and was quite polite to start with. Once I told him where I was, he said, "Janine, do not call me again!" I did not pursue it and thought, 'Right, come on that's enough now. You've bled that one dry, time to move on'.

I had fitted in really well with the staff at the hotel. The head housekeeper was a lovely woman. I can't remember her name, but I do know we got on very well. We would work together quite often cleaning the rooms. I would always be chit chatting away. What was I doing? Where was I going? What did I have planned? I was just trying to figure stuff out. I was pretty lost back then that was for sure.

When you are told you are not clever enough and your Mum has made you believe that you're worth nothing, what choices do you have available to you?

The head housekeeper did tell me one day, whatever I chose to end up doing I would be successful at it. I didn't really understand what that meant at the time. It was nice though.

It wasn't long before I was thinking about going back to Bournemouth. It was fun but it was so small. Small village, small community. My instincts were telling me to go home. I didn't see myself progressing at the hotel, although they did offer me senior housekeeper position. I thought that was pretty cool but, no. I wanted to go home. I was in the hotel for around six weeks.

This time the coach journey back to Bournemouth was done without acid.

I was back in Bournemouth. Cal was history, I had put closure to that.

# Chapter Eight
# Homeless Once Again

Mum was really happy to have me home. NOT!

Her face when I walked through the door. I was just an inconvenience. There was not a smile on her face. I had nowhere else to go so it had to be there. I knew I was not welcome but just had to suffer it until I got myself back on my feet again.

Back to Woodies I went. They gave me back my job as a bar person with plenty of hours. I got my head down and got working. Working split shifts with only one day off a week in a pub does not leave any time for a social life, that was for sure. I was earning £3.17 an hour: minimum wage. It was shit. The hours you put in just would not equate to the money you got and essentially, putting any money away. You lived hand to mouth. Drinking, partying, laughing and ultimately having the most fun at that time working on the bar. Even if it was not really conducive to looking after myself, I was having a good time. The landlord said I was a good worker. My till at the weekend made the most money.

There was a doorman that worked there at the weekend called 'Boxer!' I'm not sure if he ever boxed. He collared me one night at the door to the bar. He passed me over a bag that was full of white powder. He said, "I don't know what to do with it, you can have it." I looked at it and thought holy shit, that is a lot of drugs! It was either a massive bag of cocaine or a massive bag of speed. I bundled it under my shirt and ran off to my locker and chucked it in there. At the end of my shift, I shoved it in my bag and got that home, quick smart.

Right, thinking cap on. What am I going to do with it?

I could have handed it in to the police. I could have flushed it down the toilet. Why would I want to do that, when so much fun could be had taking some of it!

My thoughts were to get rid of most of it and keep a small amount for when I want to party. I took off to my brother's. I shared it with him. Between us, we got rid of the bulk of it to friends and fellow ravers.

The weekend shifts at the pub would always consist of the bar crew being shit-faced by the end of the shift and then piling around the corner to Alcatraz, the wine bar. We would all be shit-faced and ball out of there at two a.m., crawling up the street on our hands and knees to get home in a taxi. I recollect one night being in there when Boxer, who usually had all the shit bag banter, lost it because I ruffled his hair. He went off his head on one. Unbeknownst to me, he was wearing spray on hair! How was I to know? I mean, what is spray on hair anyway? What happens when it rains?

You see the bald guys but no one ever talks about how losing their hair might affect them? I have never asked a guy how they feel about losing their hair. I know I would be devastated. Men must feel the same but as men, they have to keep it all on the inside, not show emotion; they are tough and strong. If you show emotions, it means you are weak!

I must admit it was like ruffling straw. Oh well, that was that. He didn't speak to me much after that. Probably embarrassed!

Mum's behaviour was blowing hot and cold again. You

just would never know what was going to come through the door. One day, I was sat in the garden and I heard her come through the front door. You could feel the energy when she came through the door. She was smashing around in the kitchen and then like Captain Caveman (Google Captain Caveman if you don't know who he is), she bustled herself out into the garden talking shit, blaming me for something or the other. I said to her, "Don't start any of your shit!"

I don't know what she was going on about but I did get up and go over to her and tell her, "You are fucking mental!"

That was the worst part of her behaviour. I hadn't done anything wrong. Yes, I was out drinking but my behaviour at home was me cleaning and doing my share of what needed to be done. I was paying my rent.

I always thought she would conjure up these stories in her head, so they manifested themselves as truth. The story in her head became reality so, by the time she got home we were the ones to get it. Even if it wasn't real.

That was it, I was out of there. I knew it was only going to get worse if I stayed. I had to figure out where I was going to stay. I phoned the pub and asked the manager if I could stay in the spare room they had. He said, "Yes." So, I packed my bags and got the fuck out of there. She followed me up the stairs and was shouting shit at me in my room. As I passed out of my doorway, she stood fast and I thought, 'You lay a finger on me, I'm going to have you'. I towered over now. Her five foot nothing to my five foot eight. I knew I was stronger than her as well. I squared right up to her, looked her straight in her eyes and she didn't lift a finger.

That would be the very last time I would ever stay in that house, ever!

Kenny was a good manager. Nothing really to write about him really, especially at work. We all got on with our work and worked well together. There was a flat for the managers to live in at the top of the pub. He had a spare room and that was the first place I thought of to go. It was convenient and he wasn't going to charge me anything whilst I searched around for the next place to live. He used to watch that weird Asian cartoon porn stuff that was quite violent. Just strange. It creeped me out. I had an uneasy feeling when I was staying there. At night when I went to bed, I would wedge a chair under the handle of the door so that no one could get in whilst I slept. It's a horrible feeling when you feel unsafe and vulnerable.

It wasn't long before a local that was coming into the pub, had said that he was looking for a lodger. I can't remember his name, he was a scouser I know that. We'll call him Steve. I jumped on it. He was a bit of a sleaze, thought he was a bit of a lady's man. I was not one bit interested. I knew how to handle him though and kept him at bay.

Getting wasted was still at the top of my list of things to do. Quite often coming home early doors, forgetting my keys and waking him up, much to his annoyance. Me at the front door, starry eyed saying I'm sorry!

Leigh was in the picture at this time. We had started hanging out together and going to clubs. He was bang on it and so was I. Leigh turned up one day at Woodies with his mate Jacko. They had just returned from Glastonbury. The state of the pair of them was hilarious. They were both wearing waistcoats unbuttoned, bare chested. Thigh length shorts on. Biker boots and top hats. Leigh was in a beige top hat with a sunflower hanging off the top and Jacko's was rainbow coloured. They didn't give a shit, it was great.

Leigh was living in a house in Parker Road, Winton. It was a party house. Everyone that was anyone ended up there after the clubs had shut and we would have the best time. Smoking weed, taking E's, talking shit and most importantly, listening and dancing to the music.

Woodies was fun but I had started to look around for a job with more money. I found another bar job that paid more at a place called Chablis. It was a wine bar that attracted the more affluent type of men and women. It was very much a place where the older crowd would come at the weekend. Being twenty-one years old you are very judgemental. Especially when you see older women in their forties and fifties, wearing cocktail dresses, looking like mutton dressed up as lamb, shaking their tits and ass all around the place.

Who was I to judge! Live life how you want to live it. Shake your ass, show your tits off and wear what you like that is not age appropriate. I hate that, 'age appropriate'! Who decides that? Wear what you want and be bold and confident and ultimately, happy with who you are as a person without worrying about whatever anyone thinks. Judgement is for assholes and I was one of them when I was twenty-one!

I was getting paid a pound more an hour, which over the forty-hour week can accrue itself to a nice, tidy sum of money. I was also earning myself a good pot of tips. The punters there had a bit more money to throw around. There was a man that frequented the bar. He had taken to talking to me every time he came in. He was all right. Charming, had all the gab. He asked me out for dinner. We must have been talking about Indian food because at that time I had never been for Indian food and mentioned it. He said, "I'll take you. I know a great place in Westbourne." Let's call him Karl. I went and met Karl in Westbourne for my very first Indian meal. Poppadum's, mango chutney, that lime chili blow-your-mouth off dip, yummmmy! I went for a korma; played it safe. It was a lovely meal. He paid for the meal and then somehow, I found myself back at his house in his bedroom where he had all these pictures of him with stars around the place. I knew I was being worked and that he was trying to impress me with the connection to these people. I think he was some kind of booking agent. Fucking weird. I wanted to get out of there. I thought, 'You fucking sleaze bag. You are going to have to do more than buy a meal and show me a few photographs to get into my pants'. I did manage to get out of there unscathed. I did see him again after that night when I was walking by myself back to my flat. Karl was hanging off the railings on the side of the road in Boscombe. It would have been one or two a.m. I know walking home alone at that time of night is not the best. I used to do that a lot, walking home at that time of night. Just stupid and amazing nothing happened to me! He was hanging off the railings, a burger in one hand that he was trying to shove in his mouth with his dick hanging out trying to take a piss! He looked disgusting and I saw him in plain sight. He saw me as well and just scowled at me. What an absolute catch! Fucking, horrible dick. When I went back into work, I told everyone what I had seen and told him as well when he came in again. Shamed him, fucking piece of work.

Chablis would close around two a.m. I would walk home from there on my own all the time. So stupid but I had no other choice. I had no car. I never asked for help. I would always stay on the main road. One night, a police car pulled over and offered me a lift. I said, "No thanks." I did not trust getting into anyone's car, even if it was the police. No one is to be trusted, police included. I had my wits about me and my keys planted between my knuckles. I always made it home safely.

For some reason, I decided to get a van driver job delivering car parts. I'm not sure what prompted it. I was searching, trying different jobs out. I worked the van job during the day and worked Chablis at the weekends. I was doing all right for money at that point. Around this time, I had met a guy called Lee. He was my boyfriend for a while and he introduced me to the gym. I had looked at my legs one day and I could see cellulite. I thought, 'Errr, I don't like that. I've got to do something about that'. Lee took me to a small gym at the back of Boscombe, in a hotel called The Burlington. I loved it down there. I started to go to classes. I found I was naturally quite strong. Swim, sauna, jacuzzi, loved it. I always felt fresh and healthy. I would go and meet everyone at the party house on Sunday when everyone else had been up all night. I would turn up looking fit and healthy.

Lee didn't last long; he was taking the piss out of me. I found myself food shopping for both of us and him not contributing anything to it. He would quite happily come round and eat all my food but offer me nothing for the cost. I did not have that kind of money and that behaviour was starting to piss me off. He had to go!

After Lee, I met another guy called Fabian. Six foot three and handsome. I thought he was attracted to me. We spent some naked time together. He made me think we were an item. I then realised when we were at a party one afternoon that he was ashamed to be seen with me. He kissed me out of the way of everyone, hiding in the hallway and then when we went back into the room where everyone was hanging out, it was like it hadn't happened, to the point of completely ignoring me.

It was weird and I was not stupid. I knew he didn't want anyone to know he had been with me. I thought, 'Fuck that and fuck you', he had to go as well.

Unfortunately, the partying really started to take hold. I had no business being in that van, delivering car parts on a Monday morning. Vacant, not concentrating. I was a danger. I was getting out of control with the drug taking. We all were. I had moved out of the scouser's place and moved into a small room in a house that was quite cheap. A party house, everyone was on it! Working was not really conducive to that lifestyle. It wasn't long before they stopped giving me shifts at Chablis. Rightly so, I was turning up to work either high or looking a mess. I stopped working the van and decided to sign on. WHAT WAS I DOING? I was just lost!

In amongst all the madness, I was still trying to figure out a way to stay fit. I'm not sure if I was going to the gym at this point. I probably didn't have enough money! I do remember taking myself off down to Bournemouth Pier. I would try to run to Boscombe Pier and back, about three miles. A buddy of mine came with me to support me. I stopped so many times. I felt like my lungs were on fire. I did it though! I completed it. Getting out and running was the next best option for me because it was free.

Unfortunately, I was not working, I had no money and couldn't pay rent. Life started to fall apart and I found myself homeless, once again. Sofa hopping once again. It was horrible. I had no space to just shut myself away in.

I had to get my shit together and figure out what I was going to do next.

For some reason, I went to Bournemouth and Poole College and looked at a prospectus on courses they had there.

I found a BTech in Tourism and Leisure. I thought the course was about sport. I had my interview and they accepted me. Right, this is a fresh start on what I want to be doing.

The Southwestern was a place in town, I knew I could probably get a room in. A horrible, horrible, horrible place. I have had some low points in my life. This was definitely one of them. In the room, I could literally touch either side of the walls. It was like a jail cell. The bed was a single, about five feet in length. I had a tiny shower room and a shared kitchen with about fifty other people. I never cooked in there. My window at night would rattle. It was mouldy, rusty and really dirty. At that time, I would always fall asleep listening to music, to drown out the rattling window and to take myself somewhere other than where I was. Seal was the choice, the 'Kiss From a Rose' album. It always gave me some peace. I hated living there! I was really shameful about living there, it was such a dump but it was a space to be in for the moment, whilst I figured out my next move.

I was at Leigh's house one day. I think we had all been out partying. The partying had gone well into the next day. Most of us were still high and certainly had not slept. My mum turned up unannounced. This was before the days of mobile phones. We were both in a bit of shock as to why she was there. We had quite a few of our friends there. We all gathered in the living room just chit chatting about nothing really. I said, "Hey mum, I've got a position at College. I'm doing a B Tech in Tourism and Leisure." I was really pleased to tell her. I'm not sure what I was looking for. I wanted her to be pleased for me. Give me some encouragement, some support. Be my Mum, be proud of me. She said nothing. Gave me nothing. The look on her face told me everything I needed to know. I knew then right at that very point I needed to get her out of my life. If I wanted to get on with mine and grow and become a better person, she needed to go!

Do you know how tough that is, to make that decision about someone that is ultimately meant to be there for you, care for you and guide you? I was twenty-one years old. As far as I was concerned, she was dead to me and if I wanted to get things sorted, I had to do it of my own accord; without any encouragement or support from her. Obviously, Dad was not even a factor at this point. Who the fuck is he?

ANGER!

Angry at her. Angry at life. Angry at everyone. I had started to piece together all the incidents that we had grown up in. I started to realise that it was all wrong, what me and Leigh had been through. I went off to the Doctors at one point and said that my mum told me I needed to see a counsellor. The Doctor asked me a few questions and then told me that my mum needed to see the counsellor and that I was all right. That did reassure me a little bit but I was right at the beginning of asking all kinds of questions about myself.

College was difficult and my head was not in a place to see it through to the end. The course was not about sport at all, in the end. It was about training you up to be a manager of a sports club. I was not the one bit interested in sitting behind a desk!

I did not really set myself up at college with the right mind set anyway, the first day was an absolute shambles. Instead of staying in and being fresh for the next day, there was a party at a friend's house. Everyone was going. I said when I got to the party, "Right, I'm only going to have a couple. I've got to start college tomorrow!" It turns out, I was the last person to leave at about six in the morning, flying on Ecstasy. I started college at nine a.m.! I got myself dressed and took myself off to college. How I got through the day is beyond me. I was signing papers but I had no idea what was on them!

It just wasn't the right time. I tried to see it through but I just didn't have it in me and I was not interested in what they were teaching me. I wasn't getting the work done. The essays were terrible and I just didn't believe enough in myself to keep fighting.

Around this time, the scouser that I had lived with got in contact with me and asked me to pop round and see him. He clearly saw me as a business opportunity. He had Es to sell and asked me if I would do it. Me being me, I did. Always a yes before I think about the question. Always happy to help anyone out, without thinking about the consequences or how happy I feel doing the favour. Think about everyone else before I think about myself.

I knew enough people and our party crew was pretty big. I would have no trouble getting rid of them. Of course, I sold them but I also spent the money. What the fuck was I doing! He turned up one day at the Southwestern. He found out where I was living. He was at my door so angry and rightly so. He wanted his money. I did not have anything to give him. How he did not knock that door down, he was banging so hard. I was scared, alone and felt fucking stupid. Again, what the fuck was I doing? I managed to lose him though. It was around £300 or £400 pounds. I still feel bad about it, but it is what it is and it comes with the territory. Drugs generally means being around fucked up people, who take more than they sell, and sharks. Sharks that will use you and have no interest in how you are doing or doing right by you.

Whilst I was at college, I had seen an advertisement for a flat share. I tore off the number from the sheet and gave them a call. It was a great double room in a nice house in the back of Boscombe, Florence Road. I could not get myself out of the hell hole that was the Southwestern fast enough. I had a double bed in a lovely room, it was like luxury. I was moving up!

Being at college, I did not have a bursary or a grant for living. So, I had to get a job to subsidise my living expenses. I found a bar job at The Bournemouth International Centre (BIC). Once I had binned off the college, I then just took extra shifts so that I could afford to live in my new digs. I had befriended a girl called Kerry. She was, at the time, my brother's girlfriend. She was petite, blonde and beautiful. We got along pretty well and between us were generally getting up to no good. I never rated myself as an attractive, young woman. Never thought that anyone would be attracted to me. I thought it was great having beautiful friends because then maybe people would like me more or maybe, men would like me more. I was desperate to find someone, anyone to love me.

We were both working at The BIC, always smoking weed before work. It was nothing for the pair of us to drink a bottle of wine and drop a bomb of base (heavy-ass speed!) before going into to work. So naughty but I suppose for the most part I was self-medicating. I really didn't give a shit about anything or anyone, including myself. I did have a limit though. There was a lot of my peer group that were taking it to a whole different level. There was this guy called Zack. Me and Kerry would go and get our weed from him. One night when we were round his place, he said to go and wait in his room. We both stepped inside and saw three guys there, stooped over themselves, drooling and wasted; it terrified me! I knew they were either smacked out or cracked out. That whole level up from where I was to heroin or crack was not a place I needed to go. No way. I ran out of that room so fast. I was not going back in there. I waited outside. In fact, I shoved Kerry back in there to get our weed!

Weed, Es and speed was about as far as I wanted to take the drug journey. The heroin was never a curiosity for me. I cannot give you a clear explanation for that, it just wasn't. I suppose I always thought I was just having fun. I never questioned that I might be self-medicating. Fun was a massive part of what I was doing but I do have to recognise that I was hiding, in amongst all the partying.

Me and Kerry would quite regularly turn up to work completely spaced out. There was a manager that worked at The BIC that use to look after the pair of us and if we turned up to work in a real state, he would stick us out the back to wash the glasses. It was not long before they moved me from The BIC to the Pavilion Theatre. I think they had had enough of my erratic behaviour and did not want to sack me, so sent me across the road to be out of the way.

The Pavilion was all right to work in. I had plenty of shifts to do, daytime and evenings. If you were not working the bar between the shows, they had a ballroom out the back where they would hold tea dances and line dance evenings. They also had a great dance night called 'Bump 'n' Hustle'. When the managers would set up the night for Bump 'n' Hustle you would get assigned a bar to work with a team leader. I would be a team leader and then the younger crew would fight over who would end up on my bar, only because I would have everyone on the bar doing shots out the back. I would set the boundaries though. You can only work on my bar if you kept your shit together. If you got wasted and couldn't keep it together, you were on your own to explain the reason you were the way you were. My crew were always organised and worked hard but we would have the most fun!

The daytime shifts would be tidying up the bars and sorting the empty bottles down in the courtyard. You had to separate them into the collection skips. I one hundred percent fucking hated that job. I would always be sent down to do it. Once I got down into the courtyard, I would absolutely lose it. Launching crates across the courtyard, smashing the bottles up. On reflection it wasn't just about the bottles. I had so much anger in me it was scary.

One day I was walking in the reception of the theatre. I was nosing inside the security box. I clocked a couple of TV monitors and saw to my horror that the CCTV cameras were faced straight into the bottle yard where on numerous occasions I had proceeded to lose it. Oh, my goodness! What must they think about me? Absolute nut case! I didn't lose it again in the bottle yard, for fear that they were actually sending me down there to watch me. I tucked that anger away.

One of the managers that worked at the theatre had suggested that the military would be a good place for me to go. I thought no way! I'd be all right if I went in as a sergeant! I'd be all right if I was in a position of telling everyone what to do. I certainly was not in a place of respecting authority and I certainly did not want anyone screaming in my face. I would have lost it without any shadow of doubt. I always had a clear idea of principles and of what was right and wrong. I was never afraid to speak up and tell someone how it was. I have always been very straight talking, which over the years has lost me both friends and jobs.

My brother had taken off to the States. He has often done this over the years, usually when he has taken it too far with the drugs and needed to get out of where he was. Go and dry up. Clear his head out. I never had that relationship with my Dad. Never looked for it, never wanted it. As I have mentioned, through the stories that my Mum had told me I really didn't have a good idea of who he was, other than the man that had abandoned us and had abused my mum through physical and sexual violence. So, my opinion of him was not great.

Leigh was in America and had asked my friend Kerry to come out and join him. Before she left, she was living at my flat at the time in one of the rooms that was empty. She had nowhere to go so I let her live there rent free, like you would for a friend who had nowhere to go. I would do that for anyone I know that needs help. She had nothing really happening and no fixed abode so off she went. A blessing really because we were a bad influence on each other, the crazy drug taking stopped! I did not have that influence around me, so I was able to clear my head up a bit.

I had started going to a body building gym in Boscombe called Prime Bodies. I do not recall how I ended up there. I was twenty-one and I think someone had probably mentioned it to me. I took myself off there to check it out. It was down a back ally and was very intimidating to be in. Vern, who was the owner, set me up with a three-day split weight training program. I loved it in there. It was like going to church for me. It was like coming into the light when I was in there. I was naturally quite strong and loved picking up the metal weights. I loved the way it made me feel. I was still struggling with my confidence so I would go in at seven in the morning, even if I had been out the night before. It gave me purpose and discipline to start achieving something with myself. At seven a.m. there was no one in there. I could keep myself under the radar so that I would not have to encounter anyone that would make me feel insecure. It probably took me six to seven months before I went in there in the daytime. I remember going there on a Sunday. All I could hear from outside was the weights crashing and men talking. I walked halfway up the stairs, turned around and went home. I couldn't do it. I did not have the confidence to get up there and do a workout.

My very first training partner was Dale. He had me do this leg workout. Oh, MY! Squats, hack squats, upside down press, leg extension drop set, thigh curl, calf raises. If you have never done a proper leg session before and jumped straight into heavy sets, you are going to be in a whole world of pain for a good week. Trying to get my legs to function properly after this session was difficult. I was walking to work one night. Thinking to myself, 'I've really done it this time. I am never going to walk the same again!' I was in so much pain. I was walking like I had shit my pants. As I was trying to walk down the hill towards the beach I looked up into the sky and saw my very first shooting star. I'd never seen a shooting star before. I was on my own with no one else around. I thought, 'Okay, make a wish'. I just asked for my life to work out all right for me. I just wanted to be all right as well as my legs!

Working at The Pavilion was wearing itself thin. The tea dances and the line dance afternoons had the rudest people that came to them. Why have people got to be so rude? I cannot stand rudeness and I cannot stand someone talking to me like I'm a piece of shit, because they think they are better than me! One evening I was at work on the bar and this customer spoke to me with such disdain that I told him to, "FUCK OFF!"

"What?"

"You heard me, fuck off, go on. Think you can _,
me that way. Who the fuck do you think you are? Go on, g
up to the front of house and speak to a manger or someone that
actually gives a shit."

"FUCK OFF!"

Next day I went to work, I was sacked. I wasn't bothered.
On to the next job. I hated it there anyway.

I found a bar job at a nightclub called the Opera House. It
was the 90s and the Opera House was bouncing! It was a great
place to be. I also landed a job in the gym Prime Bodies. I was
so happy. The position in the gym definitely felt like
something I could build on. I was in a place I wanted to be.

I had since moved out of the flat I was in and into another
place with a guy that owned it. He was a live-in landlord and
rented out three of the rooms he had in the flat. He was a bit
weird but nothing that I couldn't handle. He was into dating
young girls. He would have been in his thirties at least and his
girlfriend was teenage for sure, maybe even sixteen! I would
say my hellos and goodbyes and stick in my room. Life was
pretty cool at that point. I had found my feet with the gym. I
would train most days. I liked working at The Opera House. It
was where everyone wanted to be and I was right in the middle
of it all. For some reason, the manager of the club stuck me in
the VIP bar. Only the pretty girls ended up serving in the VIP.
I didn't understand it. It was cool in there though. It took me
off the main bars and into a bar that was a bit more selective
about who went in there.

I would walk to the Opera House; it was only a few
minutes up the road from my house. I would pass a pub called
Deacons. All the scumbags would go into Deacons. I never

went in there. I would pass by the bouncer that worked on the front door. I knew he was watching me as I strutted pass. Apparently, I have been told that I strut when I walk. I don't really think about it. My walk is my walk. Anyway, his name was Graham Appleby. He had found out that I was working at the Opera House. He started to hang out at the end of the bar trying to get my attention. We eventually started chatting and he asked me out.

Graham Appleby was someone you did not fuck about with. He was volatile, unpredictable and very simple, not well-educated. I'm sure he was from a gypsy background. He was also very loyal to the ones that he held very close to his heart. Me and Graham ended up becoming very close. He wanted more but something was telling me that it wasn't a good idea. So, we were very good friends and he looked out for me all the time. It felt good having someone strong on my side at that time. Everyone was scared of him and he was my friend. I didn't feel like I was on my own, fighting the world by myself.

Big Lou was another one of my friends from back then as well. She looked like Brigitte Nielsen. Six foot, bleached blonde hair and she was amazing. Lou worked as an aerobics instructor, a door woman and also danced in the Opera House on the front stage. She was a force to be reckoned with and she was my friend. She was another friend that everyone was attracted to and I thought made me look better by just being around her.

Back at the flat, the weirdo landlord had started to play up. He would leave his bedroom door open with his TV in sight, playing porn. It was disgusting. I assumed he thought maybe one of us would go into his room to live out some kind of fantasy for him. Graham had come round for a cuppa one day.

I went into the kitchen to make the tea and the weirdo came into the kitchen with just a towel on. He accidentally on purpose dropped his towel. He was standing there with his dick out. I just looked at him, gave him no response and left the kitchen to go into my room to tell Graham what had just happened. I was howling with laughter. I mean, come on! What the fuck are you doing you fucking pervert? He must have heard us laughing in my room.

The perv landlord had this rocker-billy hair do. A big old quiff at the front of his bonce. One day I was in the kitchen again, putting together a nice fruit salad: berries, papaya, banana and yogurt on the top. As I was in the gym training every day, I had really started to pay attention to what I was putting into my body. I was all engrossed in my fruit salad when he appeared. He had no hair on his head! He was completely bald. It really took me by surprise. I had to bury my head in the fridge for a moment to contain myself from not laughing out loud in his face.

It turns out he was wearing spray on hair! Another dude with spray on hair! How the fuck do you figure that shit out? Fucking dick. He looked awful. The top of his head looked grey, where it had seen no sun! I got my fruit salad and got the fuck out of the kitchen quick smart and into my room, where I could get the laughter out of my body. Dick, such a dick!

I had started being a dick as well. I had no respect for him, so I had started to not pay my rent on time. I would leave it a week or so before I paid. I never had a lot of money to go around and had started to buy myself some nice things with the money I was earning. I would buy nice food. I could just about afford to get some nice fruit and meat. So, I did that sometimes rather than paying my rent. Fuck him, he was an asshole. It was around this time when I gave up red meat as well. Mad cow disease — who wanted that? No thanks. So that was that. I haven't had a steak, lamb, pork or bacon for twenty-five years. You can put Macdonald's, KFC, Burger King and fish and chips into that as well. I have not gone near it. I certainly do not feel that I am missing out, especially with the current obesity epidemic! I still have items of clothing now at the age of forty-seven, that I have owned since I was twenty-four, that I can still wear! So that tells you something. No fizzy drinks either. No coke, no lemonade, none of that shit!

The perv landlord eventually told me I had to get out. I knew it was coming. Homeless once again. Graham came over and helped me bag up my stuff. It was my own doing but I still stood there with tears and wondered what am I going to do now? Graham said I could come and doss at his house until I got myself sorted. I was like okay, that's a safe place to be. I knew that Graham liked me and wanted more but he was never an asshole to me. He one hundred percent respected me and would never impose himself on me. Funnily enough, I was the only one that he would listen to when he was at the Opera House and losing it. The head door-woman Amanda would come and find me and say, "Grab Graham, J. Get him out the back door before the police get here." So off I would trot, twenty-one-year-old self, five foot eight, probably around ten and a half stone and grab the six foot two, eighteen stone, thirty-two-year-old man that was in the thick of sorting someone out. Grab him and say we are off! Hustle him out of the back of the club and take him home.

Let's say I have always attracted the more mentalist type of man. I don't know why. but they always gravitate towards me.

Working at the gym I had become very friendly with the doormen that worked at the Opera House. One day, Mark who worked on the front door of the club, mentioned to me that the female security had left and they needed to replace her. Mark suggested that I would be good for the position. I asked, "How much does it pay?" Around the time in 1996 it was around £6 or £7 an hour. It was double what I was getting to work on the bar! It was a no-brainer to me. Either stand on the door or work on the bar for less money. Off I went, spoke to Amanda who was the head door woman and she said, "Sure, start Thursday night." I was twenty-one years old and I was stood on the front door of the busiest nightclub in Bournemouth. I didn't have a clue what I was doing!

The doormen were all pretty punchy back then, no licences like they have now. If you had the balls and you didn't mind getting involved in chucking dickheads out of the club, you got the job. On the front door, most of the men were geared up to the eyeballs (steroids) which meant they were really emotional and not in a teary way. Like, they wanted to punch everyone in the face for looking at them in the wrong way. I wasn't going to hit someone for the sake of it, not unless they hit me first! I never understood that. Quite often the crew would be off round the back of the club to do someone over. They would push for me to come. I never did. I would end up getting lost in the club, talking shit to another doorman or punters that were in there. I was definitely wet behind the ears when it came to working on the door. I lacked confidence in myself, did not believe in myself, was trying hard to fit in and not look like a scared chicken. I didn't know how to hit anyone, especially in the face, out of the blue. I was a fish out of water! I kept turning up though, it was double the money!

Working at the gym I had already said to myself I was going to get the most muscle definition I could! It was a purpose and the ultimate goal for right then. I had started to research what was good for my body and how I was going to go around attaining that look. Living at Graham's had given me a bit of space to really start thinking about what I wanted to be doing, moving forwards with my life. I had visited the YMCA gym in Bournemouth Town centre. I had gone with a friend and done a gym session down there. Whilst in the gym of the YMCA, I noticed an advertisement for becoming a Personal Trainer. It sparked my interest. I walked over to the desk and asked the two young men behind the counter for some information. His initial response was, "You know you have to be fit!" I said, "Just give me the information." (In my head I was saying fuck you! Who are you to tell me I need to be fit? Fucking twat! Just hand over the information, dickhead!) Begrudgingly, he gave me the information and off I went with a real spark in my belly. That is exactly what I am going to do. I am going to become a Personal Trainer.

The money to become a Personal Trainer was definitely out of my reach. I did not have the disposable income to pay for the courses. So, what was I going to do? I had to come up with a plan. I contacted the YMCA and went and had an interview with them. I offered myself as a volunteer on the understanding that if I showed my worth, they could put me through the Personal Training courses. The two guys in the interview said that that wasn't usual practice but they would think about it and get back to me. I thought, well, that's not a no! Off I went, waiting for them to respond.

In the meantime, Kerry had been in contact. My brother was back from the US but, Kerry had stayed out there. She had managed to get a job looking after kids. She said, "Look Janine, I can get you a job out here no problem. I'll look into it and I'll call you back." A week later she called me back. "I've got you a job if you want it." I took a look at the situation I was in. I had no fixed abode, I was dossing at Graham's, what did I have to lose? I thought, 'I am in'! Kerry passed the number of this lady that was looking for help in Los Altos. Me and the mother in Los Altos started talking. We spoke for at least six weeks. I made my decision to give it a go out in the USA.

In the meantime, the YMCA had got back to me. They had agreed to pay for my Personal Training course. I had to tell them I was really sorry but I had an opportunity to go to America. I thought. 'Go to America, save up enough money whilst I am there and then come back and pay for the courses myself'.

I was off. I did not even give it a second thought that I would be going into a family I knew nothing about, living in a country thousands of miles away from home. But I didn't have a home and what was I a thousand miles away from? Yes, I had my friends but really, I was essentially on my own. I was thousands of miles away from nothing!

I also saw this as an opportunity to see my Dad and find out who he really was. Not from my mother's interpretation but from my own perspective. I hadn't seen him since I was eleven years old. I was now twenty-two years old with my own viewpoint to find.

USA here I come.

# Chapter Nine
# Finding My Worth

I was off to sunny, warm California. I had my ticket and around £40 in my pocket. I was a little worried that I did not have any money on me but I was set up with a job, so money would be coming in soon enough. Kerry had paid for my plane ticket. She was meeting me at San Francisco airport.

My memory of flying out there is vague. I don't remember feeling anything. Probably excited, probably just taking it all in my stride as I usually do.

Kerry met me at the airport and drove me straight to the family's house I would be staying with. The house was based in Los Altos which is a suburb of San Jose. Los Altos means 'the heights' in Spanish. It is a pretty small town and the house was situated up in the hills. The road Kerry drove up to get to the house was pretty narrow. There was a massive cliff drop from the side of the road.

You would not catch me going up that way in the dark, that was for sure! Fortunately, there was another way down from the hills that would take a bit longer but was for sure safer to travel on!

The mum and dad were very welcoming. The kids were excited that I was there. I had bought them gifts from the UK. Mister Men books for the little girl for me to read to her and a Wallace and Gromit plasticine kit for me to do with the boy. Kerry said she would be with me the following day to show me around Los Altos.

The following morning, Kerry took me for breakfast into the Los Altos town. She also let me drive into town so that I could get used to driving on the opposite side of the road. It was a bit weird to start with but I adapted really quickly. It was warm and sunny; I was in California. I was super-happy. We changed up the small number of pounds I had, but luckily for me, the exchange rate was almost double. So, I went from £40 to $80. I felt like I was already winning. I realised when I got to the car that the woman in the cafe had given me more change back than I needed and on the way to the car I found $20. I was definitely winning. Things were looking good. After brekkie, I said to Kerry I needed to keep the gym going so we went and found a fairly cheap place to join. Kerry decided that she was going to start up as well. Sorted!

Back with the family, the mother had told me the house was a little untidy over the phone before I had arrived. That was a slight understatement! The husband was quite a bit older in his fifties and the mother was in her late twenties. They had a very sweet little boy of around nine and a three-year-old little girl that liked to scream for no apparent reason at all, at any given time!

The mother was supposed to spend time with me over the weekend to show me where the school was ready for Monday, so that I could take her son to school. It turns out going out and getting smashed up on alcohol was more important! This was my first day of work. I had been in the country for three days. No time had been spent with me at all making sure that I had all the information available to me: where the school was or how to get there. She decided to give me a map drawn on a scrappy bit of paper to take her child to school, in a van that was a bit of a death trap! I was then to come back to the house and look at the mountain of cleaning that needed to be done around the house, whilst trying to entertain a three-year-old!

It took me whole days to clean one room at a time! I started in the laundry room. I stood at the edge of the doorway deciding where to start. Every single part of that room had clothes in it. In the sinks, on the shelves, on top of the washing machine and dryer. Were they dirty or clean? Who knows? Every single part of that room needed to be scrubbed. There was a dirty scum over everything. The kitchen, the lounge and the main bedroom was the same. WHOLE DAYS to clean the rooms! What had they been doing or more to the point, not been doing? The en-suite to the main bedroom was disgusting! I was on my hands and knees trying to scrub the bathroom floor because it was so filthy! The poor little boy was wetting the bed. I know that was due to the situation, that I could see unfolding whilst I was staying there. The mother and father were constantly arguing, it was horrible! I don't even think the mother was out working! I think she was out most days just getting drunk. I was left to just get on with it and take care of everything at the house including her children, the youngest one just completely out of control with the screaming. I thought, 'What the fuck have I got myself into now'!

On my first night of staying at the house, my dad had called me. He said he was so happy I was here in California and that he had always loved me and Leigh. Of course, I wanted to hear that. What kid doesn't want to hear that from a parent that has been absent for seventeen years? It was good to hear that from him but it's not real. As I have grown up, that's just his guilt talking. That's not love, that's just him justifying his lack of parenting. His lack of input at any level.

But, as always, I would be invested in thinking that he did really love me and I was looking forward to seeing him for the first time in twelve years.

I lasted a week at the house of doom. They paid me my first week, I got that money! I did talk to the father to let him know that I would start looking for somewhere else as I was not happy. He, of course, was not best pleased. The mother came home from wherever she had been drinking and tried to make me feel bad about leaving. I recognised straight away that she was trying to manipulate me into staying. I phoned Kerry and told her to come and get me. I did not tell the family I was leaving. I packed my suitcase and as soon as Kerry got to the house, I left through the back entrance without them knowing. I did not travel thousands of miles to get caught up in a house of dysfunction. I was trying to escape that!

Where was I going to go? Kerry had spoken with the family she was working for and they agreed I could stay with her, in her den downstairs in their house. I think if I rightly remember, they were dentists. I know they were loaded. Their house was enormous. It was a mansion. Marble everywhere. Every room had an en suite. It must have had at least six bedrooms. A huge pool and top of the range cars. It was far cry away from what I had grown up in that was for sure.

My second week in the USA and I am now without work! What am I going to do?

Fortunately, Kerry knew this guy Chad who was a friend of my dad. He was working in a warehouse. He mentioned that they needed some help. It was cash in hand. Sorted. That gave me a little reprieve whilst we had started to look around for another nanny job.

Me and Kerry had decided to venture into town to have a

look around and see what was going on. There was not much nightlife and certainly no house music clubs to go to. We were in a Jack in the Box, getting some food. Some guys approached us and asked us if we wanted to go to a party. Being fearless and up for fun, not thinking about who these guys were, we said sure. So, off we went. I have no idea where we ended up but I do know that that party was predominantly black. We were blonde and white. We stuck out. Everyone was dancing really close to each other. I was scanning, trying to take everything in and keeping an eye on Kerry. All of a sudden, we were being hustled out of the door. The police had turned up and before I knew it, gun shots were being fired. I couldn't believe it. Holy shit! My second week in the USA and guns were being fired. We got in our car and got the fuck out of there quick smart. Only in America!

Whilst I was keeping myself busy with working at the warehouse, Kerry was friends with a South African woman, Sally, who worked next door to where she lived. Sally had mentioned that she knew a family that was looking for an au pair to look after their kids. We both thought it would be a good idea for me to check it out because I needed somewhere to live. I gave them a call and went for the interview. I had two interviews. The first one they wanted to check me out of course. They took all my information. The father said he would do some background checks to make sure I was not a nut job going into their house. I was then asked to go back to answer questions, to double-check I was sincere.

It turns out that I was all right they gave me the job. I was to start the day after my birthday; 1st December 1996.

Staying at Kerry's had started to wear thin. I wasn't with them long, two to three weeks max. They were trying to rope

me into working for them. It was November 1996 and my dad
had invited both me and Kerry to go and have Thanksgiving
with him and his wife. Kerry couldn't go because the family
she was working for said she had to stay and cook them dinner,
along with serving them the dinner! It was also on the
understanding that I was to do this with her. I said, "I would
rather not. Dad has asked me to go to his for Thanksgiving."
This would be the first time I had spent any time with my Dad
in over twelve years. I was not going to miss out on that. The
father of the family was less than impressed. He said that he
only let me stay in their house on the understanding that I had
nowhere to go. If I had family, I should go and stay with them.
I then had to explain that my dad had left when I was very
young. I had not seen him in over twelve years. I really did not
have that kind of relationship with him where he would just
open up his home to me. The father was still not that impressed.
I knew my time was up at the house. I had to figure out where
I needed to go.

I did not want to be a servant for them. Of course, they
had opened up their home for me but as an act of charity not
on the understanding that I would then have to serve them! I
did not want to do it! So, I ran it past my dad about my situation.
He said whilst I was waiting to start my job, I could stay with
him.

Seeing my dad again was like we had never been apart. I
always thought me and Leigh were child delinquents, until I
met Dad again at twenty-three. We were definitely our father's
children. We were at a party one night and I was watching him.
I was astonished to see Leigh's mannerisms: how he moved,
how he spoke, the sense of humour. It was so strange to watch.
We hadn't grown up around him, how could this be? He would

tell me stories of him and his mate Charlie taking acid on Bournemouth beach. He and Charlie also went to the Isle of Wight festival on acid to watch Jimmy Hendrix. I thought that was so cool. I didn't think I was so off the rails when I was with my dad. Taking drugs and being wild made sense to me. We had our dad's DNA in us. We were the way we were because of him.

I settled into being around him. He introduced me to AOL: the internet. There was nothing like that back home. Me and Kerry would sit in the chat rooms talking for hours. We would make Granny's home-made fudge and just munch our way through it. Two batches one night. Sugar, butter, condensed milk! He would ask me about Mum. I told him I hadn't seen her in a while. I would then tell him how bad it was growing up. He never really got that. I don't think it ever sunk in for him. He would then tell me how they met. My mum was a window dresser at Dolcis shoe shop. He was the manager. He said she was really beautiful. He was nineteen and she was eighteen. They got married when she was just nineteen and that was when I came along.

Me and Kerry were still making it into the gym. My dad was letting me drive his jeep. Unbeknownst to me, the car was a piece of shit. It broke down on one of the highways. The clutch cable had a hole in it. It is pretty scary breaking down on the highway in the USA. This was before mobile phones. I sat there for a while trying to figure out what I was going to do. All of a sudden, a police car pulled up behind me, bright lights on and with a speaker phone the policeman asks me to step outside of the vehicle. I was then told by the policemen that had then got out of their car and approached me, to lift up my jacket very slowly and do a turn around. It was so weird.

I'm a twenty-three-year-old female on my own, stranded on the highway being treated like a criminal. I took it all in my stride because I thought it was weird. I had nothing to hide so just got on with it. Once they had figured out that I was not a threat and that I was not a native, I explained that the car had broken down. I needed to put clutch fluid in to get it going again. The policemen did not have a first clue about where to put it. He asked me where I was going and that they would give me a lift. My first and only drive, fortunately, in the back of an American police car. I thought this is going to look great pulling up outside Kerry's family's house. Me getting out the back of a police car.

In order for me to work for the new family, I had to get my Californian drivers' licence. Off I went. I passed first time. The driver's licence was only valid for three months. On reflection I could have extended my visa. I could have gone through the correct channels to make myself legal to live in America. My dad was there. I could have got him to sponsor me but I didn't! No one was asking any questions. I seemed to be surviving okay without having to rock the boat. So, I kept my mouth shut and just got on with living out there just the way I was.

Kerry, on the other hand, was sorting out getting a fake green card. I could have done that myself really. I don't know why I didn't. I could have sorted a driver's licence but I didn't do that either. Getting the fake green card was quite a mission. We were so fearless and I was not afraid to go anywhere. Kerry asked me to go with her as back up. We drove into an area that was very Spanish and very rough. Gangs of Hispanic men were just hanging out in their cars, all wearing Nike Cortez, white vest tops, baggy shorts and braided hair. She was given a name to go and find. This person would sort all her paperwork. I waited by the car as muscle. What must we have looked like driving into that car park with all those bad asses around? I thought we were bad asses, by the way! I'd square up to anyone. That can be very unnerving to some people even if they are tough. Especially two white, blonde, British girls, although they didn't know we were British. I would have loved to be a fly on the car, to hear them talking. It was not a place that you just casually breezed into, that was for sure. But we did!

We got Kerry's green card in about an hour or so, she was sorted. I think I probably thought that it was better to be just caught and chucked out of the country, than to be carrying a fraudulent document. I thought that maybe that would carry a heavier punishment!

It was coming up to my birthday. Me and Kerry had been invited over to my half-sister's house for a get-together, to celebrate my birthday. Tim was my sister's uncle. Who, when I was there twelve years before, I had had a big crush on! I was twenty-three years old now and was not so naive. It turns out he was a massive asshole and a misogynist. He spent the whole evening putting women down. He was getting right on my tits. I was standing my ground and giving as good as I was getting. He had bought some alcohol with him. What I didn't know was that this alcohol is banned in most states of the USA. I, of course, was playing Billy-big-bollocks and he was giving it to me and Kerry. We were drinking it like it was fruit juice. It was ABSINTHE! Gods knows what proof it was. But, oh my, it was not a good outcome.

Listening to Tim witter on was getting boring, so me and Kerry both decided to go into San Jose and find a nightclub.

Both of us were in no position to be in a car driving. Not one person from the party stopped us from leaving. I made a decision that I wasn't fit for driving. Kerry decided that she was fine for driving. I was like, 'Okay, cool, let's go'. We were going down this highway into San Jose and I decided it would be a good idea to get out of the window, sit on the ledge and hold on to the top of the car whilst she was driving. It was exhilarating. Crazy, but exhilarating. The wind blowing your hair back, you are living so close to the edge of life and death that you feel the most alive. I slid back inside the car and said, 'You have to have a go'. Kerry pulled over, we exchanged seats and she did exactly the same as me. How we never got pulled over is amazing really. We made it into San Jose and found a nightclub. They let us in! We then proceeded to order drinks at the bar with no means to pay for them. What an absolute pain in the backside we both were. We then somehow made it back to my dad's house, where we collapsed and passed out until the morning. We both woke up looking very green around the gills indeed. I would never touch Absinthe again.

Feeling very jaded, I had to make my way over to the family I was going to be working for. I was pretty nervous. I didn't want them to know how much I had been drinking the night before and hoped that I would pull off a good impression when I got there. Dan, the father, decided he would take me out in the car to make sure that I could drive. I felt so ropey getting in that car but I managed to pull it off.

It was also at the back of my mind, terrified, that I was going to be like my mum looking after the kids. I had never looked after kids before. I did not have the first clue about what to do. Their mum, Jackie, showed me to my room where they had very kindly left me a birthday present. It was a burgundy shell suit with a v stripe, paisley pattern down the jacket. I am not ungrateful about the gift, but it was truly not something that a twenty-three-year-old, funky hipster like me would be wearing any time soon. I wore the bottoms around the house a few times to show that I was grateful for the gift. I then packaged it up and took it to the nearest department store I thought it was from and swapped it for a couple of sports Ts and socks.

I settled into the family really well. I was patient with the kids. Read to the kids. Played games with the kids. I also naturally instilled routine, discipline, love and consistency with my care for them. I was nothing like my mother or father. That was a good learning lesson for me. Soon enough, it was my first Christmas in California. I thought living in California that it would be sunny all year round! I remember being disappointed during my first winter there in 1996. It was pretty cloudy, very rainy but it never got below fifty degrees really. I had to be thankful for that. I never had a winter jacket whilst I was out in California.

Graham had decided that he was going to come over for Christmas. I was trying to figure out where he was going to stay. He couldn't stay with me at the house I was working in. There was no chance of that. One, there was no room and two, my room was upstairs with the kids. Tom one side and Suzy the other. It was very tight-knit, that was for sure. I certainly was not in my own annex. I was living with the family in their home. I would not want to impose myself or ask anything that might upset what I had going on. I decided to ask my dad if Graham could stay with him. I offered them money; I think around $200 for the two weeks. He agreed, so that was sorted!

Of course, in hindsight Graham could have sorted his own accommodation. I think I felt obliged to help him because he had let me stay at his house.

When Graham arrived, it was lovely seeing him. He had bought loads of cards and gifts from everyone back home. I felt super-special. I had clocked that Kerry was not impressed, maybe even a little jealous. But I ignored it and carried on opening all my cards.

I had told Graham that I would be working and getting to see him would be difficult because I lived a good forty minutes' drive away. We could spend the weekends together but seeing him during the week was going to be a nightmare. He was aware of that before he came out. Graham did himself no favours at all. He didn't go anywhere. He didn't do anything, only when I went over there to pick him up. It turned into a bit of a nightmare. He sat around my dad's house all day, watching Power Rangers and eating all their chocolate. When I took him out, his behaviour was weird as well. We ended up at a party with some guys that we had met at a bar. Graham was seen at the party putting cigarettes out on himself, probably due to the fact that I was being an absolute bitch to him! It was embarrassing though. I just couldn't bear to be around him. He was not helping the situation at all. I was young and a selfish twat that wanted him to go away. I should have dealt with it and took care of him but I didn't! I treated him awfully and wanted him to go home. I just didn't have the time to spend with him.

Really, I knew his weird behaviour before he came out to visit me. I had just ignored it when I was in England, like it was nothing that I wasn't used to living with. When you grow up in dysfunction, dysfunction is normal.

183

He was living with my dad and his wife Sarah, though. They noticed how bizarre he was being. His behaviour was exposed when he came to America. It wasn't normal. He needed to go!

Off Graham went back home, thank god. I don't think his USA experience was a great one. My dad lived off the train track. Graham could have gone out and done anything more than sit around and watch Power Rangers in San Jose for two weeks. We did remain friends though. I would often call him up and have a chat when I was feeling lonely. A touch selfish really but I did want to stay friends with him. I felt bad about the trip.

Me and Kerry were getting a little bit sick of just sitting around smoking shit weed and eating; oh my, we were eating. We would get really stoned and do pie runs. We would go to at least three different pie restaurants and eat pie. Pumpkin pie, key lime pie, lemon meringue pie, treacle pie. You get the picture. Pie!

I was starting to pack on the weight and had to make a decision on whether or not to get a size bigger in jeans, because I was out growing my clothes. A little mind check, and I was like, 'What are you doing Davis? Get your shit together and cut back on the food intake please'. Around this time, me and Kerry discovered San Francisco!

Graham had sent a newspaper through the post. On one of the pages inside was a big wrap of speed. Me and Kerry had decided to get dressed up and head into San Jose on a night out. America was weird when you went out clubbing. Firstly, I felt attractive in America. I was beating the men off with a shitty stick all the time! I would have guys coming over and asking for a dance. I thought it was super-weird! You never got asked to dance at home in the UK. I was lucky to get asked out at all, back in the UK. Let's say I am not pretty, blonde, five foot four or six and fifty-six kilograms! Such a fucking stereo type back home, especially in Bournemouth! The men in the US liked me, it was nice and ego filling. I felt like I'm not such a munter after all!

Anyway, back to the dancing, the men would ask. I would say no! Why would I want to dance with someone I don't know, weird! Then I quickly realised this is what they did. I soon started to say sure, but it was still weird. I never knew what to do. I would find myself just laughing nervously about the whole situation, while the man was getting his groove on trying to look all sexy. I just found it hilarious. On most occasions I just left the dance floor.

We visited a club called The Beehive. Me and Kerry had taken some speed. We were ready to go out and shake our booties! We met some guys who asked, "Do you want to come to San Fran?" Of course, always up for an adventure we said yes! We ended up in 1015 Folsom. This was a big nightclub in San Francisco. We had parked the car round the corner from the club. One of the guys had paid money to one of the street guys to look after it. The club was right up our street! Massive rooms, people everywhere and house music pumping in our ears. When you find a good club, without a doubt there is something tribal about everyone being in tune with the music and you are all moving to the same beat. It's electrifying!

The guys that we went with wanted to leave early. As we had gone with them, we had to leave at the same time. We got to the car and the back window had been smashed in. My passport and our massive bag of weed was in the back. I didn't care about the weed. I wanted my passport back. I didn't know the laws of the San Francisco streets. I did not care. I took off running around the streets to find anyone that might know how to get it back. The guys we were with lost it, chased after me and said, "You can't do that you will be killed!" I said, "I'm not afraid!" They enforced that I go back to the car. They would try and negotiate getting my passport back. They did a good job; I got my passport back.

We didn't see those guys after that, funnily enough. I think that maybe they thought we were too much on the wilder side of life! We didn't care, we had found 1015 Folsom. It was like the nightclubs that we went to back in the UK. We knew what we were going to be doing the following weekend!

The following weekend came around soon enough and we made our way up to San Francisco again, this time just ourselves. We always had to make sure that we had our passports on us. The clubs in San Fran were different to back home. You had to be twenty-one, no ifs or buts about it. No ID. No entry. It did not matter how old you were. I don't know how I had got into the club the week before because obviously I did not have my passport on me. I think the guys we were with had blagged us in. We found a place to park. It was always very shady around that part of San Francisco but we did our best to lock everything away and made our way to 1015 Folsom. We were in! We had a good wander around and then saw a line for the VIP part of the club. We both wanted to be up there! Two huge bouncers stood in front of a red rope keeping everyone back. The stairs behind them were lit with a red light. That was the only way in. Everyone always wants to be part of the VIP crowd. We wanted in. I made sure that Kerry was at the front: blonde, petite and beautiful. We muscled our way to the front of the crowd of people trying to get in. We made sure the bouncer could see both of us. Soon enough he waved us both through. Up went the red rope and we were bouncing up the stairs into the VIP area. It was the land of the beautiful and I was right smack bang in the middle of it all. OH MY, the men! I had never seen so many funky, beautiful looking men in all my life. Black, Asian, Mexican, Caucasian. I was a kid in a sweet shop and just stood back by the bar and soaked it all in. I was loving life. Kerry was off to see if she could find anyone that was selling Es.

We took an Ecstasy tab and made our way to the dance floor to wait for it to kick in. We were not really getting much in the way of a come up, so decided to have a wander around. I remember passing this guy and thinking holy shit you are something else. He was so handsome. I am pretty fussy with what floats my boat but this guy ticked all the boxes for me. He was Latino, which I do have a penchant for. Stocky but not too much, all the muscles in all the right places, he had his top off, that smooth Latino olive skin, yummy! The most beautiful face. How is it that you can't really explain it but there is something about a man for me that you see that just does it for you? Flips your tummy upside down. There is no talking needed. I didn't know anything about him but, oh yeah, he would definitely be the one.

There were two rooms to the VIP area. After having a little wander, we made our way back to the dance floor. I remember on this night, Kerry had a little trouble from some girls. I'm not sure why but she was my girl and we were together. I had started to put on some size with the training, which makes me bigger than most of the women I meet. Kerry came over and asked if I could help her out. I made my way over to where the girls were and made my presence known. I didn't need to do much, just let them know I was there and Kerry was with me. They soon got the message and moved away. I then realised that the beautiful guy was dancing around me. I was in a little bit of shock. He couldn't be interested in me. I ignored him. He then continued to dance right in front of me making it really obvious that he was trying to get my attention. I couldn't believe it. Me, he was interested in me. My heart was beating so fast. This was the night that I met Rafael Garza.

I don't know how many times he told me that night what his name was. I couldn't hear him. I would leave it a while and then ask again. He would very patiently tell me again Rafael. I still wouldn't hear him. I'd wait a while, and ask him again, he would tell me again. He never got angry, never brushed me off, he would just tell me again, it's Rafael.

How could someone that beautiful be interested in someone like me? I couldn't figure it out!

We spent the rest of the night together. We talked for a while; he had his friend with him, Jose. I think Jose was thinking he was going to make it with Kerry but she wasn't into him. Rafael and Jose decided to go on to a club called The END UP. The END UP opened during the early hours of Sunday morning and then stayed open all day. It was literally round the corner from 1015 Folsom. We decided to go home, get freshened up and then come back to the city to hang out with them at The END UP.

I was so excited. As we got into the car, I said to Kerry, "Have you seen him? OH my god! Let's get back, get changed and get our asses back up to the club." Obviously, I was assuming they would still be there and hadn't done a bunk.

We made it back to The END UP a couple of hours later. Rafael was still there.

We didn't stay in the club long before the boys decided they wanted to get out of there. We all ended up down on the beach. Me and Kerry were chatting, deciding what we were going to do. I could hear the boys talking about the fact they were going to go to confession. They were going to confess everything. Tomorrow was a new day as they had confessed all their sins away!

I found that conversation quite strange. Religion wasn't something I had been bought up around and really, you can just go to the church and talk about all the naughty stuff you have done and then it clears the slate clean, like it has never happened. Come on people, that's ridiculous, in my opinion!

The boys approached us. Me and Rafael got chatting again. He was asking what I was doing. I told him we were not sleeping together. I then proceeded to tell him the next person I have sex with is the person I am going to marry. So naive in my little twenty-three-year-old head. I was in a place that I wanted to meet someone and get to know them. That ultimately, they wanted more from me than sticking their penis in me. So, that's what I had decided and I was going to stick to it! Well, at least vocalise it.

Kerry drove home, and I went with Rafael. What was I thinking? We got to his place and jumped in the shower together. I had second thoughts. I didn't want to do it. I got very insecure, jumped out of the shower and said, "I'm going home". Rafael followed me, was very gentle with me and of course, we had sex. So much for waiting until I got married. I had no control over myself when it came to Rafael. Afterwards, we talked for a while. Out of the blue he started to cry. I hugged him and soothed him; I didn't ask any questions. If he wanted to talk, he would tell me what was wrong but he didn't so I just held him. We got dressed and he took me for food. He then took me all over his neighbourhood in San Fran. He showed me his church where he had not long lost his sister. She had died from cancer. I wasn't sure what was happening it was such a whirlwind, I felt like we were really connecting. Rafael wasn't a stranger to me, even though we had just met. It just all felt so right, normal. I was super-happy to be hanging out and spending time with him. He gave me his number and he took mine. Rafael was in my soul.

Going to 1015 Folsom was all part of the weekend plan now for Kerry and myself. The weekend after I had met Rafael, we both made our way back up there. Once we had made it back into the VIP area, we were scouting around for someone that was selling Es. I had clocked the guy we had bought an E from the week before that were shit. I told Kerry to go tell him that they were shit and to see if we could get a deal. When she came back, she had managed to get them for $15 instead of $20. Cool. I said, "Right, this is what we are going to do. Take the Es, set our watches and in forty-five minutes to one hour, go back and tell him that they were shit." We did exactly that, four times! Oh my god, we had so much front! We were both in such a state, I could barely open my eyes. The guy thought it was hilarious. Fortunately for us, he just ended up giving them to us. He thought we were great and couldn't believe we were doing it! We were actually having a great night but there is always a limit. A Turkish man had been watching us, he also found us amusing. He started chatting to us, started to offer us cocaine. In for a penny in for a pound, we were doing everything that night. It actually got to a point where I could not put any more up my nose. I was so high I was straight! The Turk suggested for us to go round to The END UP. We both agreed. When we got in there, we were both so sketchy, the pair of us were so paranoid. I was not having a good time. Me and Kerry decided to leave. I suggested for us to go to the beach. I had no idea how to get there. I thought it would be a good idea to phone Rafael. Lucky for him it kept going to answer phone. We tried to make our way to the beach. It was now daytime in San Francisco; a really busy city and we were not in a position to be in charge of a car. Neither of us knew what we were doing. I then had visions of us just driving round and round in circles trying to find our way out of San Francisco and not being able to find the highway. I had a slight panic; thought we were never leaving the city. We were just going to drive round and round in circles, forever! But then I saw a sign for the highway, and I said, "Let's go home!" At one point I had to pull over on to the hard shoulder because I couldn't feel my arms. I said to Kerry, "You got to keep talking to me, keep me occupied!" We then had to get off the hard shoulder because if the police pulled over, we were going to be in big trouble. It took all my concentration to get us home. I was never going to get that high like that again. That was not fun, at all.

Life at the house with the kids was pretty straightforward. I would get them ready in the morning for school, take them to school, get back, watch a bit of Ricky Lake and go and work at the factory. Gracie who owned and ran the factory took me under her wing. She really looked after me. But I was always there to help her. I ended up cleaning her house as well as working in the factory. I would then come back and watch Oprah, pick the kids up from school and hang out until Dan got home. I was then out the door and straight to the gym. Monday to Saturday was gym time. I had stopped travelling all the way over to Los Altos to train with Kerry. It was a thirty-minute drive! There was a twenty-four-hour fitness, five minutes round the corner from me. It made sense to me to go there, much to Kerry's annoyance. She did not like that one bit. Probably because I hadn't told her I was going to change gyms. I could see the annoyance on her face. I just chose to ignore it. Why am I going to keep driving thirty minutes to train, when I can get to the gym from my home in five minutes! It just made more sense to me.

It wasn't long before people had started to chat to me at the gym and a personal trainer there had collared me and roped me into some sessions with him. Ric from Texas. He wore a cowboy hat and had that real cowboy Texan twang. He seemed fun to be around and I thought all right, it would be good to get someone to train me for a bit. It wasn't long before I was a bit of a project for him and the rest of the guys that I was being introduced to. I was strong and they, meaning Ric and this other guy called Andy who was ex-military, decided they were going to see what I could do. Before I knew it, they had stacked on one hundred and thirty kilograms on the squat rack and I was trying to squat it! It was so heavy. I sort of did it. It certainly didn't bend me in half! I maintained an upright position. I was twenty-three.

I was only training with Ric once a week. The rest of the time I was figuring stuff out on my own. I had really started to pay attention to my food and protein intake. Once I had figured out the right amount for my body, my body had really started to change shape. I liked it and I was getting really strong. I used to share this information with Kerry. I could see by her face that she was not impressed, especially when I would tell her about my personal bests in the gym. She would roll her eyes and generally be very dismissive. I would continue to ignore her, note down to myself about her behaviour and just carry on.

Ric was starting to get on my nerves. He had started parading me around like his own project. 'Look at what I've done, all down to me. If you want to look like this come train with me.' I did not like that at all. Yes, I was training with him, ONCE a week but the rest of the work I was doing myself. It wasn't solely down to him! I very politely said I could not afford to train with him anymore. I then started training with my mate Andy the ex- military guy. He was full on and it did not cost me a penny. He had a friend in the San Francisco 49ers football team that was a line backer. Andy asked him to help him out with some training programs. That was when my body really started to change. I agreed to train with him at 5.30 a.m.! I did that for a year. Up at 4.30 a.m., have a little bite to eat, get into the gym for 5.30 a.m. The training was hard! Andy did not take any prisoners and would only train to maximum level, every morning! I was doing that four days a week. I was so lucky to have met these people on my fitness journey. I can't remember the guy's name from the 49ers but he was huge and he went out of his way to come to Sunnyvale to train us one morning. He took no shit and gave no sympathy if you could not do it. He was all about, 'either get your shit done, or get the fuck out'! It was scary but I loved it!

The gym to me was everything and living in California enabled me to really cement that lifestyle into my psyche. On the days I was not with Andy, I would do my cardio, either on the machines at the gym: stepper, bike or treadmill or on Saturday mornings, I would go running in the Los Altos hills. It was an amazing park area where you could hike, bike and run. I would run. The first time I went I had gone up there with Andy who took me on this trail run. Part of the run was at least a half mile climb up a zigzag hill. It was horrible! The first time I did it, I thought I was going to have a heart attack. Andy was screaming at me to not stop but I just didn't have it in me to get to the top without stopping. I was so disappointed in myself. I got myself some proper trail running shoes. I went back there by myself and practised getting up that hill until I could get to the top without stopping! I loved it up there, running through the woods. So peaceful. On a good day it was like you were floating through the woods. There were signs everywhere warning of rattle snakes and wild cats. In the three years I went running there, I never once came across either of them!

I was living quite the double life. Monday to Saturday fitness demon. Saturday night up to San Fran to live it up. I kept my private life very private and always made sure I was there for the kids. Life at the house with the family was easy. My relationship with my dad was interesting, let's say. I had not told Leigh that I was leaving to live in the USA. I think it may have thrown him a bit. I have always been the big sister and I felt as long as he knew where I was, he felt safe. I had decided to do my own thing for a change which meant he was on his own.

Leigh would phone me up quite regularly. This was before mobile phones. So, he would get himself to a pay phone. On this one occasion he phoned me up in tears. It takes quite a bit for my brother to cry. After asking him what was wrong, he said that he had been talking to Dad and that Dad had said, "Give me a minute son I'll call you straight back." Leigh had waited in that phone box for forty minutes for my dad to phone him back! I was so angry. My dad would have known that he was in a phone box. I got in my car and drove the thirty minutes to get to his house and tell him exactly what I thought about it. After fronting him out, he told me to get out of his house. He then proceeded to say, "How many times have I got to say sorry for abandoning you?" I said, "It shouldn't matter, if you actually meant it!" He never meant it. Out of sight and out of mind. He had a role to play now. I was there asking questions and wanting to know why. I suppose he could have point blank refused to see me but he was the one that had said I have always loved you, so therefore had to see it through. He never meant that either. That was all for his own purpose, to feed his own guilt. I left that night. I had said my piece that was enough.

We did move on from that outburst and nothing more was ever mentioned. It was a funny relationship really; it wasn't a father daughter relationship. I was too old for him to start parenting. We were just buddies. We would hang out, smoke weed, take cocaine, drink magic mushrooms and generally get wasted at the weekends. He would re-tell stories of him hanging out with the Hells Angels in the 70s and just generally doing his own thing when me and Leigh were back in the UK, suffering our Mother! Weird I suppose. But that's how it was and in all honestly, I enjoyed hanging out with him. It was dysfunctional but it's what I had and I was going to take whatever I could get. Would I be doing that with my kid? Probably not! It's hard today really, because I do not have any of my own children. I would want them to be honest with me about what they were doing. I know that I would have done everything I could to make sure that they had every opportunity to live with me and set them up with whatever they needed, in order to lay out a kind of life for them that had guidance and support. I know that for sure.

Dad has lived in the USA since 1976 and still has not become a citizen! Go figure. Like I said, me and Leigh were out of sight, so we were out of mind. He completely diminished himself of any responsibilities. Love, financial support, guidance, anything.

The clubbing life every weekend with Kerry was starting to take its toll. I didn't want to do it every weekend! My job was starting to suffer. My gym was starting to suffer. I was burning the candle at all ends and it was making me ill! The kids I was looking after did not deserve for me to be hung over! I had a difficult six-year-old boy and an eight-year-old madame to look after. They needed me to be on my game. After a weekend with Kerry, I was not on my game. I had started to say no to going out. She did not like that. That was another annoyance. The passive aggressive comments had really started to take hold.

I was spending a lot of time at the family's house on my own. I had no work colleagues to interact with or hang out with. It was just me and the kids. It put me in a place to really question what I was doing with my life. I was able to really ask questions about my mum and why she was the way she was. I was watching a lot of Oprah Winfrey. She was in a place with her program at the time in the 90s where she had a lot of psychologists on her program. The programs really helped me to question my life and work on my own psychological development. It sounds silly but it really did! The psychologists at the time helped me to reflect on my own personal circumstances and question my behaviour. I really started to see my journey, with much more light.

I learnt to forgive myself to a degree or even forgive my mum. Her behaviour was learnt behaviour. I realised that she was not well, mentally. I still wasn't in a place to have her back in my life but I had started to understand why she was the way she was. It was not my fault!

California also made me see life from a different perspective. I was in a job where I was getting paid to work for four hours a day (apart from when the kids were on holidays)! The rest of the time was my own. I promised myself when I returned to the UK, I was going to put myself in a position where I was earning the most money for the least amount of time. For the first time in my life, I had quality of life over working in a shit job, for shit money, for the maximum amount of time, without the ability to pursue a dream because you earned just enough to survive!

Kerry's sister had come to visit it was 1997. We had all decided to go out into San Jose. We found a small cocktail bar and started to drink and I mean, drink! We were served these margaritas in fishbowl-sized glasses. It was ridiculous. Kerry was drinking Bacardi and Coke out of one of them. The guys in the bar had noticed we were drinking a lot and started to ply us with shots that we were necking back. Oh my god, we drank so much, we were out of control! We left that bar and decided to try and hit a club. We were wasted. I don't know how we made it into the club. Kerry had found some guys that were just standing there, minding their business. She was dancing right in front of them, trying to look all sexy. She was serious about it as well. It was embarrassing. I went over to her and said, "Come on you are embarrassing yourself." She told me to fuck off and asked what the fuck did I know? I was like, "Okay, you crack on!" I went over to the bar and just stood there for a while trying to figure out what I was going to do next. With that, I saw Kerry's sister. She said, "You've got to come, the bouncers are kicking Kerry out of the club." Now we were outside the club. Kerry took off down the street. She wanted to find the car. I said, "No way!" She was adamant. We had a little kerfuffle outside the club. Kerry was being really difficult. The police came over to see what was going on. I managed to calm it down. We then got in a taxi. We had no idea where we were in San Jose or what our next plan of action was. It was just chaos. We stopped the taxi and just got out and decided to walk to find the car. Kerry and her sister started to argue. I left them to it to begin with but it was starting to escalate. I decided to get in the middle of them to try and calm it down. Big, big mistake. Kerry started on me and in my non-rational, drunk mind, a switch flipped on! I turned to her and said, "I have had enough of your bullshit." I beat her up! I mean really beat her up! This wasn't a bitch-slap fight. I laid into her. A big crowd started to form around us. Three or four guys jumped on me and pinned me down to the floor to get me off her. In my head, when my face was pressed into the concrete I was crying, not because I was upset; it was pure rage. I started to think fast. I wanted these guys to let go of me. I thought if I want to get back up, I have to look like I am calm. I repeated, "I'm all right, I'm all right." I knew though, once I got up, I was going to take them all on. They let go of me. I bounded up on to my feet as fast as I could and screamed at them, "Right, I'm taking you all on!" They all ran, scattered as fast as they could. I heard one of them say, "She's mad!" I spotted Kerry on a car being tended to by a guy. I could see she was crying on his shoulder, playing the 'poor me' victim. I ran as fast as I could over to her. I planted my right hand on her chin with as much force as I could summon up. It took her right off that car bonnet.

It was then I could hear police sirens. I do not know where the voice came from, but it said to me in my ear, 'You need to get the fuck out of here'. I slipped through that crowd of people so fast. There was no way I was going to get pulled by the police. I was out of there!

I was walking down a street in San Jose trying to figure out what I was going to do. A guy pulled over in his car and asked if I was all right. I said, "No." He said, "Get in." So, I jumped into this stranger's car. He told me that if the police saw me in this state, they would pull me over. I thought okay just go with it for now. My mind was switched on but my language was still drunk. I had explained to this guy what had happened and kept apologising for being so drunk. He said, "Look, come back to mine, chill out and I'll take you home in the morning." My predator alarm bell was switched on and I was thinking, 'No, I don't think that's a good idea. I don't know this guy; he could be anybody. Even though he's helped me out. I need to get out of this situation'. I said, "No, can you just drive me to where I think the car is and I'll figure out what to do next?" He said, "Okay, as long as you're sure?"

My instincts were telling me that's what I needed to do. I found the car and then just sat on the car thinking how the fuck am I going to get home? My house keys were inside the car. I had no way of getting inside the car. I thought maybe Kerry or her sister might show up. I don't know how long I sat on that car for but these two guys approached me and asked if I was, okay. I then proceeded to tell them the whole story and that I had no way of getting home. I had a good feel about the fact that they were good guys. One of them said, "Get in my truck and I'll take you home." That's exactly what they did.

I was now stood outside of my family's house with no keys to get in. It must have been around three in the morning. I was not about to wake them up. I went over to my car. Luckily, I had left one of the windows open. I opened up the car and pulled off one of the seat covers, and got underneath it. I fell asleep until I thought it was a reasonable enough time to ring the doorbell.

The following day I was full of shame. The passive aggressive behaviour and underlying resentment had all been bought to the surface because of the alcohol consumption. It was a horrible, horrible night. Not one that I ever want to repeat. The visit to that place I had no control over is a place I never ever want to resurface. I could have killed her!

I apologised to my family. I explained that Kerry wants to go out getting drunk all the time and I just didn't want that anymore. I explained we had had a massive fight and I had left my keys in her car. That's why I couldn't get in. The mum understood and said not to worry. I was lucky. I had to phone Kerry to get my keys back. She was at her family's house. I drove over there to get the keys. As soon as I walked through the door she started with her snide comments and digs. I couldn't believe it! She had bruises everywhere. I was shameful about what I had done to her. I said, "Look at the state of you. You want to go again?" She shut up very quickly.

Kerry and her sister got arrested for being drunk and disorderly. No charges were made against them as I am aware. The police just let them go, fortunately. She told her family that she got jumped by some Mexicans and they believed her. I took my keys and that was the end of the friendship. We never spoke again after that!

It was the best thing for me really. It was a defining moment for me. I knew that I had to channel some of that anger. The day after that fight, I found a kickboxing school round the corner from where I was living with the family. I knew I needed to get this anger under control. I never wanted to be out of control like that ever again. I was dangerous. I was lucky to have come out of that situation unscathed. I was lucky that I had not put her in the hospital.

'Women Kickin' It', that was the name of the kickboxing school I joined. I loved it. I was in the place I needed to be.

After that friendship breakdown, I felt really alone. I didn't work with anyone where I could make friends. I had guy friends at the gym but no one I was hanging out with. It was a solitary time. I didn't like it. Kerry had told Gracie at the factory that it was either me or her at the factory. She was making Gracie choose. Gracie chose me. I knew that Kerry was good friends with my dad. I thought that maybe he would take her side. I phoned him up to talk about what had happened and said that I felt alone. He did reassure me that I wasn't alone and that I could come and hang out at the house anytime I wanted to. It did make me feel good to hear that. Kerry had built up a relationship with my horrible gran. I never spoke to my gran again after America. Kerry and my gran spoke all the time. Kerry had a better relationship with her than I did. Gran chose her.

I then threw myself into the gym and kickboxing. Six days a week I was doing both. I kept myself busy with training and channelling my aggression. On Saturday nights I would go and hang out at my dad's, if I wasn't getting a phone call from Rafael.

Rafael was about in amongst all of this. Not long after I

had met him, he did invite me up to San Francisco to train with him at the 24hr Fitness just off Folsom. He was a Personal Trainer there. I was to meet him downstairs. I was so nervous. I don't know why. I suppose because he was the most beautiful man that had ever wanted to spend any time with me. He came and got me at reception. We did a workout together. I did not say a word, just smiled and giggled a bit. What was wrong with me? He never even tried to initiate a conversation. We just lifted weights. I just couldn't shake myself together. It was like I was in awe of him! I can't even remember if we went and got a drink afterwards but I do know that I kicked myself all the way home. What an idiot. What was wrong with me? He was just so beautiful, to me anyway. No one like him had ever even given me the time of day. All I could do was smile and giggle. What a douche! I thought, 'Well that's the end of that'!

It wasn't though. He did call me again. Rafael's presence would last for around three months if you were lucky. One minute he was there and the next minute he was gone. The first time he ghosted me I was devastated. I didn't know what I had done wrong. I questioned myself and looked at my own inadequacies. Then out of the blue he would call again. My heart would jump and off I would go, running like a puppy dog. If I showered him with enough love and gifts maybe he would stick around. Of course, he would disappear again. This was his cycle of behaviour. I did eventually figure it out. It didn't hurt any less when he would disappear. I don't know why I put up with it. I loved him. Maybe, I just didn't love myself enough to think I could do better. I had put him on a pedestal because I thought he was so handsome. I never questioned how he was treating me and the fact that I could do better.

As soon as he called, I would drive up to San Francisco to

meet him. We would then drive all over San Fran doing his meet-ups and jobs. I always had to wait outside in the car. I never got to go inside and meet his friends. I would sit outside in the car for ages sometimes. I would never put up with that now. I was so young and naive. We would drive over to Oakland to pick up his stash of drugs, in my car. I was a taxi service. He didn't have a car so I was convenient enough to put up with for a time so that he could do all his running around in my car. I mean, what was I doing? A massive stash of skunk and a big bag of Es. I never gave it a second thought. In my delusional mind, I was spending time with him and he wanted to be with me, so I would take what I could get.

He did take me to Reno for my twenty-fourth birthday. That was fun. We basically got wasted and gambled. We had planned to go to a show but he passed out, so that was the end of that. Bloody lightweight. We had got up to the hotel room. He then decided we should get an upgrade. I was like, "Okay, cool." But we hadn't long dropped an E. We were starting to come up and fast. By the time we made it down to the reception we were both flying! It was hilarious; we could barely stand up at the counter. The receptionist was laughing at us both and gave us our upgrade. It was a beautiful room with a view that looked out over Reno.

We were in the room partying and generally getting up to no good. He then decided we needed more vodka. He phoned room service to bring it up. There was a knock at the door, he answered it with a towel round his waist. They spoke Spanish to each other. I was positioned on the bed round the corner from the door, naked and enjoying my E high. I then realised the room service guy was walking across the room to place the vodka on the table next to the bed I was lounging on, naked. I was surprised but just proceed to smile and say hi. They then spoke again in Spanish and he left. I said, "You bastard!" He just laughed and we continued partying.

I knew Rafael had a separate life going on. I knew that there was another woman or other women. I just chose to ignore it. I never questioned him about it. I spent a lot of time crying about it but never once challenged him about it.

Rafael smoked a lot of weed. Skunk mainly. It was so strong. I was so insecure around that time. When I did smoke it, I proceeded to lose it. I became really paranoid. I couldn't speak or string a sentence together. It was certainly not a chilled-out experience. I was always too afraid to say no because I didn't want to seem like the weak one not doing it, with the group. I would buy the weed and figured that maybe I hadn't smoked enough. I must smoke more to get used to it. I did that for a while, until I woke up in my mind one evening and said to myself, 'What the fuck are you doing? You don't like it! It does not agree with your body, stop doing it'! So, that's what I did. I never smoked it again. It was so refreshing to take control of myself, just say no and not care about what other people thought.

I would end up at these parties with people I didn't know. Smoking skunk, getting all paranoid and not being able to speak. Now, I would just say, 'No thank you. I don't smoke'. It was cool. I was able to participate in talking and not hide in the corner.

One week in 1998, Rafael had phoned me up. He asked me to go up for the weekend. He had told me to bring a sleeping bag. I couldn't find a sleeping bag so I chucked in a massive, quilted throw I found. Off we went to this house in San Francisco with these people I had never met. They offered me a smoke. I declined. Felt cool. I had a couple of beers and life was good. After the visit he said, "I'm taking you somewhere." I said, "Cool." I was always up for an adventure. We drove for about three hours. It was getting pretty late, three a.m., maybe four in the morning. We arrived at this place called Harbin's Hot springs. I realise now that it was a healing sanctuary. The pools were man-made but the springs were piped in from the mountains. We sat in the car for a bit. Rafael said, "You need to have a smoke to enjoy the experience." I said, "No." He said, "Come on!" I said, "I don't want to." He said, "Just a little one." I gave in and thought I'll just have a small hit. Well, I must have the biggest lungs because when I blew the smoke out, it went on forever and ever. I thought, 'Right, here we go. I'm going to lose my shit'. We sat there for a while. Rafael said, Right, let's go. Grab the stuff from the boot." I got out and opened the boot. It felt like I just stood in front of the boot for around ten minutes just staring into it! Rafael looked at me and then said, "Where is your sleeping bag?" I said, "I haven't got one." He was pretty miffed at that. He said, "I told you to bring one," I said, "I bought this instead." I grabbed the massive quilt cover. He grabbed his and mine and we started to make our way up this really steep hill. In my infinite wisdom I thought, 'I know, let's have something to eat. Get some food in me that might straighten me up a bit'. I found an oat bar in my pocket. If you have smoked weed and understand what happens to your mouth, you understand that an oat bar is the last thing you should be putting in there! I had no saliva. I had what is called cotton mouth. I was chewing on this oat bar for what seemed like an eternity. Rafael was five metres ahead of me, so he was not aware of what I was doing. I thought I need to get rid of what was in my mouth. I was never going to be able to swallow it. So, I flubbed it out in the nearest bush to the left of me and kept walking up the hill, relieved. Rafael was completely unaware.

We got to the top of the hill. Rafael made his way to this wooden shelter. He dumped the sleeping bags and took off all his clothes. He never explained what the deal was or what I was supposed to do. So, I just followed suit. I got naked too. We got in the big, meditation pool they had. It was amazing. You could feel the sulphur bubbles all over your body. From the pool you could see the stars and the Milky Way, for as far as your eyesight could take you. Just magical. There was a dude in the pool with a tube he had his head on just floating around snoring!

Next to the meditation pool was a boiling hot pool. You had to take your time getting in that one. Once the heat was too much, you would go to the next pool that was a plunge pool. That pool was freezing cold! The pools closed at five a.m. for cleaning, to be opened again at six a.m. Once we had finished floating around, we got ourselves together. Rafael led the way to this decking area to sleep out underneath the stars. He opened up his sleeping bag and we used my quilt to lay on. He then pulled me in tight. In that moment, I felt so close to him. Protected. Loved. He had never done that before. He had never showed any level of intimacy.

The problem with me was that I never knew what was right or wrong. I loved him so took what I could have with him. I never judged him. I never asked questions. He never kissed me. He never made love to me. I know that now. He would just fuck me. There is a difference. As a twenty-four-year-old girl I still did not know what I wanted. I never thought about my own desires. What turned me on. He took what he wanted, when he wanted and I was subservient in all his desires. His dick was hard and you knew what was coming next! That was pretty much the set up with our sexual activity.

He asked me to marry him twice. The first time we were going to Las Vegas. I had told my dad. He wasn't that impressed or bothered. I really thought Rafael was going to go through with it. I ran around trying to sort wedding rings and flights to Las Vegas. It was a strange time. At the back of my mind, I did think that it wasn't real but I also did not want to believe that it wasn't. Dad wasn't going to go with me to Las Vegas and suggested that I take his wife Sarah. I didn't really care for Sarah.

Sarah was my dad's third wife. She was a snob and was used to the finer things in life. Until she had an affair with my dad. She then had to get a job because my dad could not provide the life that she was accustomed to. Sarah also did not care for any part of my dad's family or his kids. As far as she was concerned, we did not exist. There were pictures everywhere around the house of her kids but there was nothing of Leigh, or myself, or Ashley, who is my half-sister. Sarah was also a functioning alcoholic. On the dot every night at eight p.m., out comes the vodka. Neat. I couldn't figure it out at first. I couldn't understand how she was getting so drunk every night. I assumed it was water. I soon realised after observing her, that it was neat vodka. But of course, Sarah got up to work every day and continued with her life on a day-to-day basis, so therefore in her eyes she did not have a problem. Anyone in my book that has to down neat vodka seven days a week, is a functioning alcoholic.

I knew she didn't really care for me. Her daughter had visited the house one day and they both sat opposite me in the kitchen and berated me for not having an education. I knew they were being bitches towards me. Like bitchy girls in the playground at school that think they are better than everyone else. I thought, 'Fuck you two. I fought my corner and think you are just a pair of cunts'!

I could tolerate her though. I was not ecstatic about going with her to Las Vegas but I thought, 'It'll be all right, it's only four days'.

I had gone out to celebrate getting married the night before the marriage was supposed to happen. It certainly wasn't a hen night, but it was along those lines. I got absolutely wasted. I was bought shot after shot after shot. I ended up back at a mate's house drinking more and was offered what I thought was a joint. He asked if I fancied a smoke. In my drunken state I was like, "Sure." What I didn't realise was that it was crack! It didn't really do anything for me. I didn't become instantly addicted to it.

Let me tell you though, about the come down I had the following day! I have never in my life had a come down like it. I was all on my own. I didn't know what to do with myself. I was having all kinds of horrible thoughts. I phoned my friends in the UK who stayed on the phone with me for over two hours, talking me round. I managed to fall asleep after the phone call. The following day I was off to Las Vegas. In my fantasy, Rafael was going to meet me there. Of course, he didn't; we didn't get married. I spent four days with a chain smoker in my hotel room who didn't give a fuck that it was a non-smoking room and did it anyway, who also drunk herself pissed every night we were there. I did see a couple of shows but I mostly got myself out in the sun and recovered from the reckless night I had before I got there.

I was laid out in the MGM sun lounge area by the pool, minding my own business and some dude walked past me and did a walk by photo! It was so weird. Maybe he thought I was someone famous. I was stood taking a sip out of my drink, soaking up the sun and he aimed the camera as he walked by and took a picture! Weird!

I know it is hard to believe there was a second time. When I write this now, I ask myself, 'What were you thinking'? but I loved him and would do anything to be with him. I certainly had no role models to guide me in how I should be treated. Could that have made a difference in my life, having role models or parents to turn to?

The second time was 1998 into 1999, New Year's Eve. I had gone to San Francisco to have the night of my life. I had invited my friend Cassandra from the kickboxing school. I asked Cassandra if she wanted to spend New Year's with me in San Fran. She said, "Sure". I thought, "Great". I phoned Cassandra up before the night out. I had to lay out the boundaries. I told Cassandra I would be staying out all night. If she wanted to come home early, she was to bring her car because I would not be leaving any time soon before midday the following day. She said, "No worries." I also told her that I would be taking E. She said, "I want to try some of that too." I said, "Okay, we are going to have a great night!" I had £300 dollars and I was going to spend the lot on the night out. We club hopped all over San Francisco. We did not take any prisoners that night. Isn't it amazing how you can be half-way round the world and end up meeting someone who lives only up from the street from you? I met Clare and Craig that night. Clare was from my hometown. Craig from New Zealand. We have become lifelong friends.

I only gave Cassandra half an E, just to make sure she did not overdo it. We made it into 1015 Folsom, it was around three a.m. at this point and Cassandra kept falling asleep. I kept having to wake her up otherwise we were going to get thrown out. I was still bouncing around like the Duracell bunny! I then took Cassandra around to The END UP. It must have been around eleven a.m. by this time and it was now 1999 New Year's Day. Poor Cassandra, she had had enough really. But I had told her. If she wanted to go home, she needed to have bought her car. She was sat down and I was still dancing and parading around the club. This is when Rafael appeared. My heart missed a beat as it always did. He said, "Let's go get married." I said, "Okay." I went over to Cassandra, gave her my car keys and said, "I'm off to get married." She was soon very much awake and said, "Dude! What are you doing?" I said, "It's okay, I know him! I'm off to Reno. Take my keys and I'll see you in a couple of days." She said, "Okay. Dude, are you sure?" I said, "Yes." Off I went. He bought one of his friends as a witness. They were so high. I fell asleep in the back of the car. He was talking all the way to Reno about us getting married but as the high started to dissipate, he probably thought that it was not such a good idea. We arrived in Reno and nothing more was said. We partied for a couple of days and then drove home. The drive home was an event in itself. Rafael and his buddy were so paranoid. Just sketchy from all the drugs they had been taking. We were followed by police for a little while. The pair of them were losing their shit all over the place. I had to tell them to calm the fuck down, otherwise you are going to get us pulled over. We turned off down into a dirt track and laid low for half an hour and then made our way home.

Poor Cassandra drove herself home. She arrived home around one p.m. Her house mate ran out asking her if she was okay. Cassandra's hair was thick and she had been wearing it up. On the drive home she took it down, so it was like cousin 'It'. It was all over the place. She had also been wearing strappy sandals. With all the dancing her feet were bleeding! Her house mate assumed she had been attacked. She said, "It's okay, I've been out with Janine!"

After that night, I didn't hear from him again for around another three months or so. He would call, I would run. He went through a phase of wanting to become a tattoo artist. I stupidly let him practice on me! Again, what was I thinking? I ask myself all the time, 'Where the fuck were you? Why did you let him do this to you?' My friend Cassandra said he had me under the Rafael spell! It was like I was blind. Blind to his bullshit, blind with my own love for him. I let him tattoo me twice. It was like a five-year-old had drawn on my leg! I now have that on my leg as a constant reminder of him and what I let him do to me. I have since had it covered up, not with something I would have originally chosen. I had to have a lot of black over the monstrosity to make sure that it was completely covered up.

During the year of 1999, Rafael's drug taking was getting out of control. When I met him in 1996, he had told me that only the stupid, get into taking cocaine. Just stick with the weed and you'll be fine. You get into selling the cocaine, the likelihood is that you will end up doing more than you sell.

He had phoned once again and like usual I went running as fast as I could to get to him. We were driving around San Francisco in his truck that he had bought. He would have conversations about the fact that he wanted to live the homeless life. I would try and talk him round, try and get him to see that wasn't the way forward. Wouldn't you want to set up a home, get yourself a base? I thought, 'Preferably with me'. I would never say that to him though. I didn't want to scare him away. I would keep all my misgivings to myself for fear of never seeing him again.

I am what you call a giver. I think or used to think, if I love them enough, they will stick around. I ignored all the bad behaviour in the thought that I could show them how to live a better life. Of course, that does not happen. The givers meet takers and the takers, TAKE and keep taking, until you see the light and get the fuck out of there.

We were driving around San Francisco and he kept referring to the fact that there were cars following him. The FBI were watching him! I was not on a cocaine paranoid fix so could see the nonsense in what he was talking about. There were black sedan cars that were posh taxis all over San Fran. He had it in his head they were FBI and they were following him. I realised then that he was starting to really lose it. We spent a weekend in Calistoga. We drove in my car to a cabin that was just up the road from Harbin's Hot springs. On the way to the cabin was the first time I had ever thought, 'What if we get pulled over now?' We had a massive bag of skunk in the car. He was carrying a shit load of cocaine. What the fuck was I doing! In the cabin we could hear a helicopter flying outside. He then said, "The FBI, have followed me here. They know I'm here!" I said, "How the fuck are they going to know you are here? We are in my car?" He kept referring to the fact that he would not go to prison! There was no way he was going to go to prison. I said, "If you can't do the time, don't do the crime. Don't fucking moan about it There are consequences to your behaviour if you get caught, either get on with it and stop moaning about it or stop it and sort your shit out!" Yeah, he didn't like that! That was the last time I let him drive around in my car with shit in it.

One of the last times I spent with him, we had met up on Haight Street. Haight Street was cool. It was made famous by the hippie movement in the 60s. I always loved hanging out there. We met there and he then proceeded to take PCP. I did think to myself, 'You selfish bastard. You're high. I'm straight'. I'm an idiot because I should have just left him there! No, I spent the whole day with him. He took me to this house in Oakland. They were having a party. I did not know a soul in the house. I certainly did not know how to get out of Oakland. This was before Google maps or smart phones. He basically did his own fucking thing and left me to sit in the corner of this house by myself, until he was ready to leave. I thought, 'Fuck this'!

The last time he called me, he said, "You need to come to San Francisco now!" I said, "Why?" His response, "They have towed my van!"

I was living at my dad's at that point with the view of coming home to the UK. I was back in the old Jeep that was a pile of shit. I kept breaking down in it! I said, "I can't." His response was, "You can't, or you won't?"

On the inside it was killing me. He knew that I would have come running. Fortunately for me I had a shit car, so I couldn't. It was time to say no. I told him the car would never make it. I wasn't going to take any chances trying to get up there. I then asked him what he was doing? He said, "Sat in a bar getting shit faced." I said, "Well, that's going to help the situation!" He did not like that. He gave me an ultimatum, it's yes or no.

213

I said, "No." He put the phone down on me.

I didn't hear from him again. It broke my heart!

In between the drama with Rafael, I continued living with the same family for three years. As I have said, I spent a lot of time on my own. It was really difficult to find genuine friendships out in California. I found a lot of the Americans that I met to be pretty false and insincere. Whilst the time on my own was lonely, it was good because I was not surrounded by bad influences, like I was back home in Bournemouth. It gave me time to self-reflect and grow as an individual. Really figure out my mum. I still didn't like her but I had started to come to peace with the fact that she was the way she was and it wasn't my fault. I was really able to look at what I wanted for myself in life. I had started to find a small amount of self-worth.

Aside from meeting Rafael, in my quest to make friends and get myself out there, I met my fair share of nuts jobs that I went on dates with when Rafael wasn't around. I may well have been heartbroken but I did not let that stop me from getting out there and meeting different guys. The following are some of the dates that I went on.

Robert Paradise. His name was not Robert Paradise! I knew that but I didn't care. He was African American. He would want me to speak sweet nothings in his ear. If you know me, you know I just cannot do that. It was just weird. I'm British, we don't do things like that! He took me round to a house one day in San Fran. All his family and friends were in the living room. I was made to sit out the back in a box room away from them all! It was weird. I had never experienced racism before. The racism in America is prolific. It shocked me when I got there. I sat in that back room trying to figure

214

out how I was going to leave without causing a scene. I was out in that room for at least thirty minutes. That was the end of that. When I told him, I didn't want to see him again, he told me I had mental problems! Nice!

Another guy. He was African American. I don't even remember his name. He made me sit through videos of him playing football. I sat there and watched him play American football whilst he spoke about himself playing football. So fucking boring! He had to go.

I met a bouncer guy at one of the clubs me and Cassandra used to go to and watch male strippers. Oooo, there was a guy called Mike. Oh my god that boy could dance. He used to visit The END UP. He gave me my very own impromptu private dance one night. I felt very special. Anyway, back to the bouncer. He asked me out and I thought, 'yeah, sure'. He picked me up and was talking all covert. He had to do a deal and had some shit to take care of. I thought he was talking drugs! I asked him what he was going on about. He said, "Steroids." 'Oh, is that all'?

We ended up at a guy's house, they were talking and he then started to talk about me like I wasn't in the room. He was talking about our genetics and how the kids we would have would be machines! I was flabbergasted and when I chipped in to say something, he told me to only speak when I am spoken to! WHAT THE ACTUAL FUCK! I told him to take me home. The guy was huge. Six foot six easy, maybe more. Must have weighed one hundred and forty kilograms plus. On the drive home, he started to tell me about the size of his PENIS! How it was eleven inches. I said, "Is that all!" His response, "Well most women can't handle it." I said, "Oh yeah, well I am not most women!" I never saw him again. What an absolute wanker!

Another guy lived down the street from me. We had waved at each other a couple times. I am a friendly person. I'll make friends with almost everyone. He stopped one day in his car and we exchanged numbers. He phoned me up and asked me out for a coffee. I said, "Sure." I was trying to build my social circle. As we were getting to the end of the conversation he then said, "I'll take you up to a viewpoint in the area." I thought, 'Great, that'll be nice. Someone to show me around'. He then finished with, "Maybe you could give me a massage up there!" There was me thinking he was being nice. I was like, "Oh fuck off, dick head." I put the phone down. Never spoke to him again.

The final guy I am going to share is a man I met at a kickboxing event. I did think he was a bit weird at the show but I like to give people the benefit of the doubt. I did give him my number. He called and arranged to take me out for dinner. As I opened the door he asked if I was all right. I responded with, "Yes, I am well, thank you." He then asked me a further five times before I had even got in the car! Which is fine and I know that maybe he was nervous but I mean come on. I told him I was fine and to stop asking me. He kept giving me a high five! I relayed a story from Seinfeld an American sitcom. A character in Seinfeld, Elaine, had a boyfriend that kept on giving out high fives that everyone found annoying. He stopped high fives after that. He then offered me a Chuppa Chupp lolly pop! I knew it was going to be one of those nights. He had decided we were going to drive down to Santa Cruz, which was very nice. On the way down to Santa Cruz he needed to fill up with petrol. He pulled into a gas station, kept the car running and proceeded to fill up with petrol with me still in the car. I pulled down the window and asked him what he was doing. He said, "Filling the car up." I was like, "Not with me in it, with the engine still on!" I mean, what the fuck? He turned off the engine. When he got back in the car, the car would not start. He obviously had some issue with the starter. He told me to jump start the car. I was wearing buffalo shoes. They were the rage in the 90s. They have very thick soles on them, not great for feeling the pedals to a 6.21 V8 Camaro. All I could see happening was me shooting through the gas station into the side of the wall. I said, "You jump start. I will push!" So, there I was pushing this Camaro through the gas station.

We went for our meal. It was all right. He did nothing to reassure me of the fact that the guy had no issues. On leaving the restaurant, he went to floss and brush his teeth! That took me by surprise. I hadn't thought to bring my toothbrush with me, you fucking weirdo. He had taken some pictures of the kickboxing show he decided to share with me by the car. As I was looking though them, he passed me a tissue. I thought, 'Okay, have I got something on my face'? He then passed me the whole pack of tissues and told me I had some moisture on my nose. You have got to be kidding me. I told him, "Take me home now please." I had had enough. When we got in the car he asked if I wanted to go down to the beach? I mean how stupid have you got to be to not see the signals that I had had enough. I said, "No, take me home." That was the end of that. He used to phone the house and ask to speak to the English girl. He couldn't even remember my name. Knob jockey!

Leigh came to visit in 1999. It was so cool having my brother there with me. I would go over to Dad's to pick him up. Dad would be pottering in the garage. I'd ask where Leigh was. He said, "Upstairs, I think." Off I'd go to find him. There he was, stoned, laid out in his room. Leigh and Dad had been hitting the bong pipe! I tell ya, that skunk is strong! You're either present or wiped out not able to function. There is no in-between. Once Leigh had got his shit together. I'd take him off for the day. We spent quite a bit of time in San Francisco. Leigh did meet Rafael on one of our nights out. On our drive home, he told me that Rafael was no good for me. He's not a good person. I knew that, I just didn't want to hear it.

On one of our drives home one night, it was around two in the morning. I only had one drink, so I was not wasted. I had started to get a bit of conscience about being reckless. I also had my brother in the car who I was responsible for. I had made a conscious decision not to drink so much. The drive home from San Fran to San Jose was about an hour. The 101 highway out of San Fran was always busy and lit up. We then turned off on to the 880 to get to San Jose. This highway was not busy. It was also very dark. Leigh was asleep. I was starting to get tired. I slowed the car down to fifty. The speed limit in the USA is or was sixty.

I opened the window to freshen up a bit, wake me up a bit. All of a sudden out of nowhere there were lights behind me. I hadn't really registered what was happening. The car came from nowhere and before I knew it, was to the right of me up on the hard shoulder. It then lost control in front of us and swerved across the highway and hit the middle reservation. It then up turned, came flying back across the highway upside down, sparks flying everywhere. Leigh was fully awake now. My mind was racing. If we get caught in this, my Honda Civic was going to get crushed and we would die. Instinctively I just started to pump the brakes. It was enough to keep us out of the way of the car that was out of control. The car bounced across the highway three times before it landed to the left of me upside down. I do not know how I managed to keep us out of that crash. But I did! I saw that another vehicle had stopped. I said to Leigh I was not stopping. That other car had stopped so we would keep driving. They can help them. If the police turn up, I would be an illegal. They would start asking questions. The accident was not my fault. Thankfully, I had slowed down, because if I hadn't me and Leigh would be dead, for sure. I certainly didn't have health insurance. The rest of the car ride home was silent. We arrived at my dad's house, Leigh went to his room and I went to mine. We have never spoken about it since!

My dad was re-mortgaging the house that he and Sarah were living in. I wasn't really paying that much attention. He did speak to me about it but it went in one ear and out the other! It didn't really involve me and the outcome of what they were going to do wouldn't affect me, so I just did not bother listening. I think with some of the money, they had planned to give some to Sarah's kids if I am right. Again, I expected nothing less and have never expected anything from my dad. So I felt nothing about the fact that they would get money and I would not. I was twenty-five years old at this point. He had provided nothing in the way of care or financial support my whole life, why should I expect it now?

To my surprise, I turned up at the house one day and he gave me $1000! I couldn't believe it! It was a small gesture in a lifetime of being a parent but it was enough for me to pay for my Personal Training course. I had seen a poster in the 24-hour gym advertising to become a personal trainer with the International Sports Science Association. I signed myself up. In 1999, I became a Personal Trainer. I couldn't believe it. I had actually achieved something. My very first qualification. I was so proud of myself. I had my PT seminar in San Francisco with Tom Platz as my tutor. He is a legend in the body building world. There are not any personal trainers in Bournemouth where I am from that can quote that. I had Tom Platz as my PT tutor!

This is where my life now begins!

I had some credibility to who I was as a person. I was also doing really well with my kickboxing. I had made it to Black Belt status in the three years I was there. I knew that I needed to keep doing the martial arts because it was an environment where I could let go of my anger in a controlled manner, without getting into trouble with the police. Dan, the father of the family I was working for, said that I needed a manager. When are you going to start fighting? What are you going to do with it? I wasn't really sure at the time but I did know that I needed the focus in my life, to keep me out of getting up to mischief.

I was so excited about my growth in lifting weights and the martial arts. It was really empowering me and giving me a sense of belief in who I was. But I was stepping outside of the norms of what it means to be a woman. A man in the gym one evening had overheard my conversation about the martial arts. I didn't know him; he was not my friend. He felt that he could impart his opinion on what he felt. I quote, 'How do you think you are going to find a man?' My response, "It will sort the men out from the boys, now go away." I was certainly not going to stop doing what I was doing because I needed to find a man!

The kids I was looking after were getting older. Suzy was now coming up to twelve years old and Tom was now ten. I felt they needed to be hanging out with their own friends, going to after school clubs, having sleepovers. They needed different stimulation other than my own. Looking after the kids was tough especially during the summer months, when they had close to three months off! Trying to keep them entertained was a tough ask, especially when you were bound to the house because the parents did not feel comfortable with us going outside of the local area.

I had thought in my early twenties that I would like to have kids. I had started to think about maybe getting pregnant; trying to meet someone to have children with. I would have had a child with Rafael. I did at one point think that might have happened but I took the morning after pill. I was in no position in America to bring a child into the world. I never knew when he was going to be around. I was of no fixed abode. Maybe I was looking for the perfect position to be in. I don't think that is too much to ask, that I should at least be in some sort of stable position before I bring a child into the world.

The morning after pill gave me a horrendous period. Unexpectedly, Rafael had popped up again at this time. When I explained to him, what I had done, he got all self-righteous on me. It was his child too. I shouldn't have made that decision on my own. I never challenged his behaviour at all back then but every so often I would find my voice. I replied back to him, "I never know when you are going to be around. You come, you go. I'm not going to do the pregnancy on my own!" He had nothing to say because I was right!

The kids at the family certainly gave me an insight into what it would be like looking after kids. It was tough, that was for sure. I sat on the couch one day when they were being particularly difficult. I said to myself, 'This is not for me. NO

KIDS'.

The family had decided they were going to move to a new house. This was a good time for me to decide what I was going to do moving forwards. Was I going to move with them? My freedom was limited with them. Rightly so, they wanted me at the house Monday to Friday. They did not want me staying out or venturing away from the home during the week because they had to work. I had started to feel a little suffocated. I had started to do some research into trying to make myself legal. I wanted to find myself a different job and try to set up a life there outside of the family. Unfortunately for me, the laws had changed in 1999, just about when I was getting my shit together. There was no way round the paperwork. Dad certainly did not do anything about sponsoring me or helping in anyway. To be honest, I did not ask and he never offered the help. The only way I could get legal now in the USA was to wait for an amnesty day where you could put yourself forward and gain a green card. If I had just really thought about following correct procedure from the outset, I could have got all the right paperwork together.

It was really time for me to come back to the UK.

I finished working for the family and moved into Dad's whilst I procrastinated about coming back to the UK. I had bought my ticket home and moved the dates three times, before biting the bullet and getting on the plane home. I loved my life in California but I was stuck. I had no ability to progress. I was not legal and had no ability other than my dad coming forward and sponsoring me, which he was not going to do. The push for me to come home was Leigh. Leigh had been at a party in Boscombe. He was in a flat with a balcony. The balcony was faulty and gave way with Leigh attached to it. He went over and landed on his face with one of the spikes going through his right cheek. Fortunately for Leigh, he had just double dropped an E. Had he not been so high and in such a relaxed state he would be dead. Being high had saved his life.

Big sister had to come home and keep an eye on the younger brother. Dad never came back. Dad never did anything!

I was going to come back to the UK as a Personal Trainer though. I had the potential now, to earn £20 an hour! I had a qualification. I was coming back a somebody.

# Chapter Ten
## You Either Want It Or You Don't

Leaving San Francisco airport, I gave in my three-month visa that I had attained on my way out. The attendant at the check in desk did not question me about how long I had been in the country. I checked in a huge amount of luggage. I paid $150 in excess! All my new shoes and clothes, I wanted to take them home.

Gracie, who I had worked for at the factory managed to sort me a first-class ticket home! She paid all her business transactions through her credit cards that accrued flight miles. She had plenty to sort a first-class flight for me to get home. Flying first class is something else! The attendant offered me a glass of champagne as I boarded. I was then shown to my seat, that had so much space around it. The attendant then put my name in a hat to get a massage whilst we were flying. I was then shown my menu card, of which I could order food whenever I wanted. I had music, TV, the seat extended out so that I could lie down. Blankets, pillows. I had whatever I needed to make the flight as comfortable as possible.

There I was. I had arrived in the USA with nothing. I was flying home, a Personal Trainer in first class. Who would have believed it?

There was no way that I could have carried all that luggage on the coach on my own. Fortunately, my friend Lou picked me up from the airport. Having someone there as you walk through the arrival doors on your own, just fills up your soul. The drive home was catch up time. Bournemouth is not too far away from Heathrow, about an hour and half. I was excited to see everyone. It had been three years!

Whenever you drive home to Bournemouth, there is really only one route in from Heathrow. M3, M27, Spur Road. When you hit that Spur Road you are on your home straight. You drive over the Cooper Dean roundabout. You feel all the stress leave your body as you start to see the greenery and flowers. Open sky, sea air, space. Bournemouth is a great town. On reflection, I am pretty lucky that I was born here and grew up here. A small town by the sea. Whenever I go away, the one thing I miss the most about my town is the beach and walking down the promenade. I can never live away from the ocean now, ever!

We arrived at Lou's house. She had kindly said I could live at her house. I had a small room upstairs, big enough room for a bed and some drawers. It didn't bother me that it was small. As long as I had somewhere with a roof over my head and a bathroom to get clean, I did not care.

My brother gave me a call once I had arrived in town and told me to get myself down to Bar Med to meet everyone. My mate Huggy also called me as well and said, "Let's get together that night and go out into town!"

I was knackered but I was happy to be back. I got my shit together and headed into town to meet my brother. He was up and about following the accident to his face. When I arrived at Bar Med, Leigh was the first one to meet me. His whole jaw was wired together. He had elastic bands all the way round his mouth. The scar under his right eye looked fresh but tidy. I remember not feeling shocked when I saw him. I was just happy to be back and looking out for him. He kept on doing Jaws impressions — the baddy out of James Bond. It was really funny. Leigh as per usual was as happy as Larry. He was in his element, surrounded by his made-up family. I met his girlfriend, Jess. She was beautiful. Leigh has always had a way with the ladies. They love him! He has a wonderful charm about him but he also has that vulnerability as well, that women will want to take care of. I, on the other hand, maybe have a little bit of charm mixed in with a don't fuck with me attitude. If you do, I'll fucking rip your head off! Doesn't bode so well with the male species.

Leigh started to show me off. Apparently, he had been telling all his friends I was coming home. What he hadn't told them was that I was five foot eight and had been spending quite a bit of time in the gym. I sit quite comfortably at eighty kilograms (twelve, point six, stone). I never see myself as big. I'm just me. But I have been told numerous times that I am built like a brick shit house or that I am very masculine!

Because of course, women are not allowed to be strong in our society without the association to being masculine. Strength has everything to do with being a man. I mean what was I thinking, becoming strong? How dare I! All of the discrimination that I have sustained over the years about my sexual orientation or the fact that I look masculine has just fed fuel to the fire. I will do exactly what I want to do and I will not conform!

I strut into Bar Med. Tank top on, arms bare, shoulders pumped. Tight jeans, so my quads are showing off nicely through the denim. All of the young women that were so looking forward to meeting me because Leigh had been talking me up, all did a double-take and basically said, unbeknownst to me, "Oh my god she is huge!" They did their quick hellos and then ran away.

Bournemouth is a rich town. There are a lot of very pretentious people that live in the town. There are a lot of people that like to play the socialite game and buy into all the designer gear, because of course that makes you someone interesting! Not! There are a lot of very superficial people in the town. They pretend to your face that they are being your friend but really, they all talk shit behind your back. I couldn't and cannot stand it. I sussed that out really quickly. I caught up with Leigh and then got myself out of there quick smart! A quick rest up at Lou's house and then out with my mate Huggy.

I met Huggy before I went to the USA. He was one of Graham's good friends. Huggy did the security at The Pavilion when I was working there. He was so handsome. I used to check him out all the time. He had given me his address before I left. I would write to him all the time. Nobody does that anymore; write letters. It's so nice receiving letters, there is something very personal about it. I had written to him as a friend. I knew he was having a hard time at home with his ex-partner who was stopping him from seeing his child. I wrote to him to send him hugs and support through the post, let him know that I was his friend. I'm not sure if he thought I was cracking onto him but my agenda was always friendship and that I cared.

Being back in Bournemouth was like a whirlwind. Everyone wants to catch up with you all at the same time. Huggy was showing signs of wanting more than just friendship. We tried that out for a moment; we ended up being friends. He did, however, tell me about a martial arts gym in Bournemouth town centre called the Bulldog Gym. He said I should go and

227

check it out.

I knew that martial arts were an activity that I needed to keep doing. It was a place where I could vent out all my anger and frustrations in a controlled environment. First week back I was straight down there and got myself sorted with their timetable. Even though I had come back a black belt I went to the beginner's class. There was no way I thought of myself as something special. I certainly was not going to put myself in a position of being tested. I went to the beginner's session to figure the club out first.

Living at Lou's was interesting to say the least. When I had left Bournemouth, she was an aerobics instructor, who worked the doors and danced in the Academy on the rave nights. On my return she was now working as a dominatrix! I never have any judgement with anyone on what they do or how they earn their money; their life, their choices. It is none of my business what they choose to do. Lou was my friend and she had kindly opened her home to me so that I had a roof over my head. I was in no position to judge her or even wanting to judge her. The dining room had been converted into a dungeon. Let me tell you she had all walks of men coming to see her. Some of the men drove down from London, to see her on the same day!

There are a few stories that have stayed in my I mind from when she was working. A man had phoned up and asked if she could piss in his face. She said sure, told him the hourly rate for her time and then made the appointment. When they were set up, she asked him if he was sure? He replied yes. She then emptied her piss all over his face. His response (*classic!*), "I did not like that one bit!" So, funny! What possesses them to think that it will be an enjoyable experience? That of course is just my opinion. If you get off on that, more fool you. No judgement here. I certainly do not want anyone pissing in my face, thank you very much.

Another time we had been out in town and had a few drinks. A mate, Paul that I worked with on the doors, had come back to ours. His mate had come back with him. I'm not sure where his mate slept that night but Paul fell asleep in my bed. We had stayed up chatting. In the morning, his mate was furiously banging on my door. He swung that door open as fast as he could. "Dude, we have got to get the fuck out of here!" I started laughing. He repeated it again, "Dude come on! Someone is getting the shit kicked out of them downstairs! Please, come on!"

Lou had a client early that morning, who clearly was getting a proper dealing with. Paul's mate looked so scared. It was really funny.

We would often be sat in the living room chilling out, whilst she was torturing some man next door. She would leave them tied up and wonder in, in her latex gear, have a cup of tea and a quick chat. put on her rubber gloves and go finish them off.

Another man had called her up and asked her if she did teeth extraction! She declined that one. There are some crazy, crazy fetishes out there that are just not for me. Thank you.

Lou did try to get me involved. There was one punter that she had that liked to be crushed. She would sit on him and crush him! Lou asked if I would join in one time. I thought, 'He's fully clothed. I don't have to put the rubber glove on at the end to finish him off. All I have to do is sit on him at the same time as Lou and crush him'! I can't remember what I got paid for thirty minutes of sitting on a man whilst he lay on the

229

floor. It was pretty easy money earnt though, that was for sure.

It was weird and awkward. I felt insecure, although I may have carried it off as though I wasn't. But usually when you are trying hard to cover up how you feel, you are usually showing how you feel! After that experience I knew that I just wasn't interested. I've always been insecure around my sexual prowess. Not that you have to be sexy to be a dominatrix but if you are stepping into the sex industry, I feel you have to have a level of confidence about who you are as a person on an intimate level. I just don't have that in me, being all sexy and that. It just feels foreign. I knew I did not want to do any more than have that one experience. I certainly did not want to finish someone off with a glove on a regular basis, that was for damn sure. Men that go to titty bars, prostitutes and dominatrices I just see as a bit sad. They generally do not have a good perception of women from my observation. When they sit there leering at the women like they are just pieces of meat without being human, I find very difficult to get my head around. So, that was the end of that.

The week after my return from California. I was walking into Boscombe. It was a twenty-minute walk from Lou's. Just as I was arriving at the pedestrianised shopping area. I had a panic attack.

The panic attacks had started in California. I didn't really understand what was happening to my body. They always seemed to happen in the car, especially when I was out on the highway going up to San Fran. It got to a point that I did not want to be inside the car.

They are really hard to explain, other than there is an overriding fear running through every vein in your body. It's like you can't breathe. Like death is imminent. All rationality leaves your thinking, as if something really awful is going to happen.

I managed to keep myself on my feet into Boscombe and talk myself through it. I found somewhere to sit for a minute. I felt I had no strength in my legs. I didn't trust that they were going to hold me up. I made it to the shop where I was going. Then managed to get myself home and didn't speak about it. I did go to the Doctors and ask to see a counsellor. I wanted to understand what was happening. Why they were happening. What was going on with my body. The counsellor didn't come up with anything for me really. She was nice to talk to but she explained nothing.

My mission on my return to the UK, was to concentrate on my lifting and martial arts. Lou initially was going to pay me to look after her daughter. She did for a while but, on reflection, I was being lazy. I was depressed. I thought I had made the biggest mistake of my life coming back. I was surrounded by the people that I had escaped. They were all still taking drugs and living that lifestyle that I really couldn't say no to. It was easy to fall straight back into taking Es, getting wasted and feeling like shit for the rest of the week. I can see how I was. It had started to wind her up. Of course, it would. I would get upset with someone if I felt they were not pulling their weight.

I was also back working the doors as a bouncer at The Academy, which was now called The Opera House, as well as working a coffee shop in the mornings, seven a.m. to ten a.m., for extra money. Friday mornings at the coffee shop was debilitating. I would finish work at three a.m. at the club, get home around four a.m., have two hours' sleep and then get into the coffee shop for seven a.m. It was horrible. I was like a zombie. I would get home from the coffee shop, have a sleep, get back to work at the club for nine p.m., to then finish again at three a.m. It was tough. In the middle of doing all that I was training in the gym, lifting weights and making it to the Bulldog to train in my kickboxing. I was not happy at all. I wanted out! I wanted to go back to the USA.

My gym work and martial arts kept me sane though. My body was changing all the time. My arms and body were getting bigger. Me and Lou would have conversations in the kitchen at home about how big my arms were getting. We'd get the tape measure out; fourteen or fifteen inches. I don't know what that means. I just wanted to be strong. My body was just doing what it was doing with the training. There was talk at the time about me getting on some kind of steroid, Winstrol, I think it was. I could have got massive but I just wasn't interested in that. It was not about body building for me, it was about strength. I am addicted to being strong. My body is a product of my strength training. Getting bigger was never an issue to me. So, taking steroids was not really on the agenda for me. Thankfully I stayed well clear of that. Had I gone down that route, I would have certainly ended up being one hundred kilograms, fifteen stone in weight in no time!

Being eighty kilograms is enough and comes with its own discrimination as it is. 'You're a big girl', 'You're built like a bloke!' 'You're very masculine!' and 'I always thought you were a lesbian' were comments I regularly heard, because clearly lifting weights means that I must be a lesbian. People are weird!

When I stepped into the Bulldog gym, I kept a very low profile. It's quite difficult to do when you are a female carrying eighty kilograms of muscle! But I started out in the beginner's class and stayed at the back. I didn't say much, did the work and got out without mingling too much. There were a lot of women in the beginner's class. They were not built like me nor did they have any of my strength. They never looked best pleased to be partnered with me. I was always very respectful. I never pushed my weight around but I did like to work hard. The instructor, Shaun, would usually come over and hold the pads for me. After a few sessions he said you should step up into the advanced session.

The Bulldog gym was a proper boxing gym: a little bit grubby and everything in there was well worn. There was a box at the end of the gym that had used boxing gloves in that you could borrow if you did not have your own. When you put those gloves on, your hands would heat up pretty quick. The gloves stank and inside it felt like all the used up sweat from everyone else that had been using them would start to fizz. It was disgusting.

I had seen some of the men that would come in after the beginner's class. They looked pretty tough and serious to me. I didn't see any other women go into the advanced session. I certainly did not feel like I was ready for that at all. I might have been a black belt in the USA. That was semi-contact sparring, this was full contact. Shin guards if you were lucky, gum shield, you were not allowed to spar without it and no head guard. Get in the ring and go. It was a very daunting step up to get my head around. I just wasn't good enough in my eyes. I stayed put in the beginner's class. I felt safe there. I was in control of the environment. I needed to be pushed but I was going to do it when I wanted to.

Back at the house, it was going from bad to worse. My relationship with Lou was really starting to break down. She was struggling with work. The punters were not always coming in. We were all doing too many drugs! I was depressed about being back in the UK and working at the Opera House as a security person; I hated it!

Working on the door as a security person, you get to see people at their worst. I had to really show my worth there as well. There was a head doorman, Chris, that was known as a bit of a twat! He liked to make fun of people in front of all his mates that he worked with on the door. They would then gang up together, making the person they were bullying, essentially feel very small. If you did not stand your ground, you were going to get eaten up and that was just with the men you were working with, never mind having to deal with drugged up, pissed up wankers in the club.

I was a different person when I came back from the USA. I had grown into myself. I wasn't going to get pushed around anymore. I certainly wasn't going to be bullied anymore. I wasn't afraid of not fitting in anymore. I was in a place where I was comfortable being myself. I did not care what people thought about me *anymore*! I knew Chris was a twat and he liked to single people out. I just made a point at work to stay clear of him.

One night, the whole team had to meet at the end of the night. All the men and then me, the only woman on the team, were stood by the front door. Chris passed me a clipboard with a sheet on it to sign. As I passed it back, Chris failed to grab it. The clipboard fell to the floor and the paper that had been on the clip board flew everywhere. He barked at me, in a belittling manner, "P*ick it up!*" in front of all the door staff. If I had picked that up in fear, I would never have gained any respect in front of those men. I stood back and replied with aggression,

*"You fucking pick it up!"* I stood strong and was not going to back down. My face was strong and was not about to be fucked about with in front of all those men. Fuck you! Chris picked up the clip board. He left me alone after that.

In 1999, you could still smoke in the clubs. That's what I hated the most. I hate cigarette smoke, it has to be one of the most disgusting habits any person can have. Along with the amount of dry ice smoke the club was pumping out on to the dance floor, I would just stress about the amount of shit getting into my lungs. Yes, I could have left the job. But I was earning £13 an hour. Minimum working wage back in 1999 was £3.60! How the fuck are you meant to live on that? You have to work like a dog to get enough money to live on at £3.60 an hour. So, working in the club was shit but £13 an hour made more sense to me.

I saw in the year 2000 in the Opera House. What a night that was. The manager Paul had said we could all have a drink at midnight to celebrate the New Year in, as it was a pretty special one to be seeing in. The security team had only been at work an hour and Paul the manager, who was also a bit of a dick, decided he was going to change his mind and retract the offer of a drink. We were to get nothing! Of course, that does a great job at making people feel respected and worthy in their job. It did put a dampener on the evening.

At home, my brother had been round. Lou, Jessica and my brother were all off to a house party. Leigh dropped a pill in my hand and said don't take it all at once they are really strong. I thought, 'Cool', dropped it into my pocket and trotted off to work.

Once Paul had made that decision not to let the team have a celebratory drink, I thought, 'Fuck you. I am going to get twatted'. I found Marcus, another doorman that I was working with. He was on the stage and I was on bar one. Bar one was situated right by the stage. Marcus had also decided he was going to get twatted. We made a pact together. We were going to look out for each other and if we got too bad, we were to let each other know, which is just ridiculous because as you get twatted, your vision and perception gets twisted. The blind leading the blind.

Marcus would just appear buzzing, eyes wide and say, "What do I look like?" I'd say, "Great, dude!" He would then disappear like a whirlwind, up the steps to the back of the stage! I had dropped half of the pill and thought, 'Fuck it, I'll take the other half'. I had different punters coming up to me giving me pills. I had about five of them down my boot! I suddenly got a call over the radio to go and do a drug search! I thought, 'Oh shit! What if someone searches me?' I stood there for a while trying to figure out what I was going to do. I came to the decision, 'Fuck it. I don't look too bad. I feel pretty together. I reckon I can carry this off'. Off I went to the office to search a girl for drugs, knowing full well I had drugs on me! I managed to keep my shit together, searched the girl and did not find anything. Whether it was paranoia, or the manager did know, I saw him look at me and just smile. I knew he knew but who was there to search me? No one! Once I was finished searching the girl, off I went to enjoy the year 2000 New Year's Eve. Myself and Marcus had a top night!

Living at Lou's I was so unhappy. I didn't see any future here back in Bournemouth. I just saw the old behaviour surrounding me, everyone just living for the weekends, getting their substances sorted: Es, weed and cocaine. Getting twatted every weekend, the same old merry go round. I wanted out. I wanted back to California. I had a nice life there. I was an illegal but I had a nice life.

I had thought about changing my passport. Stupid, I know. As if changing my passport would make any difference in me getting back into the USA. It may be a different passport number but all my details are the same, stupid! Date of birth, etc, etc. I didn't change my passport, I used my old passport and applied for a six-month visa. I thought that could buy me some time once I had arrived in USA. At least give me more time than three months to try and get sorted. I filled in the form. There was a question on the form that asked if you had visited the USA before. If you had, how long had you been out there? I thought what harm would it do if I put three months? Of course, at that point, I was an idiot. I wanted out of my situation and was willing to do anything I could do to change the circumstances I was in. I posted it and it returned with a six-month visa in it. I thought, 'Great, I'm in'. I then phoned Gracie my ex-employer in California, the women that owned the factory. She said she would help me. I can't even remember where I was going to stay or what job I was going to step into. I was blagging it all the way. I thought, I'll sort it when I get there.

Gracie sorted me out a first-class ticket back to California. Amazing! I paid $65 for it. The rest she paid for with her air miles. I did not pay attention to the fact that she had only bought me a one-way ticket. Stupid. I had a friend, Ben, from San Fran come and visit me in Bournemouth. I had planned to fly back with him. He was a massive dude that was stuck right at the back of the aeroplane. I was in first class again with all the room I needed. Of course, I was an old hat at this now, flying first class: music, films, menu, blanket and pillows. I knew the score. I had asked if my friend could come and visit me. The steward said no! I thought, 'That's a shame, oh well. I'll see him when I land'. I had everything going on: music, film and stuffing my face. There was a tap on my shoulder. I looked up it was Ben. He said, "Dude, what the fuck is going on here, look at you!"

"Hey Ben, what's up!"

"Come on, we are going to the bar!" We sat at the bar for a while, Ben then informed me that he didn't care about what I was doing. He was going to stay at the bar for the rest of the flight! I did not blame him one bit. We both stayed there for the rest of the flight.

Going through customs at any airport is stressful. You always feel like you've done something wrong even though you haven't. I pulled up with my bags and passed over my passport. The officer looked at me. "Miss Davis have you been to the US before."

I said, "yes!"

He then asked, "For how long?"

This moment in time felt like it went on forever. Do I lie, do I tell the truth? Really, either one I was not winning. I replied, "Three months!" An outright lie. He put a big cross over my paperwork and said to go over to the customs section. I knew from that moment I was not winning, although there was a small amount in my brain that thought I may be able to pull it off.

I was put in front of a gentleman. Another customs' officer. He said, "Janine, how did you get this visa?"

"I applied for it. Not a lie. I did apply for it!"

"Janine, how did you get this visa?"

"I applied for it." Again, not a lie.

"Janine, I am going to ask you again and if you do not start telling me the truth. You are going to get in a whole lot more trouble than you are in now!"

I thought at that moment, 'Give it up'. I replied, "I lied on the visa application form."

His response, "Do you know that is fraud? You can get into some real serious trouble for that. Take your bags and go and sit over there."

I knew then I was in real trouble. I was taken out the back into a booth. Two guards sat me down and then proceeded to stand over me. I am assuming to intimidate me. They both started reading me my rights. Talked about asylum. If I was in any position of dying should I return home, I could seek asylum.

Just for a moment in my thoughts I did give that some thought. But it was the UK. I wasn't escaping a war-torn country. So, that quickly vanished. They were still shouting at me, reading me the riot act. I looked at them and thought it was a load of nonsense. I stopped them in their tracks and said, "Look. I'm not an asshole. I'm an idiot. Just put me on the next flight home." They both looked at each other, stopped their shouting and left me in the booth. I was allowed to make a few phone calls. I phoned Gracie. I didn't even think to call my dad. He would not have helped anyway. Gracie tried to get them to agree to let me stay at her house for the night. That was definitely a no go. There was no way I was leaving that airport.

Whilst I was sat in the booth, they pulled in this Filipino woman. She was handcuffed to the chair, in a booth next to me. The officers were going mad. They threatened to throw her in jail if she did not co-operate. The Filipino sat fast, did not say a word. Within a few hours, she was signing papers and was off, making entry to the USA. How the fuck did she do that?

In my case, the officers were debating where to send me for the night. Marin County Jail or Oakland, a predominantly black and dangerous County Jail? I know where I wanted to go. Marin County. I also knew at that point I had to start getting my head together. I couldn't show any signs of weakness. If I did, I was going to get the shit beaten out of me.

Once they had made the decision, I was going to Marin County, I was carted off through the airport, in handcuffs! Not only was it embarrassing, I said, "I have not been arrested for anything!" The officer replied, "It is just general procedure ma'am." I thought it was ridiculous and a crock of shit! The tears had started at this point. I'm not sure what I was so upset about. I didn't care about the situation I was in. I was more worried about what I was going back to. I was literally homeless. I was going to be living on the streets. Phoning my dad was just not an option. He'd never been there for me, so why would he be there at that point!

I sat in the back of the meat wagon. Fortunately, I was on my own. I curled myself up in the back and thought, 'Well, this is the closest I am going to get to being back in San Francisco'. The meat wagon took me across the Golden Gate Bridge which was cool. I took it in for a moment but then I had to get my thoughts back together again. I did not know what I was going to be going into. What if they put me in a cell with a lunatic? I said to myself, 'Get your shit together, Davis. Stop your crying. If you get into that cell and she starts on you. You beat the shit out of her'! I was ready!

Once we arrived at the County Jail, the officers took me inside and I was directed to sit on a bench by the reception. I was then told to take out my laces from my shoes. I suppose, just in case I tried to hang myself with them. I could not have felt any lower at that point in my life than when I was sat in that jail. How the fuck did I end up there? I could sense the officers on the other side of the desk kept looking at me and talking amongst themselves. They asked if I was hungry. I said, "Sure." They passed over a brown paper bag. I opened it up. A warm, soft apple, a spam sandwich, made with nibble bread. I could not eat that. Is spam even real food? It also had a carton of milk. I drank the milk. To be honest I was not that hungry.

The officers were trying to figure out a place for me to sleep. The holding cell opposite me had a drunk guy in it that was passed out. They said they were not going to put me in there, thank god! They then figured out a cell they were going to put me in. Before getting to the cell, I was questioned. Some kind of prick test was done on my wrist. I was sure I had my retina taken. I know I had to eyeball something! All that interrogation was pretty tough. I was tired, emotional and I just didn't know what I was going to do when I got home to the UK. What the fuck was I going to do? I had nowhere!

I was then asked to follow this officer to a shower unit where I was told to take off my clothes and bag them up in a black bin liner. I was given blue prison uniform. The plimsolls were a bit small but I didn't think I was in a position to complain about them. I was then given two pillows, two big white pants, toothbrush, toothpaste and socks that were on top of the pillows. I was taken through to a hall. I am assuming the hall was where all the prisoners sit during the day when they are let out of their cells. The officer then pointed at a cell I was to make my way to. For me it was like I was walking the plank. I kept repeating to myself, 'Keep your shit together, keep your shit together'. The door to the cell was buzzed open and I walked in. I chucked my pillows etc on the side and jumped up on to the top bunk. The woman on the bottom bunk said, "Hi." I was on my guard, until I had figured her out. She had a quick chat with me. Asked me what I had done. I explained I had been hauled in from the airport. She then told me not to worry and that it wasn't a big deal. She's been locked up this time for eight months. She had been stealing clothes from Bloomingdales and then returning the clothes to Bloomingdales to get the money. I did feel a little relieved that she was nice. I was not in a position where I was fighting for my life. I did have a panic though, I thought I was never getting out of there. Why had they put me in prison uniform? Also, no one knew I was there. I remember sitting bolt upright on numerous occasions. I could see across the hall to a big clock. I would lay down to try and settle and then sit bolt upright and look across at the clock to see what the time was. I also remember sitting bolt upright on one of the occasions and saying, 'Okay, okay, I'm listening. What the fuck am I doing inside this cell? This is not who I am! How the fuck did I end up here? When I get out and get home to the UK, I need to sort my fucking life out'!

Fortunately for me I was only in that cell for a few hours. An officer came and got me around five thirty a.m. I was given a black bin liner with all my clothes in. Once dressed, I was put in a holding cell until they were ready to take me to another holding cell in San Fran city.

In the first holding cell I was put in, I met an Asian woman. She was on her way to an appeal. She had already served five years of a twenty-five-year sentence. She was twenty-four years old! I asked her what she had done. She replied she was not allowed to talk about it. For a twenty-five-year sentence it either had to be murder or drugs. I reckon it was drugs! She did tell me though that she had lived in the USA since she was two years old. She did not speak Chinese. America was her home. Unfortunately for her, once she was let out of prison she was going to be deported back to China, a country she knew nothing about!

The second holding cell I was in was right in the city centre. There were a lot more women in this one. Most of them were Hispanic, wearing orange uniforms. I wasn't sure what that meant. I was sure that I wanted to be left well alone. One woman did ask me if I was from England. I said, "Yes!" That was the end of that conversation. I kept myself to myself. That is where my size comes in handy. I am assuming I look a bit more foreboding, than a five-foot, forty-five-kilogram woman. Five feet eight and eighty kilos, are a bit more to mess around with. I have been told many times over that I look strong. Good is what I think to that. Good! It means the fuckers, won't want to fuck around with me.

There was a telephone inside the cell. I had managed to get hold of my brother. He was never really in a position to help me out. He was doing his best to try and survive himself. Anyway, I thought that's my only option. Leigh said, "Don't worry Sis. I'll get you somewhere to stay for a couple of nights when you get back." My relationship with Lou had broken down completely so that was out of the question. I thought, 'Okay. I've bought myself two nights. I'll figure out the rest when I get back'.

It felt like I had been in that holding cell for hours. An officer came in and got me. He informed me that they were ready to take me to the airport. He took a look at me and said, "Do you work out?" I said, "Yeah!" He was then like, "You must be starving? Do you want some food?" I said, "Sure!" He took me into this room where there were proper sandwiches, made with proper bread. Boxes of cereal and drinks. He said, "Take whatever you want." It was really weird. All of a sudden, I wasn't being treated like a criminal anymore. The officer was being really super-friendly, like we were just hanging out!

I filled up my pockets with as much food as I could fit in there. Once we had arrived at the airport, they took me back to where I had been held the day before. One officer had to take a picture of me. He kept telling me to step back. I would step back. He would say a bit more, a bit more, a bit more. I thought what the fuck is he doing?

I had a jumper on with the American flag on it. He wanted to make sure that the flag was in the picture! What a dick! This particular officer then made a comment saying that he reckoned I would look good scrubbed up, fucking sleaze. He was looking at me like he was already fucking me. Fucking asshole. I was glad to get out of there.

I was chaperoned by another officer to the plane, I suppose, in case I made a run for it! He seemed a nice guy. I started asking him questions about the Filipino woman the day before. How did she get in? He told me she had a kid with her. They had nowhere to put the kid. So, she was signing paperwork and was allowed to enter the country. It's all about knowing how to work the system, in everything you do in life!

The flight home was horrendous. There was no first class privilege this time. I spent the whole flight crying and sleeping. No one was there at the arrival gate. This is it; I am on my own! Really on my own.

I phoned Leigh when I arrived in Bournemouth coach station. Bedraggled and glad to be home in Bournemouth, I didn't even know what day it was or how long I had been away! I just wanted to get a cup of tea and figure out what I was going to do next. He told me to come to Olly's. Olly was one of his closest mates. He said that I could use his couch for a couple of nights.

Work! What was I going to do for work? A mutual friend of mine and Leigh's managed a bar in town called Cafe Paris, it was situated on Old Christchurch Road. You get a lot of foot traffic at night along that road. The bar crawls would start at the top of Old Christchurch Road and work their way down past Cafe Paris. Meaning, you would get all walks of life coming in and out of the bar.

Froot, that's the name of the manager of Cafe Paris. She phoned me up and said they needed a door person Friday and Saturday night. The bar closed at eleven p.m. and it was cash in hand! Great, that will get me going. I would be working the door on my own. I didn't give it a second thought. I never even questioned working on my own. I needed work and I needed the cash coming in. A few pissed up wankers didn't intimidate me. I also managed to get my job back at The Opera House. I was able to go up to the club once I had finished at Cafe Paris and finish the night at the club. Great, work sorted, we're on a roll.

Where to stay? I couldn't be fussy. I was in a vulnerable place. I was happy to be anywhere where I had a roof over my head for a moment, just until I got some money together to get into a flat. This is where Sarah came in.

I didn't really know Sarah. She was a security woman at The Opera House. She didn't really do security. Sarah's position was just a female presence. She never really dealt with anything. She never got involved with chucking people out of the club. She was there to check the female toilets. Do the random searches of the women and their bags on the way in. Stand on the VIP door and get completely off her tits on E!

Apparently, she was adamant that I was to go and stay with her, unbeknownst to me. I just needed somewhere to stay so didn't question her agenda. As always, I genuinely thought she was helping me out. What I hadn't known was that a woman from The Opera House called Ri, had a room she was looking to rent. Ri had mentioned the fact that she had this room but Sarah was pretty persuasive in saying, "No! Janine can come and stay with me. I will look after her!"

Sarah had a studio flat at the top of a block of flats. It was pretty small, a tiny room, with an alcove bit where all her bookshelves were. There was a tiny bit of floor space right by the books. That was where I slept on the floor, on rolled out camping mats. There was a tiny galley kitchen and a small bathroom that had a bath in it. It was so nice to have a bath and disappear in the water for a moment. In the first days of staying there I would sit and talk about my time in San Francisco. I would talk a lot about Rafael. How much he meant to me. I would discuss if I was ever going to see him again. Facebook wasn't around then. I had no idea how I was going to try and find him.

I didn't want to take advantage of staying there so suggested that I pay her £35 a week, for sleeping on her floor, along with putting money on her gas and electric key. She must have thought all her Christmases had come at once. If it was me and I knew that someone needed help, I would have let them stay and just got them on their feet. Sarah, on the other hand, was happy for me to owe her money. I didn't have any at that point so had to wait until I got paid, to then try and pay off what I owed. What a cunt! When I think about that now it makes me so mad. Fucking leech. These fuckers that see people that are in a vulnerable state and then prey on them. I was in a place where I thought I was being helped out. What I didn't realise was that I was being preyed upon.

Sarah had a budgie as well! The bird shit everywhere! She never cleaned it up. There was bird shit over everything. I tried not to spend too much time in the flat if I could help it. I ate there, slept there and washed myself. I tried to keep myself out of the flat as much as possible. I got myself back into the gym. Fortunately, the flat was right by the beach. I would take off running down there to try and clear my head, as much as possible.

Sarah was a recovering heroine addicted. Whilst she may have been off the heroine, she was now doing a very fine job of taking as much Ecstasy as she could. I was back in and around these dysfunctional people. I needed out, but where the fuck was I going to go?

Working at Cafe Paris was starting to take its toll. Really, I needed to be with at least another person on the door. Trying to deal with pissed up wankers on your own is not much fun.

The worst part of working the door is the end of the night. Last orders are given. Lights are up. The bar is closed. You, as the security person, go around and very politely start to tell people to drink their drinks up. The bar is shut, it's time to go. What you then get is mostly men telling you that you need to check my law! That, by law, they have twenty minutes to drink their drinks up. I mean what the fuck! These fucking assholes that you have to deal with. I've asked nicely. I then politely tell them that it is at the bar owners' discretion as to whether they can have the time to drink their drinks up. The bar and premises are now closed, you have to go. The men then look at you like you are a piece of shit, pick up their pint and take the tiniest sip they can out of the glass to make a point. Depending on what type of person you are, you are either going to respond to it violently or just walk away for a moment, let them think that they have one over on you and then drag them out by the scruff of their shirts, creating a scene that would not need to take place if they had just done what you had asked them to do in the first place!

On one particular occasion in Cafe Paris, there was one guy that I had told five times, it was time to go. I knew he was going to make a scene. I had to really think about how I was going to deal with this. If I did not assert my authority, he would be able to come into that place and do whatever the fuck he wanted to. I was not about to let that happen. I went over for the sixth time, asked him politely to finish his drink and he looked at me with such disdain, as if to say, 'What the fuck are you going to do about it'? I thought fuck this. I didn't even give it a second thought. I punched him full on in his face. Fuck you! It's time to go mother fucker. It kicked off a bit but before I knew it he had been bundled out of the door. Fuck off, dickhead! This is when my reputation as a door woman started to get around the town.

There were a couple of door men that worked a couple of doors down at Sharkey's. They would pop up every so often and They said if I needed any help, to give them a shout. I said, "Sure, if you need any help give me a shout!"

I needed out of Cafe Paris. I took on three nights at The Opera House. It was just a little bit safer for me to be there, just because I had a team of men to work with. So, I wouldn't be working on my own anymore.

Around this time, I was working a night at The Opera House called Nuts and Bolts. It was a gay night; those nights were always really fun to work. It was a late finish though: Four a.m. I had met Ri that night. She was working on a bar upstairs in The Opera House called Benedict's. We got chatting and she mentioned the room she had to rent. I said, "Cool. Yes, I need somewhere to live!" She passed me her number. I said, "Great I'll call you tomorrow." I tucked that number away in my pocket. I finished the night around four thirty a.m., once we had cleared the last of the partygoers out.

I was looking forward to my bed! I walked home, knackered! I put my key in the door. It wouldn't open. I tried again. The doorknob wouldn't turn. I stood there for a minute and tried to think about what I was going to do. I could hear Sarah in there snoring. I tried knocking but I was going to wake up the rest of the block if I knocked too loudly. I went downstairs and tried pushing the buzzer to see if that would wake her. I eventually got someone on the speaker telling me to FUCK OFF. I said, "I'm trying to get in!" They didn't care. It was five in the morning and I had woken them up. I went back up the stairs and tried my key again, nope it wasn't going to work. Sarah in her fucked-up state, had come in and put her key in the opposite side of the door, meaning that my key wouldn't work and then proceeded to pass out. There was no way I was getting in any time soon.

I sat down on the stairs and contemplated sleeping there in the foyer. I felt the lowest of the low, again, just another situation to make me feel like I was a worthless piece of shit. There was no lower. I'm now going to sleep on the stairs in a block of flats. I had nowhere to go and no one to call for help. Fuck, I felt alone.

I then suddenly remembered that I had Ri's number in my pocket. I took a chance and walked to the nearest phone box. I dug out her number and phoned her up. Thankfully she answered. I was pretty upset because of the situation I was in. It was horrible. I was running out of resilience. Emotionally, I was at my brink! I explained what had happened with Sarah and asked if I could come and crash at hers. She said sure, she was just pottering around at that point anyway. Ri only lived five minutes up the road. I felt just a small amount of relief. I had somewhere to go. A roof over my head! Ri made me a cuppa and we chatted for a while. She showed me the room that she was renting and said that it was available straight away. It was small but I didn't care. It had a door and it was mine, for £50 a week. I said, "I'll have a little snooze, make my way back to Sarah's, get my shit and move in straight away!" Thank god for that! I was out of there, out of Sarah's. Paying £35 a week plus gas and electric to sleep on her bird shit covered floor.

Moving into Ri's I shut out all the people that I thought were no good to be around. Ri had told me that she had originally told Sarah about the room she had. I could have been in that room weeks before I moved in. Fucking leech.

In the weeks following my move into Ri's, Sarah would come and loiter around me when I was getting paid from working at The Opera House. We would get paid cash every two weeks on a Friday night at the club. She would loiter around me expecting the money she thought I owed her. There was no way I was paying her any more money. The cheeky bitch was using the money to go to dance festivals and get twatted on E. I was trying to get my life together and that bitch was trying to get as much as she could out of me. She could fuck right off. I phoned her up. That was the best thing for me to do. I did lose my shit down the phone. Had I been in front of her, I may well have got hold of her and ragged her around a bit. I told her in no uncertain terms that she was getting no more money out of me. That she was to fuck off hanging around me when I was getting paid. That she had been getting £35 a week out of me for sleeping on her bird shit floor and that I was now only paying £50 a week for my own fucking room. She left me alone after that.

It was important to put one hundred percent focus into my training. It was what I needed to keep myself disciplined. I also wanted to keep pursuing my education because I knew, the more I studied, the more credibility I would have as a personal trainer. I worked three nights at the club. That gave me plenty of time to concentrate on my martial arts and getting strong. I figured out a budget where I was living on £5 a day for food. It is not much but I made it happen. Where there is a will, there is a way. I put my C.V. together for my personal training. I then went round all the gyms in the local Bournemouth area and introduced myself. What I hadn't realised is that they were not interested in the USA personal training qualification. I hadn't thought about that when I was taking the qualification. Some of the managers suggested I take the PT course again, with a relevant qualification that they would recognise. I was to conjure up £3000 to take another PT course that I already had. No way! I would find another way.

At the Bulldog gym, I had stepped up from the beginner's sessions. I was now in the advanced fighting sessions. I shit myself the first time I went. The men in the session all looked like pretty seasoned fighters to me. I was the only woman in the session. What I hadn't realised was that they had taken one look at me and thought, 'Shit, she looks scary'!

There was a guy in the session called Indi. He was my partner. I was taking it easy. I was afraid. I didn't know how hard to go. I wasn't ready to find out what the consequences would be should I land a shot that was deemed to be too hard. We were finishing the session with body shots to each other. You stayed in real close to each other and just walloped them into the side of your body. Indi said to me in his Spanish accent, "Come on, you look strong, hit me." So, I did! He then hit me back, it was all right. It didn't faze me at all. He let me open up a bit. Helped me build my confidence in the session.

There were three flights of stairs to get up to get into that gym. Every time I walked up them it was with fear and trepidation. I suppose I should have asked myself what kept me going there. I didn't need to go to the gym and keep sparring men but I knew it was something I needed to do. I am extremely competitive, that is just inherent. I can't explain it. It is just in me. I am naturally strong. At the time I had an abundance of aggression, due to my mother and father being absolute losers for parents! I wasn't afraid of getting hit. I never thought I was good at anything. So, I keep going back and trying to achieve the unreasonable heights that I had set for myself. Of course, within myself I never achieve. I am never good enough. I am better these days but starting out in the competitive field of full contact fighting, I would put myself down all the time.

Taking a full on shot in the face for the very first time, I was like, 'Okay, it's not great but I don't care'. That was easily gotten over with. Being kicked in the head is not that much fun either. I soon discovered I could take a good shot without it rocking me too much.

Some of the early sessions in the advanced classes I was just trying to figure stuff out. Dave had said, "J get in the ring." I was unsure but said, "Okay." Off I went and climbed through the ropes. My sparring partner was a taekwondo guy. He was leaping about all over the place. I was doing good at staying away from his shots. He kept dropping his head, really low. Like, waist height. I watched him do it again and dropped my kick in on his head. It wasn't that difficult. I timed it just right and my foot caught his head, flush. He stood up and rocked backwards and forwards and then fell on his arse. I stood there, a little surprised. Dave came over and got in the ring trying not to laugh. He said, "J, go and get on the bag," while he tried to sort out the dude that I had just knocked out! I said, "Okay," climbed back through the ropes and wandered down the gym, got myself on a bag and got to work. We never saw the guy again.

It was generally the same guys in the session, week after week. Luke, he was a good Thai boxer but couldn't get his shit together the night before a fight. From what I understand he would go out and get shit faced the night before a fight. When it came to the fight the next day he couldn't perform. Rick, he was another great Thai boxer. Really tough. I'm sure he became British Champion. His knees! He dropped me once with his knees. One minute I was stood up, the next I was on my knees just trying to catch my breath. Not knocked out, just unable to move. Teddy Therese. Teddy was French Algerian. He was another great Thai boxer. He was a bit of a bully to me to start out with. I was a kick boxer. Kicks above the waist and punching. Thai boxing is kicks to the legs and everywhere else. Knees to every part of your body. Punches and elbows. It is a martial art that is not for the faint hearted. Teddy would grab me and say, "Janine, sparring." I would say, "Okay, but kick boxing. I'm not a Thai boxer." He would then say, "Well, it's time you learnt." He would then smash my legs, knee me in the body and sweep me so I would then be on the floor, trying to pick myself up again. It was a little unfair because I didn't know at the time how to defend against the attacks. It really started to piss me off. Of course, I could have said no. I'm not sure why I didn't at the time. I had started learning a little bit of Thai boxing. There is a move where you can stamp on the knee. We were sparring one day and I saw my move. I shot through with my right foot and stamped on his knee. There was definitely a crack. That was the end of that and the end of him asking me to spar with him. In fact, he stopped speaking to me all together. He phoned me up when I was on my way to work one night. I only had forty-five minutes to get ready because I would go training before work. I certainly didn't have time to be apologising to Teddy. I told him to fuck off and stop bothering me. He would also come into the fight shop and make a point of standing in front of me with his back to me, so it was like I wasn't in the room to speak to everyone. Over the years that passed we became good training buddies. He didn't push me around at all after that.

Matty was another guy that was a regular in the Bulldog. When I saw him, I thought, 'Great, he's a fucking dick'. Matty went to my school. He was a year above me. He would go out of his way to make fun of me at school, get everyone laughing at me. I did not like him one bit. We were in the gym one day, just talking shit. Fight banter. I may have said something along the lines of knocking him out. He did not take that so well. We were partnered in a fighter's session. He did actually try to knock me out. He was hitting me as hard as he could. You always know when someone is going too hard. I am not a soft touch and I knew he had a point to prove. The coach, Tom, had set a task of only having five punches. We had to make sure that those punches landed. If we used them up, we had nothing else.

Those first two punches he threw in were meant to hurt me. They landed so hard round my head, I had a headache from the start. I thought. 'You fucking wanker'. I could have said, "What are you doing?" I could have asked him to go lighter but that's not me. I dropped my hands to my side and said, "Do it again." I let him punch me full on in the face. He did not pull back on his punches. He threw it in again with everything he had. I said, "Do it again!" I knew there were only two punches left. He did it again. I then said, "Again!", knowing it was the last punch. I was furious. What a complete and utter wanker. The round finished. It was now my turn. I laid into him with as much power as I could, using my five punches. I left that session with my head gone. I was so mad.

When I got home to the flat, I walked out on to the balcony and cracked my head on the door frame accidentally. That was the finishing touch. I had concussion. With the full-on punches, I already had a headache and then the door frame; I couldn't speak properly for a couple of days. I did not like that, it was weird. That was the only time I had brain injury, fortunately.

We never worked together after that session and he was a shit fighter. Dick!

I had to spar the men all the time. There just weren't any women strong enough to push me. It was tough. I always felt like I was drawing the short straw. I would come out of the sessions battered. I would constantly ask myself, 'Why is it so hard? Why do they feel the need to beat me up'? On reflection

I think it was maybe they were trying to survive, keep their ego intact. Of course, they did not want to lose out to a woman.

Whilst it was hard, it was good for me though. All that tough sparring meant that when I started fighting the women, it wasn't so hard.

The year 2000 was when I had my first fight. I hadn't joined the gym to be a fighter. I just knew I needed to be in that sport at that time. It seemed to happen naturally. Dave put his arm around me one day and walked me through the gym. He spoke to me gently and suggested that I think about having my first fight. My first reaction was, 'I'm not sure about that. I don't think I am good enough for that.'! But Dave was a master at manipulation. He talked me into it and said that I should think about getting down to seventy-two kilograms. I was and do now walk around comfortably at eighty kilograms. It is very difficult to find women to fight at eighty kilograms.

In August 2000, I set about my own training camp. I figured out what I needed to be eating. I filled in a food diary every day, making sure that I was eating the right percentages to make my weight. I was running on the beach for the first four weeks. Three times a week at seven a.m. I would plod down Sea Road, down to Boscombe Pier and run to Bournemouth pier and back again. Nice and steady. I would then get into the gym and do a weights program four days a week. The martial arts, I would get into three to four times a week. If I was going to do this, I was going to put everything I had into it. NO drinking, NO drugs. One hundred percent focus. Dave had arranged a fight with a woman called Gina Stone. I didn't care who it was with. I just needed to keep to my own game plan. You would get the same old questions. You gonna win? Do you know she is a British Champion? I would always say, "I'll do my best! Is she? I don't care either way." I didn't either. It was what it was. I'll do my first fight and see where it goes from there.

The first fight was a freestyle fight. Kick boxing with low kicks. No shin guards but you could wear foot shields. I don't really know why. You might of well as worn nothing. Gum shield and gloves, that was it. I never wore breast protection or groin protection. I didn't care about that either.

Leading up to the fight, I was doing a lot of sparring. There was a young lad in the gym called 'The Bubble'. 'Nic the Greek' — 'bubble and squeak' — 'The Bubble'! He was a feisty little fucker. He always wanted to spar with me. It was supposed to be light sparring. He decided that it wasn't. The Bubble decided that he was going to smash in my left leg. That first kick I took was not light. It was intentionally meant to hurt me. I could have told him to go lighter, but that would have shown weakness. On the inside I was fuming. I thought fuck you, I'm not even going to block them. I took them for the whole three rounds I was in there. I thought, 'Fuck you shit head; you'll have to kill me to stop me! FUCK YOU'!

My left leg was as black as black could be from all the bruising. At night when I was trying to sleep, it was like someone was playing guitar strings on my tendons it was so painful. But fuck him, he didn't stop me and I did not go down.

Four weeks before the fight and I was running five days a week now. Three of those were sprint sessions. Run to Bournemouth. Sprint, jog, sprint, jog, in-between the groynes back to Boscombe. Lifting weights still four times a week. Training in the fight gym five days a week. I was on target for seventy-two kilograms.

A week before the fight I was training with The Bubble

again. It was supposed to be light sparring again. Technical work. He decided otherwise. He threw in a spinning heel kick to my left breast, bruising the ribs underneath it. That fucker! Every time I took a breath in it was painful. I kept that to myself, I had a job to finish. At the back of my mind, I worried about it a little. I thought. 'What if I can't breathe in the fight'? But I just tucked that thought away. I'll deal with it after the fight.

All my friends were there. Everyone I knew on the door was there. My brother and all the party heads were there. The fight was the last thing I was thinking about, really. I had so much to prove to myself and to show everyone else in that auditorium, that I was more than just a pill head.

My come-out tune was 'Who Let the Dogs Out?' The music was playing; it was show time. I was ready.

As I walked out, the whole place erupted. The show had just been tinkering along, no real atmosphere. There were more demonstrations than fights. Demonstrations can get a little dull to watch. Then, I came out and the roof just came off! Everyone was cheering. It was a bit of a shock but I swaggered myself into the ring. It was show time.

I climbed into the ring and took a quick peek at the woman in the opposite corner. My first thoughts were that she was a bit lardy. The referee called both of us to the centre of the ring. The ref. usually talks about keeping it clean and if he says 'break' make sure you 'break'. Ultimately, he is in charge in there and we are to listen to him. I never used to hear anything they said in all my fights. I would stand there and bury my soul into their eyes, try to get right inside their head. I was up for it! They needed to know, were they ready? The ref. then asks you to go back to your corner and then the bell goes.

The first round was a blur. I do not remember anything from that round. It was chaos in my head. I know I was working. I was getting my punches in, throwing low kicks and getting my rib kicks in. I wasn't getting hurt. The bell rang and it was the end of the round. I got back to my corner and sat on the stool, trying to get my breath back. Dave was talking to me. I couldn't hear a word he was saying. I knew his mouth was moving but my brain was moving too fast to understand what he was saying to me. Something about a push kick, I don't know. I'm told to stand up, bell goes, second round. I forget what Dave has said to me. I can't figure it out anyway. I just needed to keep working, keep the pace up and keep landing my shots. The bell goes, end of the second round. Back to my corner, sat on my stool. Get my breathing down. Dave was talking to me again. I still couldn't figure out what he was saying to me. That's when Tom gets in the ring. Tom was the other coach in the gym. He said, "Stand up. Right, how much do you want it?" I say, "I want it!" He said to me again and louder, "How much do you want it?" I say louder, "I want it!" He says, "Again!'" I say even louder, "I want it!" The bell goes. I am so hyped up I come out rib kicking, punching and driving her back on to the ropes. I knew I couldn't sustain that tempo for two minutes. I backed off. Gina clouts me with a left hook. Oh my god, it was painful. I say to myself in my head, I do not want to take another one of those. I punched her back but every time I finished my combos, I pull her in to me; tied her up so that she cannot work. For a fighter that is so frustrating. I did that for the rest of the round. I was scoring the points and letting her do nothing. I said to myself in my head, 'Where is the fucking bell'! The bell goes! I had survived my first fight!

The first person I see from the ring is Leigh, my brother!

He's crying. He was so proud of me. I was shouting back at him. I was so happy, I'd done it!

Me and Gina were then pulled to the centre of the ring for them to announce the winner. It turns out it was me! I couldn't believe it! I'd won! I embarrassingly burst out into a dance. It is cringe-worthy watching that back. 'Who Let The Dogs Out' was playing through the hall and everyone that was in that hall was cheering for me. I'd really done it. I'd done it for myself and I had proven to everyone else in there, that I was more than just a recreational drug user!

Right from that moment, life changed. It turned out that Gina was the current British Champion. She hadn't fought in a year but she had twelve fights to my no fights. A novice against a twelve-fight champion is really unheard of. It propelled me onto the fighting map, really quickly. Dave was even talking about me becoming a British Champion!

I phoned my dad. I wanted to share what I had done. I suppose I was like a little kid showing my parent, 'Look Dad, look. Look what I've done'. He said all the pleasantries. "Amazing Janine. I'm so proud of you," blah, blah, blah. He should be proud of me. I'd done it all on my own!

Dad did make a guest appearance with Ashley, my half-sister, in April or May, 2001. I don't remember a great deal from that trip. He peeked in at where I was training. Didn't really stick around. On reflection, I don't think his ego could carry it. I wanted him to be proud of me but he just didn't know how to just be there for me. He was in Bournemouth around three days. It's about all he could manage.

Me! A British Champion. I'd never been a champion at anything. This was my opportunity. I was twenty-seven years old. It was now or never to give this a shot. Really do something with myself. Get myself out of the shit pool that I had been wandering around in. Really give myself some respectability. I knew that this would help with my personal training as well. It would help to build my persona, so that I could generate more business.

'Janine The Machine' was born.

On my return back to work at The Opera House, I was getting a different kind of attention. The people that ordinarily would ignore me, now wanted to be my friend. It was a bit weird. I was still the same person but now I had some credibility about me. I was a small-town celebrity. I knew who these people were and I could see it was fake. I found it all very amusing. Even Leigh said that the guys that used to bully him a bit and make fun of him, were now really nice to him. They all wanted to be his friend. Fucking idiots! Good! There is nothing wrong with a bit of fear. Leave me alone and leave my brother alone.

I had mentioned to my head doorman about maybe becoming a British Champion. He scoffed down his nose at me and then proceeded to laugh in my face, like I was an idiot for mentioning such a thing! I looked at him and thought, 'Fuck you! I'll fucking show you, you fucking dick'. It wasn't going to happen overnight, I knew that but I would train and keep training until I had reached the point of becoming a British Champion, it did not matter how long it would take.

Dave had sorted out my second fight really quickly. I had four weeks to keep my shit together. I was to fight on a show in Chippenham. I just ticked over with my fitness, kept my weight under control and kept my head down. That was, until my friend Clare had come home from San Francisco. I went down and met her in a pub called Casa in Bournemouth town centre. I thought, 'I'll have one drink. It won't hurt'. One drink turned into a session which turned into taking pills.

One night at work in The Opera House a couple of weeks prior to this day, I was walking across the dance floor clearing everyone out at the end of the night, when I saw a plastic money bag on the floor. I picked it up. It must have had sixty pills in the bag. I tucked them away in my pocket really quickly and took them home. I sold most of them to a buddy of mine and kept the remnants of all the broken pieces for myself for a rainy day. This rainy day was the night I met Clare! Before I knew it, it was eleven a.m. the next day. I crawled through the door, put myself to bed and then spent the next two weeks chasing my guilt and my tail trying to make myself feel better about the night I had had out. I was a fucking dick!

I couldn't afford to take the night off work the night before the fight. I finished at three a.m. I then had a kids' class to go and teach at nine thirty a.m.! I thought, 'I'll go back and get some sleep before I go to the fight'. That did not happen. We got to Chippenham. Dave was warming me up and asking me how I felt. I remember saying, "I do not want to do any more warming up." He said, "What!" I replied, "I don't want to warm up anymore!" He told me to go over in the corner of the hall and have a word with myself. I thought, 'Fine, as long as I am not warming up anymore'.

The woman that I fought on that show was certainly not seventy-two kilograms in weight. She looked more like one hundred kilograms. I didn't care. The bell rang. I get to moving around. I certainly was not on my game. After the first round, I sat on my stool. I could hear her telling her corner man from the other side of the ring, "She hit me really hard in the face!" I laughed to myself on the inside. Dave was doing his nut; you need to do more work. I just didn't have it in me. I could hear him in the round banging on the ring, more work, more work! I wasn't listening. The final bell went. I won by the skin of my teeth. I knew that I had just got away with that. If I was going to take myself seriously, I had to knock all the drinking and drug taking completely on the head. That was the day I became sober; November 2000!

I pretty much stayed sober for fifteen years. Apart from, I had a weekend trip that consisted of a Friday night *Slinky* dance night at the Opera House, up to Camden Palace on Saturday and then straight out of the club to Waterloo Station to get on the Eurostar to spend the day in Paris 2002. It was an amazing weekend! I also got talked into drinking Thai whiskey for one night, when I was in Thailand. In fifteen years, that is the only partying I had done.

I was taking one fight at a time, seeing how it went and working on my self-worth. There were numerous times when I was getting ready to fight in the gym that I would climb out of the ring and say, "I can't do this. I'm not good enough!" Dave would bark at me. "Shut up with that shit. I don't want to hear that again. Get back in the ring!"

Dave would really put me through it. There was one day I turned up to the fighter's session. There was no warning of what he was going to do. He put these coach sparring pads on. They are like boxing gloves but they have pads on them to hit. The bell went and Dave hit me around the head as hard as he could. It took me by surprise. I could see white lights in front of my eyes. I couldn't see anything for a few seconds. I backed off out of harm's way so that I didn't take another one. I could hear him saying, "Get yourself together and get back in to range." I did what I was told to do. He smashed me round the head again. This time I was ready. I guarded up. The shots kept on coming and really hard. My head had started to hurt. I was starting to get angry. I was on the third of two-minute rounds of this and had had enough. I started to miss the pads on purpose and punched him right in the middle of his chest and his throat and I'm sure I caught him on the chin. Fuck you.

That's how the sessions were. Hard! I would regularly go to work at The Opera House with my legs covered in analgesic Thai boxing cream because they had just been smashed to bits. No one ever said that I stank of Deep Heat. I was building a reputation that you just didn't fuck around with me. The guys would just give me a wide berth most of the time.

At the beginning of a work shift I would have to stand just inside the front door, randomly checking women's bags as they came in. My legs would be in pieces and I would just have to put the pain to the back of my mind. I had six hours on my feet to get through. Suck it up and get the work done.

Standing inside that door, I would ask the women very politely if I could just check inside their bags. They would look at me like I stank of shit. They would then huff and throw their bags in my direction. So, fucking rude! I would then, on purpose, turn the bags upside down and empty the entire contents onto the table. Fucking bitches. I'm only doing my job. I would then shoo them away with my hand.

Working in that environment never brings out the best in you, because you are dealing with people that are either wasted on alcohol or fucked up on drugs. Human beings generally become complete and utter wankers when they are on alcohol. There are too many stories to tell of incidents of what I had to deal with but a couple that stick out in my mind are: one night I had been placed on the balcony of the club. The security had to stand at the top of the stairs and keep the stairs clear, for obvious reasons, so that pissed up idiots would not trip and break their necks by falling down the stairs! You would spend the whole night trying to keep people off the stairs. At the beginning of the night, I had a word with myself. I am not going to get angry tonight. I am not going to let a fucked up little wanker ruin my night. Okay, I'm set. I'll stay calm.

With that, I looked down the stairs at a couple of guys that were busting shapes off the stairs to the people down on the dance floor. Off I went to move them on. I asked them nicely. They completely ignored me. I asked them again, nicely. I got ignored again. I asked them again with a little bit more force. I got shooed away. Now, I was getting angry. What the fuck is wrong with these people. I've asked nicely twice now! There was an advert at the time for Budweiser, where the dudes were saying 'what's up?' to each other. Everyone was doing it. Well, one of these guys thought it would be a good idea to scream it in my face. I could feel his breath on my face. What a fucking asshole! I got hold of him and threw him across the landing of the stairs. He got up to run back to me. Fortunately, his mates got hold of him and held him back. I told him, if he didn't get the fuck out of my face, I was going to throw him out. They disappeared very quickly. Now, I was angry at myself, because I'd promised myself I was not going to get angry. Door work, it was horrible. But I needed to do it because it paid me the money an hour that I would not get in a minimum wage paid job.

On another occasion, I was on my way to the stage and saw a lad with a cap on. For whatever reason, the club's policy was no caps on inside the club. I'm not sure why but it was a rule. I told him to take it off. I stood up on the stage surveying the club and saw the lad with his cap on again. I called him over. I said, "Take your cap off, I've just told you!" He took his cap off and wandered off. About twenty minutes later I saw him again, cap back on. I called him over again. I said, "If I see you with your cap on again, I'm going to chuck you out!" His response, "What the fuck is wrong with you? You fucking lesbian!"

So, I jabbed him really quickly in the throat, not so hard as to choke him but enough to make him pay attention.

The fucking little shit. He stood there for a minute holding on to his throat, shocked. I told him he had better fuck off and reminded him to take his cap off. I didn't see him again for the rest of the night.

There was a position in the club that everyone hated, it was standing on the entrance to the diner. If you were placed there, you would spend the whole night saying to people, "There is no smoking in the diner." I never got that really. There was smoking everywhere else in the club. It wasn't like there were doors on the diner. The smoke from the club was everywhere but that was the requirement. So, that is what you had to do.

I was stood on the diner this one particular night. At nine p.m. you are communicating with the punters with jokes and friendliness. By three a.m. you are tired, you want your bed and you are done in, telling the same people there is no smoking in the diner. I had told this one guy probably six or seven times. I had tried to be his friend and have a laugh but by three a.m., my patience was non-existent. I caught him down the end of the diner, smoking away like it was not a big deal. I lost it. He'd seen me coming for him. He tried to hide the cigarette inside his fist, so he knew what he was doing. I reached over the table, got hold of his fist and crushed it as hard as I could, knowing full well that he had a lit cigarette inside his hand. I repeated in a calm tone, "I said, no fucking smoking in the diner!" I let go and he screamed, the whole table got up and quickly vacated the diner.

The security team would all have radios on them. If we needed back-up or there was something going on, we could put a call out. At the end of a shift one night, I had a call over the radio. "Security Janine, you need to get down to the front door!" I thought, 'Shit, it's going off and they need my help'. They radioed again. "Security Janine, you need to get to the front door!" I ran down to the front door. I couldn't see any commotion. Neil the head doorman said, "It's your brother, he's OD'd, overdosed!" I didn't panic. I just thought, 'Right! I need to get to the hospital'. There was a girl there that had been out with him that night. They had a car waiting. I jumped into it. They took me down to Bournemouth A and E. I had told him before he went out that night, not to fuck about. I had given him a talking to about the group he was going out with. I knew the group he was with. They were all into taking GHB. GHB was big in the 90s on the rave scene. On the club scene, they called it liquid Ecstasy. It was dangerous, dangerous stuff. In the 00s, men were using it to rape women. If you take too much of it, it will slow your heart rate down until it stops. I told Leigh to stay the fuck away from it. Famous last words.

Apparently, he had done a pill so he was already off his head. He then grabbed a bottle out of one of the group's hands and finished off whatever was left in the bottle. I'm not sure if he knew what was in it. I know he would not be thinking rationally about how much he should be taking. He then proceeded to lose his shit. He had got behind the DJ's console and pissed all over the amp. The security threw him outside, for him then to pass out. One of his so-called friends said to go and put him in my car to sleep it off. Thank goodness they didn't, because at that point his heart was about to give up. The club called an ambulance and that's where I enter. Leigh was laying on a gurney. He was conscious at this point, rubbing his toes together, repeating, "I'm bad, who's bad!" I said, "You are a fucking twat. I fucking told you!" The nurses told me there was nothing I could do. He was in a safe place. They would keep him until he was ready to go home tomorrow.

I got a phone call from Leigh the following day, in tears. His heart had stopped twice in the night. The doctors had jump started him both times. I told him that there was nothing I could say that he didn't know already. I told him to call me when he got home.

Back to work at The Opera House. I was carrying women down the stairs because they had passed out in the toilets, as a regular occurrence. The guys I was working with would often ask, "Do you need help?" I would reply, "No!" as I was more than capable of doing it myself. This did mean that there were a few urban myths going around about me. Knocking out men and carrying them out on my shoulders was one of the myths that was going around at the time. That was always fun to hear.

Dave had suggested that I start looking around for sponsorship for my fights. I approached the manager of the club, Dick. I'm not sure what I was thinking. He is the most despicable human being you can ever have the misfortune of meeting or having anything to do with. One night when I was working on the front door, he had come balling in, off his face on cocaine. That was a regular occurrence. When he was really twatted, he would get on the mike in front of three thousand people and start talking absolute bullshit, off his face, thinking he was rocking it. It was embarrassing to watch. Dick, who was a fucking dick!

I was standing there doing my job one night and Dick was balling up the entrance of the night club. Dick started talking shit to me and then got hold of my ponytail and dragged my head back, still talking absolute shit. I was completely humiliated in front of the security crew. I couldn't just leave; I needed the job. I just had to suck it up. Before this incident I had approached him thinking, that he would be interested in sponsoring me. Before I had even finished talking, he had butted in and said, "Don't even think about asking me for sponsorship. I don't waste my time with bullshit operations like that." Like I said, 'What was I thinking asking him? We all knew he was a complete cunt'.

I did leave The Opera House not long after that incident. I got myself another job in the town centre at a club called Elements. It was still only three nights a week. It also meant that I had to get a taxi home. When I was working at The Opera House, I only lived across the road; five minutes and I was home. Elements was a good twenty-five-minute walk or £8 in taxi fare home. I could have asked someone for a lift in hindsight but I didn't like to ask for help or be a burden to anyone. £8 out of my already very tight budget was not good. I decided to walk home. It was on the main roads but at three in the morning, let's say the more predatory type of people are hanging around at that time of night. I was walking past a group of Middle Eastern origin men. One of them asked me for a light. I replied I did not have one. His response was," Why not?"

I didn't reply and kept on walking. They decided to start

following me. I thought, 'Right. Sort your keys in your pocket. Get them through your knuckles. If they grab you, slice their face open. Walk with urgency but not afraid'. My heart was pounding so hard. I didn't look back and just kept moving. They stopped following me and went off down a side road. I made it home in one piece. I needed to leave Elements. I could not be walking home at that time of night on my own.

I went back to The Opera House and asked for my job back. The head doorman Mark Metcalf said, "Sure. Do you want to be head of security inside?" I said, "Sure!" It paid a little bit more money as well. I was in charge of the guys inside the club. I spent my nights wandering around chatting to the punters and making sure everything was running ship shape.

Dave, at the Bulldog gym, had asked me to come in and have a meeting with him. He asked me where I saw my future going? I was just trying to build my profile and ultimately sort my personal training business out. Dave suggested if we all worked together, we could help each other build our businesses together. He made me believe that we were in it together.

At the time, I bought in to it. I still believed that there were good people and that if someone said to me that they were going to look out for me, I genuinely believed it. As I was only working three nights over the weekend at the club, it did mean that I had some free time outside of my training during the week. I had started daily to go into the fight shop to help Dave out with his banking and administration. This was every day. I didn't ask to be paid. I did it off my own back. I like to believe that if you do good, you get good back. I figured if I did that for him it would pay off down the line. I would also clean the gym for no payment either. I did that for a year and a half at least. Dave never once offered anything to me. Money, food, asking if I was all right. Am I doing all right. I would never let on how poor I was. I was too ashamed to say anything to let people know.

I would watch them all coming into the shop collecting their money after the shows. I had fought and earnt nothing from it, especially in the beginning. It was never about the money for me. I knew there was no money in it but it did piss me off when I would see people from the shows getting paid and I would get nothing. I would sit there, cashing up the money, sorting the memberships out and living on my £5 a day.

Greed is one of the worst human behaviours along with dishonesty.

Tom, who worked in the shop alongside me, was a five-time World Champion. He bought some credibility to the Bulldog gym. He would coach the boxing and the kick boxing over in the gym. That's when he bothered to turn up. When he was present, he was a great coach. I learnt a lot from him but when he was sat in the office with a girl on his lap, shouting instructions through the window, he was not such a great coach. He accused me of stealing money when I was banking.

Tom, I was on my ass!

Whilst everyone was getting paid from the shows, some of them I was fighting on, I had no money and really did not have the funds to feed myself. I probably should have asked for help. I was ashamed. I was embarrassed to let people know that I was struggling but really, they could have bunged me the odd tenner or something, when I was coming into that shop day after day.

I will own this.

On one of the days I was banking, there was an extra £20

271

floating around. It was extra, over from the banking. I had done all the cashing up. It was just spare and I took it, so that I could get myself some dinner. So that I could feed myself whilst I was fighting for your gym.

I was ashamed. I never did it again. But sometimes you see an opportunity and you run with it, especially when you are desperate.

Having a relationship with a man was out of the question for me. I did not want anything getting in the way of my training. I certainly didn't want anyone telling me what I could and couldn't do. Men in my experience do not understand the life of a female fighter. It takes a special kind of secure man to get involved with a female athlete.

However, I did have a few encounters. None of which ended well.

I had met a guy, let's call him Paul. He took a fancy to me. We had spent the whole weekend hanging out. When it came to him staying over, we were 'getting down to business'! and he started acting weird. I asked him what the problem was. He said that he was having an inferiority complex. When I asked him what about, he said because your muscles are bigger than mine.

What a fucking dick! I said, "Get your shit together and fuck off! Go on, get out." It's not like we had just met. I don't wear clothes that hide the fact that I have an athletic body. Idiot! He got his shit together and left. As I was falling back to sleep, I could hear stones being thrown at my window. I opened my window. He looked up hesitantly. "I forgot my keys!" I threw his keys down to him and swiftly shut the window. Goodbye, dick face.

Another guy called Dave started working at The Opera

House. I had shown him around and set him up in his station. He was all right looking. He had started coming down to the fight store, just turning up out of the blue. I am completely naive to anyone showing me any kind of attention. I just don't think anyone is attracted to me. Dave started coming to my Thai boxing sessions. I still didn't get it. That was until he said, "Janine do you want to go for a coffee?" I was like, "Sure" I didn't want a relationship but I wasn't opposed to some sexy time. We hung out a few times. It was all right. Like I said I wanted nothing serious. Dave said, "I like you Janine, can we become an item?" I said, "Well sure, we can have some fun! I am busy at the moment fighting. I am not going to let anything get in my way." After three days he was round my house talking engagement and marriage. He asked me to cook food for him, knowing full well I did not have time in-between PT, Thai sessions, training for my fights and working the door. He was at my house doing nothing whilst I was running around doing everything, expecting me to sort out food for him before work. If he had thought about it, he could have done it for me. Taken care of me! I said, "Hold up a second. I told you I don't have time for this! We've only been seeing each other a few days." What the fuck. He had to go!

I had another little fling with one of the doormen I was working with at The Opera House. A very cute, muscular, Portuguese man. That olive skin and dark hair, I do have a thing for. It didn't go anywhere. Just a little bit of sex.

The fights were pretty consistent after the first two. The third fight was when I had got concussion. I should not have been in the ring. I didn't tell anyone that I had concussion until after the fight. I should have won the fight but my head was all over the place. Tom started shouting at me from the corner.

"How much do I want it!" I didn't need to hear that right then. I got hold of him and threw him out of my corner. The whole crowd gasped. Tom was a five times world champion! What was I thinking? I knew what I was thinking and Tom shouting at me was not what I needed. I didn't win that fight. It was a draw. I spoke with Dave after the fight and explained the concussion. He said, "You never said!" I replied, "You never asked!"

Fourth fight won.

Fifth fight won in Milton Keynes against a woman that was ten kilos heavier than me. She growled at me when we stood facing each other. Apparently, it was her first fight. Dave had decided to get me a fight under an assumed name. I was to be called Janine Diamond. Dave was having difficulty finding women to fight me. I'm not sure why. I just knew we had to take this fight under an assumed name. I felt bad because the woman I was fighting was a novice. I had made the decision to take it easy on her. Suss her out in the first round and if she wanted to fight, I'd take up the level. Never mind that I was giving away ten kilos in weight. I weighed in at seventy-one kilograms, she was eighty-two kilograms! There was a load of argy-bargy about how long the rounds were going to be. Dave and the promoter of the fight were arguing between one-minute rounds and a minute and half. I didn't care, I just wanted to get the fight done and out of the way. We were now both in the ring. The ref. was talking to us and that's when she started to growl at me. As I turned back to walk to my corner, I said to myself, 'Fuck you, it's on!'

I stopped her in the second round. I had put her down in her own corner and she had started to cry. Her corner made her get up and try to carry on. As she got back up, I went in and finished her off. Job done. I mean, growling! You can fuck right off with your growling. On the way back from this fight I was passed out in the back of the car. I farted! I was mortified. It was a silent but deadly. Dave in the front, driving, piped up and asked, "Who was that?" I kept my mouth shut. Dave then said, "Winstanley was that you?" He said, "Yup," knowing full well it wasn't. Bless him. Lee Winstanley was one of the kids I use to train. He would probably have been around twelve or thirteen. He took the wrap for me. Nothing more was said.

Sixth fight win. Alex Reid, who was married to Katie Price, was the ref. in this one. What an absolute doughnut. He didn't know any of the rules and stopped the fight in the middle of the first round, to ask Dave in my corner what the rules were! At the end of the second round, he told me I had an attitude problem. Funny that really, when I'm in the middle of getting my face punched in, you twat. I'm not going to be singing bells and roses. Idiot!

In 2001 I had my seventh fight which was a shot at the Southern Area title. WIN. I am now Southern Area Thai boxing Champion. That was at the BIC in the Purbeck Hall.

Eighth fight — win.

Ninth fight — win.

Tenth fight — win.

After this fight it became harder for Dave to find me opponents. No one wanted to fight me. It was also difficult to find me opponents in my weight. Dave said, "You need to come down to sixty-six kilograms." I replied, "I don't want to, it's too light for me." Dave's response," You either want it or you don't." Dave was my coach and I did what I was told. Of course I wanted it.

Living at Ri's was starting to fall apart. It was a tiny flat.

I had her bedroom. She had converted the living room space into her bedroom. We shared the kitchen and bathroom. It was all right when it was just us two. Ri had met these group of guys. These guys were heavily into taking drugs. It wasn't long before they were all in the flat. I was shut out and the space that was once an open space, was shut down to me. I was in my tiny room with them on the other side of the door getting twatted.

I just wasn't in that place anymore. I was so focused and disciplined with my fighting. I was not about to let all my hard work go to shit because my home life was now being invaded by a load of druggies. It was time to move out.

I moved into a client's house. Because I was now Janine The Machine around town, my notoriety was building. I had people approaching me for one-to-one training which was awesome. The hard work was starting to pay off. I had finished giving up my free time to Dave in the shop. Sacked that right off. I was now earning £15 an hour with my personal training. Life was on the up.

Karl, who was a tattoo artist in Bournemouth, had a room free in his house. He said, "Sure, come and rent with me." I had a massive, big, double room in a big, four-bedroom house. Space and no druggies!

Dad was calling me quite a bit around this time. Listening to him moan about his life was starting to grate on me. Him and his wife had upped-sticks and moved out of California to Ohio. I think it was to try and escape paying money he owed for child support. Let's get one thing straight here. HE NEVER PAID A PENNY TOWARDS MINE AND LEIGH'S UPBRINGING. NOT A PENNY!

It would amaze me that he would phone me up and

complain about the money he was going to have to pay to Ashley, my half-sister. I wondered if he even realised who he was talking to. Tina, his second wife, took him to court. The court ordered him to pay £35,000 dollars in back payment. It would make me sick to my stomach. I don't know why I just didn't say anything to him. I just stopped answering the phone calls. I had enough to be getting on with. I did not want to listen to that selfish twat moan about shit he should have been taking care of as a parent!

Living at Karl's, I had started to feel like I was really on my own. Maybe the stress of the fighting all the time had started to take its toll. Trying to drop down to sixty-six kilograms was emotionally hard as well as physically hard. It had really started to get me down. I would spend numerous evenings crying about the fact that I just wanted to be with someone, find someone that would love me. Not take care of me, just be there for me. I was tired of fighting life on my own. This is where Scott entered my life.

I'd not long got back from my trip to Thailand. I went and stayed on a Thai boxing training camp in Koh Samui. Dave thought it would be a good idea to drop weight. A couple of the fighters before me had been out and dropped loads of weight. I think being in the heat and the intensive training would mean I would drop weight faster than staying here in the UK. It was also a good idea just to go out there and experience the culture of Thailand and staying in a Thai camp. It was an amazing trip. The first holiday I had taken since coming back from America in 1999. It's August 2002. I took my friend Deb, who had only been training in Thai boxing for three months. Off we went. Deb was shitting herself. I, of course, was right up for it. As soon as we land and we are walking through the airport, Thai men were all commenting on the fact that I look strong and do I do Thai boxing?

Koh Samui is a beautiful place. We were collected from the airport on the island in a jeep and driven to the camp. The room was basic but luckily it had a western toilet, thank goodness! The training facilities were pretty basic as well. There was a ring but the bag section was all on concrete. So, your feet needed to be tough, because you were barefoot. My days consisted of training at seven a.m. for an hour or so. I'd get Debs up after training. I did try and get her up but she growled at me, "I'm on fucking holiday, who the fuck gets up at 6.45 a.m. on holiday? Fuck off!" She rolled over and went back to sleep. That was my cue not to push it. We'd go and get breakfast, lay on the beach, go back to our room and have a little nap, then get going for the six p.m. training session. That was every day. I loved it! The perfect holiday.

There is a serenity in Thailand. I never once felt unsafe. We had gone to watch the fights that take place every week. I had made sure that I had used the toilet before we left for the fight arena. I was sure that there would be toilets. I just wasn't up for a hole dug in the ground. Deb on the other hand, needed to go. We had a whole debate about whether or not she was going to go. She then bit the bullet and took off, only to come back traumatised by the whole situation. I was sat there laughing as she was telling me. Apparently, it was just like an open shower block that people were just doing their business into. I couldn't figure out where she put herself or even how she was meant to squat down. I certainly didn't go and find out!

On another occasion, we were on the beach topping up our tans. Deb loves a chat, even if the people have not got a clue what she was talking about. You have local Thais wandering up and down the beach, trying to sell you stuff; the women especially. "You wan' massage, you wan' pedicure?" I said, "No way, get away from my feet!" Deb, on the other hand is always up for a pedi'!

As I sat there watching her get her feet done, I was curious to know what the fuck the liquid was they were putting onto cotton wool and then leaving on her heels. Some kind of acetone? It was certainly something that was stripping her skin off! I then thought, that's not going to be good training on concrete! Fresh, soft skin on concrete; not good.

I was right. Deb ended up looking like a character out of a cartoon with two big bandages wrapped around her big toes because all the skin had come off from training that night after the pedi. They were raw!

We had a great time though. In Thailand anything goes. You would see whole families on a scooter, along with a dog, building supplies and shopping. Just going about their business like it's just another normal day, not one of them wearing a crash helmet. Men walking up and down the beach all day long with massive yolks on their shoulders. I'm not sure what they were carrying but it looked heavy as shit. It would be thirty-five plus in the heat and they didn't look any heavier than fifty kilograms themselves, not breaking a sweat.

Me and Deb had decided to fly back to Bangkok the day before we were meant to leave. We had met a guy, Matt, on the camp who was living in Bangkok. Matt had said if we make our way to Bangkok, to give him a shout and he'll show us around. When we landed in Bangkok, we had been set up in a five-star hotel by the owner of the camp. We jumped into a taxi and gave him our address. Driving through Bangkok is a sensory overload. The sights. The smells. The cars. The chaos.

The tuk tuks weaving in and out of the traffic. Elephants just wandering down the busy city street! I felt sorry for the elephants. It's not where they belong.

We arrived at the hotel and it was posh. Oh, my goodness it was posh. I asked Deb, "Are you sure this is where we are meant to be?" We phoned Matt and told him where we were. He invited us to come and stay with him as he had a spare room. We both agreed, even though staying in that hotel would have been epic. Hanging out with your mates at their home is, I don't know, a bit more homely, comfy and chill.

Matt decided to pick up some Thai whiskey that apparently has amphetamine in it. We ordered a takeaway and went back to his apartment, where Deb and Matt decided to start drinking. I was still very much in my sober head. I knew I had a big fight coming up when I returned. I was fighting for a Commonwealth Title shot. I needed to keep my head together. If I fell off the wagon now, I would feel guilty about not staying sober. As the night wore on, Matt and Deb were working on me to let my hair down and have at least one drink. "Come on J, one drink is not going to do you any harm." The fight was not until November. It was the beginning of September so I still had time to recover. I had been training solidly for two weeks, twice a day. Running twice a day, as well as doing my weights in between. Maybe I could have a little drink. I gave in and I did have a few drinks. It didn't really do that much to me actually. It was just nice to let go of the control I had over myself and feel free for a moment.

The following day, Matt took us around Bangkok and we did a little bit of shopping. He took us to this shopping mall. The first floor is all the fake goods. Nike, Adidas, etc. If you wanted the real goods you were to go on the next floors up. It was crazy. You would never find that back home in the UK. Matt then took us to the top floor, to a food court. All I wanted was some chicken and rice. How was I go to ask for chicken and rice? Thai is not an easy language to speak. I found myself pointing at the food on the boards. I felt so ignorant. Fortunately, some very kind soul asked me in English if I would like some help. I couldn't thank them enough. I sat down with my chicken and rice. Me and Deb were talking about getting back to Bournemouth, getting out on the town with our tans, looking fresh and fit! It was now Saturday afternoon in Bangkok. We had assumed our flight was two a.m. on Saturday, thinking Saturday night. What idiots! Matt pointed out that there is a time difference but I don't think you can go back in time! We both suddenly realised we had missed our flight. What the fuck were we going to do?

We got back to Matt's place and got our shit together. I tried to phone the airline. They suggested we make our way to the airport. Matt ordered us a taxi and off we went. Me and Deb were already in a state of stress so we were not really talking. So, sitting in the back of the taxi was pretty quiet. I soon realised that the back end of the taxi was wobbling from side to side. It was like we were in a different compartment to the front of the car. I thought, 'Shit we are going to die'! I looked over at the dials to see how fast we were going. Nothing was working, at all! I then thought, 'Okay, this is it. Just hope that the car stays in one piece until we get to the airport'. I mentioned nothing to Deb. I did not want to alarm her. I think she was probably thinking the same. As soon as we got to the airport, I got out of that taxi as fast as I could. We were safe. For now.

We got to our check in desk and explained our situation.

The woman behind the desk said that the next flight to the UK was in two weeks. I thought well, I can draw it out. I'm my own boss at this point. I think at this point I had stopped working at The Opera House, so taking another two weeks would cost me but I wouldn't lose my job. Deb, on the other hand, was employed and needed to get back. We asked if there were any other options. The woman behind the desk said, "I can get you to Doha but there is no guarantee that you'll get any further!" We had flown in through Doha. That was our stop over on the way out. I made the decision to go for it. I said, "Come on Deb, let's do it."

As soon as I got on the plane, I passed out asleep. We hit a massive air pocket or something because it literally lifted me out of my seat. I woke up, saw Deb and her white knuckles holding on to her arm rests. I said, "You all right?" She didn't even look at me. She said, "Yes!" I went back to sleep. Debs did say that me falling back to sleep meant she calmed down. It's scary being up there sometimes when you hit big pockets of turbulence.

We landed in Doha, made our way to the check in desk and explained our situation. The gentleman behind the desk was not helpful in anyway. He suggested we leave the airport and go to find a hotel and come back the following day. I said, "No way!" Debs was pleading with me, "Please J! Come on, we can go get a bit more sun." I said, "No way! We go out there we are not coming back alive. I was dressed in short denim shorts, with a bright, yellow vest top. Debs was in a denim jean mini skirt and a small, bright red T. We were surrounded by women in Burkas. This was not a country to be baring flesh. I felt that the safest place for us was in the airport. We were not about to leave any time soon. I would get us on a flight home, by hook or by crook.

There was a seven hour wait for the next flight to London. Doha airport in 2002 was not very big. We went upstairs to the cafe. The women in the cafe just stared at us, like we were some kind of novelty! We then went downstairs for a change of scenery, more women, more staring! We circulated like that for seven hours, with me going back and forward to the desk to see if we had a chance of getting on the London flight. We had, at one point, tried to phone British Airways. That was the only other airline that flew into Doha. British Airways informed us that a flight back to the UK from Doha was going to cost us £1500 to get home. So, that was a no go!

We were both sat by the boarding gate of the London flight. They had started calling people to board. Both Debs and me sat there watching people board to get to London, without a hope in hell of getting on it. I said, "Fuck this!" I flew up to the desk. There was a lot of commotion going on. The London flight had been over booked. People were angry that they were not boarding. I heard the guy behind the desk mention Germany. I thought, I would rather be in Germany dressed like this than here in the Middle East. I dove in front of the desk and barked at the man that I wanted to get on the flight to Germany. He didn't argue. There were eleven Japanese men there that were trying to get on to the same flight. For some reason, the man behind the desk decided to put me and Deb along with the Japanese on the same ticket. I didn't care. I had got me and Deb out of Doha. We were flying to Germany. We can sort the rest out once we had landed. We would certainly have more options getting back to London from Germany, that was for sure.

When we landed in Germany, we had fifteen minutes to

get across the airport to our gate to catch our next connection flight. Stress levels were up. I'm not sure if we even knew what day it was. How long we had been travelling for? We were both really tired. Matt then called and asked if we got home safely. I laughed and said, "No we are still travelling, we are in Germany!" He said, "What the fuck?" I said, "I'll message you when we land in London!"

We made it to our gate just on time. Deb's was feeling completely bedraggled and said, "J, I've got to have a fag." I let her get on with it and took our ticket up to the desk. I wanted to know about our luggage. The very angry lady behind the check-in desk was not at all helpful. In a very angry, blunt manner she proceeded to tell me, "We don't have that information. You go to baggage claim when you land in London." She also then went on to say there are eleven of you on the ticket and only ten seats available. I thought, "Fuck!" I shouted at Debs. Poor Debs, her little face had had enough. I beckoned her over, explained the situation. I said, "If they call your name, go for it. I'll figure out a way home from here." Debs said, "No way, if your name gets called, I'll do the same." We spent the next five minutes arguing over who was going to get on to the plane. Suddenly, her name was called. I said, "Run!" Then my name was called so I ran too. We both took off. I felt bad for the Japanese guys but we both wanted home. We sat in our seats and waited for take-off. I have never been so happy to land in London.

We both decided to go and check to see if our luggage had made it home. Our luggage was the first, off the plane! We hadn't paid a penny for any of those flights. We were both really lucky in that sense and for the fact that we had made it home in one piece. We did though, pay a London taxicab £200 to take us home. I could not sit around and wait any more for transport. I just wanted home and bed.

One week after my return from Thailand, I went into the fight store. Monday morning. Dave called me into the office. He said, "Right, there is a fight that has come up. It's a fight against Jan Young." I had already fought her and won. "Her opponent has pulled out. They have offered it to you. It's a British Title shot. It's kickboxing and it is on Saturday!"

My initial thought was I'm not ready, that's only four days away to train. Dave then said, "Look we go down there, we do the fight. If we lose, we know what to work on for the upcoming Commonwealth title shot. If we win, you walk away being British Champion."

After my little bit of negative thought, I said, "Yeah sure, I'm in." I was still fit from Thailand. Let's do it. Four days of training. Saturday I was on my way to Chippenham to fight for a British Title.

On fight day I was always the same. Jokey, laughing and having fun. That's how I dealt with the nerves. Once I got to the venue, I would stay out the back. I could not be doing with small talk with all and sundry. It would do my head in. The same perpetual questions: Are you ready? Are you going to win? All I would be thinking is, 'Will you just fuck off'! So, best place for me was out the back where I could focus and chill out. An hour before, is when I would really start to get my head in the game. No talking, just simple instructions, pad work and tech drills. One of the corner guys, Jas, kept coming in whilst I was warming up and talking to me. I suffered it for three or four times. Then he got told to fuck off out of my face. I knew what I was doing. I did not need him in and out of my face telling me what I needed to be doing! Dave jokingly said it was probably a good idea for Jas to now leave the building. Jas took the hint. If I wanted to know anything I would ask.

I am back in the ring. Ref. has moved his mouth. I'm back in my corner. Bell has gone. I start moving around. It's going okay. Probably about thirty seconds into the first round, I sit back on the ropes and have a flash of, 'I can't do this'. I jumped out of that thought as quick as it had arrived. What the fuck am I doing? I want to win. I step into a different gear. Jan catches me with a right hand, all I can see is a white light. I'm blinded for seconds. I can hear the crowd cheering. I cover up and turn her on the ropes. I am now in control. I can see again. I offload a flurry of punches. I suddenly hear Dave shouting to calm down. I thought, 'Right step back. Gather yourself. Back to the game plan. Don't get caught like that again'. The rest of the fight felt like I was fighting in slow motion. I could see everything she was doing before she was doing it. My thoughts were so clear in what I wanted to do. It was like I was having an out of body experience. Five rounds. Every time I went back to the corner, Dave, Jas and Les were all arguing over what to tell me to do. Really, there was nothing to tell me to do. Dave just said, "Keep doing what you are doing." That's exactly what I did.

In Sports Psychology they call that Peak Flow.

After my eleventh fight in September 2002, I am now British Middle Weight Kickboxing Champion.

The twelfth fight was a shot at the Commonwealth Title. I was sixty-six kilograms and against Louise O'Donnell.

The fighters were now earning commission on ticket sales, which was more than I was earning on my first fights. The more tickets you sold the more commission you could earn. It was never a great deal. But at least I was earning something now for being the top of the bill. I would sell to my friends, to the security crew and to everyone I knew at the weights gym.

There was a guy that would come into the gym called Scott. He was a bit of a character. Very strong. I got chatting to him and said, "Do you want to come and see me fight?" It certainly wasn't a come on. I just wanted to sell tickets. He said, "I don't have any money on me." I said, "No worries, take the ticket. I'll collect the money later. Give me your number." That wasn't a come on either. We exchanged numbers. I wanted the ticket sales.

It was November 5$^{th}$ 2002. I was at a fireworks party at a friend's. Scott had started to text me. I replied. We were flirting with each other over the text messages. I felt flattered. We started to hang out a bit. Nothing sexual. Gym, drinks with mates, movies. Scott asked me, "If I asked you out on a date would you go?" I told him he needed to sort it out with his girlfriend as I did not want to be part of being the other woman. When you have sorted that out, come and speak to me. I remember thinking that I don't really fancy him. But, same as before, he was paying me some attention and I was lonely. He seemed all right. I knew that he had gone through A.A. He had the date on his arm of when he went into recovery. I thought that he was out the other side. I thought that he was working on his recovery. I'll support anyone. I have no judgement. Everyone has a past. Everyone has a story. Everyone deserves a chance.

Scott's behaviour right from the outset was a bit erratic. We would be texting all the time. I would get tired of the texting and try to ring. It would go straight through to answer phone. Then we would go back to texting again. I would try to call again. It would go straight to answer phone. It was like he would text and then switch his phone off. I started to think that it wasn't him that I was talking to. The behaviour was weird. I stayed with it though. No judgement. There is obviously a valid reason for it.

Scott drove up to London the same night he had asked me out and finished it with his girlfriend. He came straight round to mine on the way back, to tell me it was all over. That was the start of my relationship with Scott. I wanted to take things nice and slow. I was busy training for my Commonwealth Title. I also didn't want to jump straight into having sex. I wanted to spend some time getting to know him. These days everyone is so quick to jump into bed. I just wanted some time to figure him out before I gave that up. I wanted a bit of foundation to the relationship as friends. It's just how I wanted it to be. I didn't see anything wrong with that.

I made weight for the fight. It was so hard getting down to sixty-six kilograms. I looked emaciated but I did it. I had a twenty-four-hour weigh in. I spent an hour in the sauna just before weighing in, just to get off those last couple of kilos. After weighing in, I went home and had a nice big feast. Nothing bad. Energy food that was going to fill me up for the following day.

I made it down to the BIC. This time I was fighting in the Windsor Hall; the biggest hall in the BIC. It held three thousand spectators. It was a big one. I was my usual self. Joking around. Keeping myself upbeat. See the doctor, eat my food. Get my head together. I was top of the show. It was now time for me to fight. I had got through my warm-up fine, no issues. I made my way down to the stage. I was out the back waiting to get into the ring. Dave was holding me back, waiting for my tune to come on. I don't even remember what it was. All I know is that in that moment, I had an overriding feeling of panic. I was now in the middle of a panic attack. The last one was when I was walking through Boscombe when I had first returned from the States, two years before this fight. I couldn't believe it. What was I going to do? I told Dave, "We have to go. We have got to go now!" He said, "Wait, in a minute!"

I couldn't share with him what was going on. There were three thousand people waiting for me to come out and fight. Suddenly, my name is called, 'Jannniiine The Machine Davis'. The crowd is cheering. I have to walk out like nothing is happening. My legs felt like any minute they were going to give way. I climbed into the ring and proceeded to do my Wai Kru. That seemed to settle me a little bit. I was just trying to get my body to do what it needed to do.

The ref. calls us to the centre of the ring. I square my opponent down. I am giving nothing away. I look her straight through her eyeballs. Really, on the inside, my body is a complete and utter mess. Back to my corner. Bell goes. It is fight time. I throw a leg kick. She blocks it with her knee. I show no pain. On the inside I think, 'Ooooo, that fucking hurt. I won't do that again'. I'm moving around and getting my shots in. I know I'm doing well and that she is on the back foot.

Before we had gone out into the ring, the ring owner had bought the wrong canvas. He had bought a canvas that was from a show the night before. It was covered in sponsorship from the previous night. He had to turn the canvas over, meaning, it was like a fucking ice-skating rink in barefoot. Dave had mentioned this before going out and then in the corner sprayed my feet with water, like that was going to do any good! Every single fighter that night had slipped or gone over and landed on their arse.

I had Louise in the corner of the ring. I had just off-loaded punches and kicks. I stepped to my left and my foot slipped out from underneath me. I put out my right hand to land on the floor. When you have boxing gloves on, you are not going to land on your palm. I took full weight on my right wrist. I didn't think anything of it. Got back up continued with the fight. I felt pain in my wrist but thought that maybe a ligament was out. I didn't think for one minute that I had broken my arm. I finished the round. Sat down in my corner. Dave started to talk tactics to me. I said, "I can't feel my hand." He said, "What do you mean?" I repeated, "I can't feel my hand!" I knew something was wrong. Dave's response, "What do you want to do?" I said, "I don't fucking know, I can't feel my hand." I thought, 'You're the fucking corner man. You make the decision'. Otherwise, what's the point of me having someone in the corner? Dave called over the Doctor. I now was in quite a lot of pain. I definitely knew something was bad. They managed to pull my glove off. You could see straight away that my hand was hanging off. I had snapped the top of my radius. I was devastated! I started to cry.

Nick Stone from the Bulldog gym in Australia came over to see what was happening. He said, "It's a no contest then." You can't judge a fight over one round. Louise O'Donnell did not break my wrist. I had slipped on the fucking canvas and landed on my wrist.

On the way back to his corner, Nick Stone changed his mind. He said, "Well, there were a lot of kicks thrown. I think we should give the decision to Louise." What an absolute crock of shit. She didn't stop me. She didn't kick my wrist. I fell on the slippery canvas. They gave her the decision. She was gifted the Commonwealth Title and did nothing for it.

Am I angry about it? Not really. I didn't kick up a fuss. I took it like a real sports person should and sucked it up. It was what it was but let's have it straight, she did not win that fight. She got handed that on a platter!

Scott came down to the hospital. I knew then that he was socially awkward. Dave's wife was with me. I tried to make Scott feel welcome. Try and take his nerves away at being around people he didn't know. One of my character traits: help other people before I help myself.

Scott drove me home after my arm had been put in a cast. I did not sleep a wink that night. Scott stayed up with me the whole night. I felt so wired and pumped. I was also in a lot of pain.

The following day I wanted to get a roast. Scott came with me and cut all my food up for me. That was it. Just the small amount of kindness paid to me hooked me in. It doesn't take much. I thought he was a good guy. That evening we both went back to my place as I was starting to fade a bit. We chilled out in my room. Out of nowhere he started crying. I didn't understand what was going on. He didn't really explain it either. I think he blamed it on the David Gray music I was playing. Anyway, I let him get on with it and lay there with him so he didn't feel alone. He then took off. Said, "I'll send you a text." I thought, 'Okay, cool'. I didn't hear from him for over a week.

This pattern of behaviour started to repeat itself. I would notice when I went to visit him at his place, there were times that he wasn't even communicating with me. I thought, 'He must want to be on his own'. I would leave and get on with my own life. He would then get in contact with me again.

Knowing that something wasn't right I started to ask questions. He then started to open up about depression and that he suffered with it. I also realised that the doctors were giving him medication that he would take for a period of three weeks. He would go through all kinds of panic attacks, anxiety and wanting to be a recluse, before the tablets settled in and then go through the same behaviours coming off them, because he would fail to get the repeat prescription in time to keep him on an even keel. He was all over the place. One time the pharmacy had given him triple the dose that was recommended. He was completely out of it!

This is the start of me taking care of him and feeling that I should be helping him. I could teach him how to do better. Get him dressing better as he had a pair of jogging bottoms that were for the gym, going out casual and going for dinner. They had a massive split through the crutch. He was a state really but I felt like he needed someone. That someone was me.

One night when Scott had stayed over, Rafael came to me in my dream. It was so clear. The background was white. He was walking towards me. We sat down. He asked me if I was okay. We sat and talked. I told him about Scott. He said, "Is he good?" I said, "He seems all right." We spoke for ages. I then woke up and I sat bolt upright. That wasn't like my usual dreams. That was as clear as clear could be. It shook me up a bit. I thought, 'Rafael must have died'. That was the only explanation for it. That is when I started to look for him on the internet. I went to the San Francisco obituaries. I started to look through those intermittently. Not every day, but certainly when he was on my mind.

Even with my arm in a cast, I was in the gym training. I felt like I was missing out. The journey didn't feel complete. I felt like I was surplus to requirements. It's a horrible feeling when you have been right in the middle of a so-called family, to then feel like you've been pushed out, looking back in.

It wasn't long before Dave had started talking about the re-match with Louise O'Donnell. This time it would be for a World Title!

Scott had started talking about us living together. I had initially said yes, like I always would do when people ask me to do things. I need to think about it before I give an answer, because once you've said yes, you then don't want to let people down. That's how I have always been: don't want to let people down, never thinking about myself and always thinking about how everyone else feels.

Scott's flat was, let's say, kept in chaos. He would clean it once a month if you were lucky. I would find myself doing the cleaning up when I was round there. At twenty-nine years old, he really had only just moved out of his mum's house. He said he was going to A.A. meetings. I did go to one of them with him when we were first together. It was interesting and I understand the importance of them but I did feel like it was a breeding ground for self-perpetuating need, for going over the same share all the time. I suppose you can go over it and over it and over it until you are done with your share and found your light out of it. My only thought is, 'How do you start to move forwards'. If you keep going over the same old ground, where is the light out of it?

Scott had suggested that he was not keen on the fighting, that I would end up looking like Jane Couch. I didn't know what that meant. All I know is that Jane Couch laid the foundation for women to box. These women are long forgotten about. You never hear people referring to the female boxers like they do the men.

My response was that he better get his head around it or fuck off. I am not changing anything. This is what I do. You either like it or you lump it.

That was the end of that conversation.

I don't know why I felt so responsible for him from the outset. Maybe that's my trait. I feel like I need to take care of everyone. If I love them enough, I can show them a better way and they will love me back.

I know that he had borrowed his mum's push bike. He had ridden it down to Christchurch to spend the evening with his friends. Instead of locking it up, he threw it in a bush and left it there. Just threw it away. Never mind that the bike was his mum's!

I was at his mum's house with him, when his mum was asking for the bike. I knew full well what he had done. He made up some story to her about the bike being at his flat locked up round the back. I watched him lie his way out of telling her that he had actually dumped it in a bush.

When we left. I said, "What the fuck! You need to replace that bike."

Scott was working as a care worker, as well as working as a security man at a pub called O'Neil's on Friday and Saturday nights. I remember being over at Two Rivers meet gym and Scott turned up. I said, "I thought you were at work?" He said, "I am. I've left Gary in the car." I looked out the window of the gym. I couldn't believe it. He said, "Don't worry I've left the car in eye shot, he'll be all right." He had left Gary, the special needs individual in the car to wait for him, whilst he went into the gym and had a quick workout! Un-fucking believable!

Scott then bought up again about us moving in together. I told him I had changed my mind and would like to wait a bit. When he asked why, I told him I just want to wait a bit, I feel like if I moved in, I would end up doing everything. Scott did not like that. I went home that night and thought 'I'll catch up with him tomorrow'.

The following day, I couldn't get hold of him. I went round to his flat. The front door was not locked so I was able to let myself in. There were bottles and bottles and bottles of drink everywhere. Wine bottles, beer bottles, vodka bottles. Ten maybe fifteen. I found him passed out in his bedroom. What I should have done right there and then is walked away but I didn't. The guilt was there. I was responsible for this. My decision for not moving in with him made him do this. I was now invested.

I didn't understand at all back then about manipulative behaviour, but, let me tell you, I have had a master class in it now. I know all the signs.

The cast was off my arm. I was back in full training. I had a World Title to start training for. I needed to be sixty-six kilograms again. I needed to train, train and train!

For Scott's birthday in February 2003, I decided to book a few days in the Lake District. I booked us a cottage out in the sticks. We were to drive up on the Saturday and come back on the Tuesday. The pickup was from my house at ten a.m. Scott was always late and I don't mean five or ten minutes. I mean twenty to thirty to whatever time he decided to turn up. I would always be in the foulest mood by the time he would turn up. He would always have shaved at the very last minute. He never used a mirror. I'd look at him and say you look like a mental patient. He would have strips of hair on both sides of his face that he had missed. It would be the same on his head. Massive clumps of hair missed on the back of his head.

I am sat in my kitchen. Ten and eleven a.m., twelve and one p.m. all pass by! He turns up. I am fucking furious. "What the fuck have you been doing?"

His Jaguar XJS had broken down. He was trying to get it fixed. I thought, 'You have a phone. Why didn't you call me?' I said, "Okay, we'll have to rent." Do you know what it is like trying to rent a car on a Saturday!

We found a place over on the Ferndown industrial estate. It took us thirty minutes to get there. Once we had arrived, he pulled out his driver's licence. The car rental said we need to see the paper copy as well. So, we had to drive all the way back to his mum's house, thirty minutes, to pick up the paper copy. Go back, get the rental car. It's now five p.m. There is no way we are driving up to the Lake District now; from Bournemouth it is a six-hour drive.

We decided to leave first thing Sunday morning. It took us six hours to get there and just as well that we took the rental car: a nippy Peugeot 206. The Jaguar would not have made it over the back roads and through the fields to the cottage. The cottage was right in the middle of nowhere. The scenery was beautiful. Open fields, fresh air, blue skies. We ventured down to Lake Windermere in the car, had a little mooch about, stopped off at a V.G. to pick up some snacks for back at the cottage. Scott got his usual tins of tuna and rice.

As we sat on the lake taking in the beautiful view, I proposed that we head back and go out and have some dinner. He said, "Oh, I thought we were going to eat at the cottage?" I replied, "I haven't come away to eat tuna and rice, I'm on holiday. I want to go out for a meal!" I then suddenly thought,

'How much money has he come with?' I asked him, "How much money have you got on you?" His reply, "Five pounds!"

What the fuck! Five pounds. What the fuck are you going to do with five pounds? In fact, how the fuck do we get home on five fucking pounds? I said, "Don't worry. Luckily, I have come with money. I'll take care of everything." He did look a bit embarrassed. He said, "I put all my money in the Jag. It took £100 to fill it up! I thought then, thank fuck we never came up in that thing. It would have cost us £200 plus just to get around."

Why did I not walk away then? I just didn't question it. The thing is and what I have come to realise is, when you have spent your most informative years growing up in dysfunction, it just seems normal to be around it.

Scott had gone on holiday to Magaluf with his mates. He had told me some woman had stolen his money. To be honest he had probably gone without any money. He was like that, look at the Lake District! I would not have put it past him to come up with some elaborate story so everyone would take care of him. He then mentioned we should get married. I didn't say anything, I just laughed. I didn't say yes, but I also didn't say no.

He had moved out of the flat he was living in and moved into a shared flat with a woman. I can't remember why he had done that. I had changed my mind about living with him so maybe his lease had run out and he had to find somewhere else to live. His behaviour was really starting to get demanding. He would question how much I loved him all the time. I would turn up in the middle of the day to find him in a bath, drunk, asking me how much I loved him. I didn't know what to do with the behaviour. I did feel that I could not tell him the truth for fear of him falling apart. His demand for sex was on the rise. I would turn up after a heavy training session, knackered. I wanted to chill out. He wanted sex. I would, most of the time if not all the time, fall asleep, much to his annoyance. He would see that as rejection. So, more questioning of my love for him. I had started to recoil a bit. The more he pushed the more I retracted. I knew back then really, I did not want the relationship. I just didn't know how to get out of it. The more we didn't have sex the more he pushed for the fact that I didn't love him.

He had moved out of the house share with the woman. I'm sure he blamed it on her, that she was hard work. I would imagine that she had had enough of him. I just didn't see it at the time.

He moved in with a friend of his. He had a box room that was empty. His mate was growing weed in every single space in his house. It was crazy. Every time I went round there, he was drilling holes and making air vents for the plants. He worked out that he had thirty thousand pounds worth of plants when they crop.

The relationship with Scott was still tough. I would go and spend time with him, with not a word spoken by him. What am I meant to do with that? I had tried to come up with ideas to spice up the sex life. I don't know; make it fun. I was blaming myself. I thought maybe some porn would sex it up a bit. I got nothing. No response, nothing. There was no romance. I was to lay back open my legs and get on with it, as and when he wanted it.

Why didn't I leave then?

I had now given in to the fact of living with him. We found a flat in the West Cliff. It was a lovely flat during the summer

But miserable in the winter, because the only heating it had was under floor, which sounds lovely. But, it's only lovely for your feet. There was no insulation and the under-floor heating cost an absolute fortune. He did present himself to be working and I honestly thought when we were moving in there, that he was sorting his shit out and had money coming in.

I was training hard now. The World Title fight was in August 2003. I was selling my tickets and gathering sponsorship. I know I wasn't well liked in the gym amongst the girls and maybe the boys too. I know that the women were all talking about me behind my back, wishing that I was not going to turn up to training. I didn't care. It was a common occurrence for me to be without a training partner in sessions because no one wanted to work with me. Yes, I did have an ego. I'm sure if I was to watch myself back from then, I would cringe. But when you are fighting you have to take on a persona, if you don't get inside your own head and believe you are great, you are going to get eaten alive.

I was in session one night and Bushy, a six foot three Antiguan who was very muscly, turned up to train. Bushy was a fighter but hadn't been in the gym for three months. His fitness would have been a little rusty. Dave said, "Bushy get in the ring." "Davis, in the ring!" Bushy said, "Ahhhh Dave, come on, she fights like a bloke!"

All I was thinking was that he is massive, he has a longer reach than me and if he catches me it is going to hurt.

The bell goes. I am fully focused, moving around, defending well and working my shots in. Bushy, all of a sudden, sits back on the ropes. His belly is wide open. I step to the left side of him and drop a right, rib kick right across the front of his stomach. I stepped back and watched him fold in half. Bushy was now rolling around on the floor. Dave booted him out of the ring. I thought, 'Phew. Survived that one'.

Dave had a bad back. I'm not sure what was wrong with it. I do know that if he did too much training he would suffer with pain after. When we would spar, I would always take it easy. I did not want to hurt him. I mentioned this to him in the fight store one day. He said, "What, you take it easy?" I said, "Yeah, I go easy, I don't want to hurt your back!"

A couple of days later we were in the gym training. He had set us up to do a round of sparring. He came over to me and said, "You take it easy, do you? We'll see about that." I was taken aback for a moment. I then thought, 'Fuck you it's on'! I walked back to my corner and waited for the bell. Ding ding. It's on. We were moving around. Dave sat back on the ropes. I did this move where you grabbed round the neck. I would pull them back, then pull them forwards on to my knee. But, instead of going to the body, I dropped the knee in the middle of his quad. I let go and stepped back, to then drop a right, low kick right where I had just dropped the knee and stood back. We finished the round. I wasn't pushed or breathing heavy. I walked away unscathed and not hurt. Dave, as usual went to the pub. I went home to get fuelled up.

The following day I went down to the fight store to see Dave on crutches. I said, "What's happened?" He said, "When I was in the pub my leg started to seize up. I had to be carried out!" He had a massive haematoma in the middle of his thigh. He spent six weeks on crutches.

This was the start of him getting kitted up when he was training me. He started to wear head protection, as I had accidentally head butted him in sparring, nearly knocking us both out. I remember me looking at him and his face was full of surprise. I said, "You okay?" He said, "Yeah!" Dave never sparred with me again without putting on a head guard, body protection, leg protection and shin protection. He looked like the Michelin man!

Living in the flat with Scott to start out with for the first few months was okay. Scott was Scott which was chaotic but he was working and we were able to pay all our bills on time. Before we had moved into the flat together, he had come up with this idea to grow weed. I listened to him whilst he laid out this plan: to get a loan from the bank, buy a flat and then grow weed in it. He thought he had it all figured out. When I questioned him on how he was going to pay the mortgage, he became very defensive and could not see any holes in the whole situation.

Borrow ten thousand: buy a studio flat, use at least two and a half on paying the mortgage and the rest was for the down-payment. Of course, the first studio flat he was going to buy pulled out. So that was fifteen hundred lost through stamp duty and agents fees. I know that he lost fifteen hundred. So, now he is fifteen hundred down!

I said, "I do not want to know a god damn thing. Do not tell me anything. I do not care. I think you're a fucking idiot for doing it!" He did it anyway, because what do I know?

His mate that he was doing it with ended up going to court for growing weed in his house. He got six months in prison. The thirty thousand he thought he was going to get was gone. You think Scott had any idea what he was doing? NO!

So, he had a flat that had weed in it that he did not know how to grow and he had to find the money to continue paying the mortgage.

Why didn't I leave then?

He bought in this horrible man called Jaxon from Manchester. I had had a fling with him when I first got back from the US. He was a spiteful, horrible man. Jaxon, still to this day, thinks I fancy him. He believes because I will not speak to him that means I still fancy him. I'll tell you what it means. I don't fucking like you. You stink like shit. You are a horrible, sneaky, possessive, jealous individual.

So, Jaxon is in my house. I can't tell Scott that me and Jaxon have slept together. Scott needs to get this weed taken care of. So, Jaxon is in the picture. Scott just hands over the keys to the flat and trusts that Jaxon has got his back! You know Jaxon had not got his back because he is a sneaky cunt. Scott is an idiot! I did not want anything to do with it. I had other shit to be getting on with: like training for the World Title fight. I know that I would not have let somebody I didn't really know in on a scam I was running and think that they would take care of it for me. I would have been in the flat every time he was in there; but that's me. It's not Scott, the brain of Britain!

I had noticed that my money that I was saving in my drawer had been taken. He had just helped himself to it. I didn't say anything. Why didn't I say anything? I was so caught up with him and thinking he was vulnerable, that I hadn't realised right from the beginning I was being taken for a ride.

I'm not sure if he got the sack from the care home or he left. All I know was that he was no longer working at the care home. He was now working full time as a security man in town at the club: Elements. This is when the money really stopped appearing. Sometimes he would have the rent, sometimes he wouldn't. I'm not sure what he was doing. I know I didn't challenge him on it in the beginning. I was too stressed trying to make rent because I did not want to be late paying it.

I also noticed that my garlic that I would use for cooking would have pieces nibbled out of them. I did think for a moment that we had mice. I thought, 'That can't be right'. But of course, he was eating the raw garlic when he came in to disguise the smell of alcohol. I would also find needles left in the toilet. I would say, "What the fuck is this?" "Oh, oh, that's an old one."

Old one what mother fucker? I am the only person cleaning this place. It wasn't there when I cleaned it this morning! He would brush it off. I didn't really know then the extent of the steroid use. I would just carry on in amongst the dysfunctions. When you have grown up in it, it just seems normal!

Why didn't I leave then?

I had nowhere to go and no one to turn to for help. That's one of the reasons I stayed.

Scott had asked me to meet him at this French cafe we used to go to. As we sat there having a cuppa, he said, "Look what I've done!" I watched him pull up this magazine. He passed it to me. He then proceeded to tell me he had booked this holiday where we could get married. I didn't know what to say. My first response was, 'Okay'. On the outside I stayed calm. On the inside I was thinking, if I say no, he is going to fall apart. What do I do? He said, "I haven't bought you a ring, I'll get you some trainers." I said, "Trainers! What the fuck am I going to do with the trainers when they wear out? No, you'll get me a ring at least!"

So, that was that. I didn't know how to get out of it. I was now set up to marry Scott in October 2003. I did try to get him to wait. We were in the travel agents. He had set it up in Greece.

The travel agent was saying there wasn't enough time to get the paperwork sorted. I said, "Let's just wait then," hoping I could buy myself some time. He aggressively said, "No, we are doing it now!" What the fuck was I to do?

I was pushing myself really hard, training for the fight. I was having breakdowns on the beach. I was running on empty trying to make sixty-six kilograms in weight. I was exhausted but I kept on pushing; got to keep pushing.

I had a training session booked with Dave. I had no business being in that training session that day. I was over-training. I was exhausted but, my head said, 'No. You miss this, you lose the fight'.

A couple of weeks before this session. I was training in the gym with a novice. We were grappling. He went one way, my knee went the other. I screamed out and fell to the floor. Everyone stopped what they were doing. I laid there for a bit and let the pain subside. I got up. I could still walk. Everything seemed okay. 'Phew, okay, I'm all right'. I took myself off to the physio just to get it checked out. He did all the necessary checks. He gave me the all-clear.

Two weeks before the fight I was knackered but I was ready for my session with Dave. We start working on the pads. I was moving well, hitting hard and I then go in for a jumping knee strike. I place my right foot on the floor, ready for the jump. I hear this almighty gunshot go off. I think, 'Where is that coming from'? It was coming from me!

I immediately think, 'Okay, there is no immediate surging pain in my knee', which was weird because that sound was immense. I stumble back towards the back of the ring to get to a safe spot. I start to cry because now the pain has kicked in. There is no let up. Dave gets me moving round and makes me finish the round. He doesn't ask if I'm okay We finish the session. I take myself home. I have got two weeks before my World Title fight. I have just got to get on with it. I am fit enough, so no more running. I limit my pad work. I'm ready to go.

Scott pointed out that I should not be fighting. I completely ignored that advice. In my mind there was no way that I wasn't going to fight. This was a World Title fight. This wasn't a three round novice fight. I had to do it! At The Bulldog, In his mind, as the promoter of the night, he had paid for the tickets for the Aussies to come over. The venue had been booked; tickets had been sold. Dave had said after I had broken my arm in the last fight, he didn't care what happened. Break your hand, foot, leg, whatever. I was going to fight and that was the end of it. No questions asked.

I don't remember a lot from the day of the fight. I do remember the fight though. I didn't want to let anyone down and knew that my leg was not right. Dave had asked me when we were warming up, "What do you want to do, as far as the knee?" I said, "I don't know. Strap it up I suppose?" What the fuck did I know?

Before a fight, you go and see a doctor before stepping in the ring. He takes your heart rate and checks you over to make sure you are fit enough to fight. You always sign a declaration saying you potentially may die today. As a fighter you do not give it a second thought. If you were worried about dying, you would never get in the ring.

The doctor asked me how my arm was. He was the doctor at the last fight when I broke it. I said, "All good! I never mentioned my knee. I was all fit, so he signed me out. I was ready to go.

I'd strapped my knee up as best as I could. I was in the ring ready to go. The ref. had said his blah, blah… I never listened. I was too busy squaring up to my opponent. Back to my corner. Ding ding. We are ready to go. We come out. We are in reach of each other. The first shot Louise throws is a right shin kick to my jaw. I was suddenly awake. My reaction was to drive forwards with as many punches as I could throw. She was now on the back foot. We move about. I am taking the fight to her. I kept my dominance through the first round. I remember moving laterally and then feeling my whole right knee slide to the left, inside of the joint. I knew that was bad. I knew that if I tried to kick with that leg, it felt like it was going to snap in half. I couldn't and wouldn't let this fight be taken away from me again.

I locked that knee in and tensed my right thigh so that I could keep some tension and fought on. The bell goes and I am walking back to my corner thinking, 'Why is Nick Stone in my corner'? That was Louise's trainer. I looked back and realised I was walking back to the wrong corner. I saw Dave's face. I knew he was thinking, 'What the fuck is she doing'? As soon as I got back, I said, "I'm all right, I'm all right."

Second round in. I decided that she is not going to knock me out. I can't move my head because I can't move my right leg. So, I decided to take the punches to the face. I manage to block some but quite a few got through. I am still taking the fight to her. I am the aggressor in this fight. There is not one minute that I am not moving forwards. Second round done. Third round repeat the same as before. Keep surviving. Do not let this knee give way. Coming out to the fourth, Dave says, "You're not using your legs, it is shit or bust now!" I thought, 'Fuck! Okay, let's try the left. Tense that right leg kick with the left. I throw that out, follow with a left hook'. It works. I'm still standing. Right, I've got that. I make it through the fourth.

Fifth and final round. I just need to stay on my feet. I get through the round. I've made it. I know I've not won but, in my heart, I keep saying to myself, 'Please don't let me lose, please don't let me lose'.

The ref. calls both fighters to the centre. The fight is called a draw. I said, "YES! YESSSSSSS…" I am so happy. I can't walk. I needed to be carried out of the ring. I don't know where Dave is. Scott and his mate Adam carried me to the warm-up room. I sat there for a while. I didn't lose!

We get home. My face is battered. I didn't have a black eye or any welts around my eye sockets and no broken nose. So, more for me as far as that goes. I had obviously blocked more than I thought but my face felt bruised; like I had just done five rounds! I was in so much pain with my knee. It was unbearable. I ended up down at A and E at two a.m. getting it checked out. It turns out I had completely ruptured the ACL and the slide I felt in the first round, was my meniscus tearing. The hospital sent me home on crutches with further appointments to see specialists.

The following day I am at home feeling sorry for myself, reflecting on the fight. I was content with the draw under the circumstances. My phone goes. It's Dave. "Janine, you are the World Champion!"

I said, "What?" He said, "You are the World Champion!" I said, "No fucking way!"

Apparently, the Aussies had kicked up so much fuss. The WPKL representatives that had sanctioned the show and judged the show went back to the score cards. Two judges had scored it a draw. The chief judge had scored the fight to me.

TO ME!

August 2003 I was the new cruiser weight WPKL World Champion!

Me, a World Champion.

I went down to the office on my crutches to pick up my belt and my trophy. I bumped into Nick Stone who did not look best pleased. I didn't fucking care. He started bleating on about how happy Louise was when she won the Commonwealth the year before. But she didn't win it, did she? She was handed it on a fucking plate. I didn't say anything though. I behaved like a true sportsman should and agreed. I then fucked off with my belt and my trophy. I sat at home, bruised and in pain but happily content, looking at what I had won.

Janine Davis World Champion 2003. I thought to myself, 'You know what? I can do anything. I have achieved this all on my own. Who needs the imbeciles that are my parents? Fuck them, their loss'! They never saw any of my fights, not one!

I will not be defined by their inability to parent. I will use my anger and aggression in a more conducive way that will produce a more positive outcome for my life to lead.